Ex
Libris

Monica Zierhut

PIRATE ALLEY

PIRATE ALLEY

Commanding Task Force 151 off Somalia

RADM TERRY McKNIGHT, USN (RET.), AND MICHAEL HIRSH

Naval Institute Press
Annapolis, Maryland

This book has been brought to publication with the generous assistance of Marguerite and Gerry Lenfest.

Naval Institute Press
291 Wood Road
Annapolis, MD 21402

Library of Congress Cataloging-in-Publication Data
McKnight, Terry.
  Pirate Alley : commanding Task Force 151 off Somalia / Terry McKnight and Michael Hirsh ; foreword by Jim Miklaszewski.
    p. cm.
  Includes index.
  ISBN 978-1-61251-134-4 (hbk. : alk. paper) — ISBN 978-1-61251-135-1 (e-book) 1. Pirates—Somalia—21st century. 2. Piracy—Somalia—21st century. 3. Piracy—Aden, Gulf of—21st century. 4. Combined Task Force 151 (International Naval Task Force) 5. Hijacking of ships—Somalia—Prevention. 6. Hijacking of ships—Aden, Gulf of—Prevention. 7. Somalia—History, Naval—21st century. 8. Aden, Gulf of—History, Naval—21st century. I. Hirsh, Michael, 1943- II. Title.
  DT403.2.M37 2012
  364.164096773—dc23

                                                                                    2012027964

♾ This paper meets the requirements of ANSI/NISO z39.48-1992 (Permanence of Paper).
Printed in the United States of America.

20 19 18 17 16 15 14 13 12   9 8 7 6 5 4 3 2 1
First printing

For my wife, Lisa
and for our two wonderful children
T and Tyler

Also, for all the dedicated men and women who have served our nation

especially those who made the ultimate sacrifice in the cause of freedom.

Never give up laughing and loving

CONTENTS

FOREWORD

> Good morning. We're coming to you live from the deck of the U.S. war-
> ship *Vella Gulf* in the heart of Pirate Alley.
>
> —*NBC News, 10 February 2009*

By early 2009 piracy off the Horn of Africa had exploded. Pirates in small skiffs and armed only with AK-47s were brazenly hijacking huge merchant ships, seizing cargo and crews, demanding millions of dollars in ransom. Remarkably, these small bands of pirates operated with such impunity that those crowded shipping lanes in the Gulf of Aden became known as Pirate Alley.

The story was a reporter's dream. Never in my wildest imagination as the Pentagon correspondent for NBC News did I see myself caught up in a high-seas hunt for pirates. Yet there we were that February, broadcasting live from the Gulf of Aden, using the latest in twenty-first-century portable satellite technology to report on a pirate threat as ancient as seafaring itself.

From the bridge of the guided-missile cruiser *Vella Gulf*, Rear Adm. Terry McKnight had a front-row seat. He had just taken command of the newly formed Combined Task Force 151, an international alliance of naval forces whose sole mission was counterpiracy. In this book McKnight pulls no punches. It's a straightforward, honest account of the daunting challenges, bureaucratic hang-ups, and tough choices facing the international community in combating piracy.

The largely lawless coastal region of Somalia at the very tip of the Horn of Africa remains a perfect breeding ground and safe haven for pirates. And as ransom demands have soared to $8 million, investors have poured huge sums of money into pirate operations in exchange for a 60 percent share of the take.

For the pirates themselves, the reward/risk ratio is through the roof. Their cut of the ransom in a single hijacking can set them up for life. Even if captured, they know there's little chance they'll end up in jail. Most pirates are simply disarmed and set free in what military officials derisively call "catch and release." Few countries are willing or able to jail pirates, and in many cases criminal prosecutions and convictions can be difficult.

But the tide is gradually turning. While pirate attacks have dramatically risen over the past several years, successful hijackings are down. Aggressive counterpiracy operations by a multinational mix of naval forces have pirates on the run. And the shipping industry itself has finally stepped up to confront the threat.

The simplest defensive measures—steering an evasive course, posting watch, or stringing razor wire along deck railings—have thwarted countless pirate boardings. But the most effective deterrent is also the most controversial.

Armed security forces are now deployed on board many merchant vessels. Out on the open seas it may be impossible to ever know how many pirates have been killed by these private security contractors. In March 2010 a gunfight broke out between security forces and pirates attempting to board the cargo ship *Almezaan*. One pirate was killed; six were captured. The International Maritime Bureau immediately warned that such action may only increase pirate violence. McKnight himself is torn. He writes that he prefers merchant ships not be armed but then concludes, "No civilian ship with an armed security team on board has ever been successfully boarded."

On our embark aboard the *Vella Gulf* we discovered that hunting pirates can be much like fishing: "You should have been here yesterday." We didn't encounter a single pirate. But we did witness what could only be described as a fresh take on "gunboat diplomacy."

All eyes were on a Russian destroyer, *Admiral Vinogradov*, escorting a convoy of merchant ships through Pirate Alley when the radios on the *Vella Gulf* crackled to life. It was a distress call from a cargo ship about to be attacked by pirates. But the cruiser's SH-60 Seahawk helicopter was already on patrol and could not respond in time. Without hesitation, the skipper, Capt. Mark Genung, barked, "We've got to talk to the Russians." Admiral McKnight was on the radio in an instant. In no time, in a very heavy Russian accent, the commander of the *Vinogradov* responded: "American warship, we will launch our helicopter in ten minutes."

In the end it was a false alarm, but the irony and significance of what had just happened was lost on no one. These former Cold War enemies had cooperated in a joint military operation at sea. Any past rivalries were pushed aside as the Russian Helix helicopter circled the *Vella Gulf*, so close you could see the smiles on the faces of the Russian crew. A grateful Terry McKnight invited the Russian skipper to lunch the following day.

Washington, however, was not nearly as excited as everyone aboard the *Vella Gulf*. The lunch date with the Russians was approved, but orders came down through the chain of command that "Miklaszewski and his cameraman" had to be off the ship before the Russians arrived. Seems that news video of American and Russian commanders embracing at sea might fight the hard-line positions the two sides had taken on such issues as missile defense in Europe, Iran's nuclear program, and human rights in Russia.

Nevertheless, this counterpiracy mission may offer some unintended opportunities in military-to-military relations. In its latest report on the emerging military threat from China, even the Pentagon acknowledges that the Chinese navy's participation in counterpiracy operations is a positive step forward.

Despite progress on several fronts, there's no illusion that piracy will ever be eliminated or even reduced to the point where once again the potential threat can be ignored. The ultimate solution to the explosion of piracy off the Horn of Africa would be the elimination of those safe havens in Somalia. But in a country that's struggling to end more than twenty-five years of civil war and that faces a growing threat from al-Qaeda affiliate al-Shabaab, pirates are well down on the list. Until then, vigilance remains the watchword.

—*Jim Miklaszewski*

PREFACE

Why write a book about Somali piracy? More precisely, why did I write such a book? The answer is surprisingly simple. I was bitten by the piracy bug while working the mission in the Gulf of Aden. Pirates are fascinating, and I don't mean the Disney kind, although Johnny Depp is a very cool customer. But at times, I felt like Peter Pan chasing Captain Hook in the Neverland of Somalia.

I'm definitely not trying to romanticize what pirates do because, as a mariner, I find their actions reprehensible. But it does take guts. Most of these pirates come from the hill country of Somalia; they've never been to sea. A lot of them can't even swim. Yet, in the spirit of the pioneers who opened the American West, they get into tiny boats and head out on one of the earth's great oceans, oftentimes hundreds of miles toward the unknown, gambling their lives on very long odds. In the early days, no more than a third of those who set out actually captured a ship. Today, with merchantmen carrying teams of armed guards, the success rate has dropped significantly. And I suspect that the pirate death rate has risen, although no one has publicly said so. Yet they continue to venture forth because, I suspect, they see it as the only way to break away from generations of hopelessness and poverty.

When I was out there, I was in the catbird seat. I had the equivalent of a field box at Yankee Stadium to watch the game. When I came home and then retired, I discovered that I missed it. As I said, I'd been bitten by the bug. So I began reading everything I could get my hands on about Somali piracy. And because a retired flag officer usually gets his calls returned, I took advantage of the situation and started calling the experts, just to chat.

Eventually, I became friends with a small handful of people for whom keeping track of Somali piracy is a way of life. I discovered that I'd just scratched the surface. So I read more, spoke more often about the topic, and then it dawned on me: there are probably many people out there fascinated by the subject who don't have the access that I do. Don't have the firsthand experience that I do. Even among my expert friends, there isn't anyone who can say that they actually chased and caught pirates, who personally saw them on the high seas, experienced the cognitive dissonance of both admiring their fortitude and condemning their actions. That's what led to this book.

I hope you enjoy *Pirate Alley* as much as I relished going to sea and chasing those feisty buccaneers.

PROLOGUE

I can tell you the precise date, place, and time the event occurred that I believe caused the U.S. Navy to get serious about Somali piracy. It was Friday, 1 June 2007, at 1015 hours at latitude 01°50' N, longitude 50°06' E, a position in the Indian Ocean 205 miles off the coast of Somalia, roughly 140 miles north of the Equator.

That's when MV *Danica White*, a twenty-two-year-old, 200-foot bulk carrier hauling a thousand tons of drilling supplies from Dubai to Mombasa, was hijacked by pirates. She was making six knots against a southerly wind and current. The five-man crew was oblivious to the fact that the ship was being trailed by fifteen pirates in three boats. Although the master had been warned about pirates before leaving port, he set no special watch, and none of the crew saw the pirates climb over the stern rail. The ship's freeboard was less than five feet. The only thing missing was a "Welcome Pirates" doormat.

According to the report prepared by the Danish Maritime Authority (DMA), "Suddenly, the master heard screams coming from the outside. First he thought that it was the ordinary seamen who were joking around. Then he heard a few crashes and realized that somebody was pulling the door to the wheelhouse. . . . Suddenly, there were 10–15 men with weapons in the wheelhouse. The master put his hands up in the air and said they could take whatever they wanted and that the crew would do as they said." One of the seamen told the DMA that shots were fired; the cook said a machine gun was pointed at the back of his head when the pirates told him to locate the rest of the crew. The report says that the pirates had boarded the ship from three fiberglass boats, one large boat with an inboard motor and two smaller boats with outboard motors, all of which were then towed behind *Danica White*, which was now headed toward land.

It was that heading that made no sense to the watch team aboard USS *Carter Hall*, which picked up the ship on radar, read the automatic identification system locator information, and determined that *Danica White* was supposed to be heading due south to Mombasa, Kenya, not transiting a course perpendicular to its intended line of travel. *Carter Hall*, an amphibious assault ship operating as part of Combined Task Force

150, the multinational coalition established to support the fight against terrorists in the Horn of Africa, was in the area to maintain a covert over-the-horizon watch on already-hijacked ships anchored off Somali pirate villages.

The skipper, Cdr. Jim McGovern, had his OPS (operations) officer contact the task force commander, a French admiral, as well as Fifth Fleet in Bahrain. His orders were to remain covert, outside the radar range of the ship. Just seeing another vessel on radar from their position about twenty-five miles off the Somali coast was unusual, much less seeing one closing on the beach. Most merchantmen were staying several hundred miles off-shore to avoid the pirates. McGovern said crewmen spotted the ship early on Saturday afternoon, when they had been looking forward to a relaxing steel beach party. The transition to alert status was stark. "I thought to myself, no days in the Navy on deployment finish the way they start."

To McGovern and his team, it looked as though they were watching a hijacking. That supposition was confirmed as fact after a call was made to the shipping company's office in Copenhagen to tell the owners that the U.S. Navy had just observed *Danica White* headed toward Mogadishu with three boats in tow. "Is this correct?"

The company sent a private "captain's message" to *Danica White*. No response. Copenhagen then notified *Carter Hall*, according to the Danish report, "that *Danica White* was not supposed to head towards Mogadishu, and that it seemed not to be under the shipping company's control."

Initially, McGovern was ordered to maintain covert surveillance. *Carter Hall* brought up all engines and, making twenty-four knots, flanked the hijacked vessel, staying outside of her radar range. Then McGovern got orders to move in. "We started to close the ship; it maintained the same course and same speed the entire time. They didn't even flinch."

McGovern told me that his staff had been put through antipiracy classroom scenarios at Tactical Training Group Atlantic, so there was no question they were trained to handle the situation. He gave the conn to his executive officer (XO), Cdr. Nathan Strandquist, an excellent ship handler, and had his OPS officer, Lt. Tina Dalmau, handle communications with higher headquarters. That gave the skipper the ability to be hands on with the gun crews.

Carter Hall called *Danica White* on bridge-to-bridge radio. "The master said the men on board were Somali fishermen and he's helping them out. We knew they weren't fishermen—unless they were fishing with

AK-47s." There was at least one armed man on the bridge wing, and others were very quickly taking strategic positions on the ship. McGovern said, "When you think of Somali pirates, you think of a ragtag band. That's not what I saw. I saw guys that maintained muzzle discipline—at no time did anyone point a gun at our ship, even when we were firing at them."

When *Carter Hall* and the hijacked ship were still about an hour from reaching Somali territorial waters, the task force commander began asking McGovern to take more aggressive action. While preparing to do so, the skipper got another request from TF 150. "They wanted to know if we could ram the ship. Or shoulder it."

"I'm thinking, easy for you to say," McGovern recalls. Instead, he ordered his XO to get as close as he could to *Danica White* and see if they could force the pirates to change course. "We came up close, then crossed the bow. My ship handler said it wasn't the closest maneuver he'd ever done to another ship—but it was pretty close."

He'd already mustered his boarding team members and, despite rough seas, said they could have put a boat in the water without a problem. In fact, he was asked if they could board the ship. "I said, 'We could, but I think it's risky—and here's why.' The pirates had guys in well-covered high positions that could have easily engaged the boarding team. Would they have done that? I don't know."

Instead of launching the visit, board, search, and seizure team, they were given authorization to fire warning shots, and did so using a GAU minigun mounted on the bridge wing. McGovern said they put out about five hundred rounds, tearing up the water fifty yards in front of the pirated ship. Zero effect.

Daylight was running out, and they were now getting uncomfortably close to the twelve-mile territorial limit. That's when they got authorization to sink the three skiffs towed out behind *Danica White*. They maneuvered into position and opened fire on the trailing skiffs with their 25-mm chain gun and the twin-50s. McGovern said they were about five hundred yards away and the moonlight was pretty good when they began shooting. "It took us a while to get dialed in. We engaged the first skiff, the line breaks, there's a small fire and it began to sink. Then the second skiff, we fired for maybe twenty seconds. The forward skiff had a bunch of fifty-five gallon drums on it. It was three shots—*Boom! Boom! Boom!* And the thing exploded. By that time the gunner had dialed in the elevation and range—he just nailed it. It was pretty spectacular—like New Year's Eve."

But the pirates never slowed down, never changed course. And the navigator on the *Carter Hall* bridge was counting down the distance to Somali territory. It was about three miles away and they were doing eight knots.

That's when the notion of disabling fire, which had been mentioned by the ship's owner, was discussed with higher headquarters. McGovern did not see it as a reasonable solution to their problem. "We could have tried to go to disabling fire. At that point, if you can't get them off the ship, they'd have five hostages. Firing at the ship was a non-starter. From a preservation of human life perspective, it doesn't make sense. The last thing we want to do is harm an innocent sailor. Sure, we could have tried disabling fire, but at what cost? Now you have a ship that's got no propulsion. You've got ten to fifteen bad guys and five good guys. You've seen in the past what happens when the bad guys get antsy, get defensive. They kill the hostages. To escalate it any further than that may have resulted in loss of life of innocent mariners." He was referring to the tragedy during an attempt by Navy SEALs to rescue four American hostages held aboard their sailboat, SV *Quest.*

Captain McGovern's recommendations were never questioned by his command. He said, "Their response was always measured; their handling of the situation and the escalation of it was spot on."

To their disappointment, the crew members of *Carter Hall* could do nothing more than watch the hijacked ship head to the pirate's anchorage. They turned away at twelve and a half miles and stayed offshore for the remainder of the night. McGovern had sought permission to follow *Danica White* into Somali waters but his request was denied.

From where I sit—from where I sat—that troubles me. Never mind that there was no effective government in that country. Never mind that there was really no one to ask for permission. Never mind that our warship was in hot pursuit. It was just like that damned kid's game, olly olly oxen free! They got past the line without being tagged. They're free to go. Who was going to get angry with us if we went into territorial waters to try and save those hostages? The nonexistent government of a failed state?

But *Carter Hall* had fired some serious weaponry in an effort to break up that hijacking, and in my mind, that represented a real commitment to the fight. I figured the diplomats and politicians would work out the niceties sooner or later; at least our navy could use the gear we'd been issued to begin dealing with this scourge.

Anti-Piracy Planning Chart
Red Sea, Gulf of Aden, and Arabian Sea

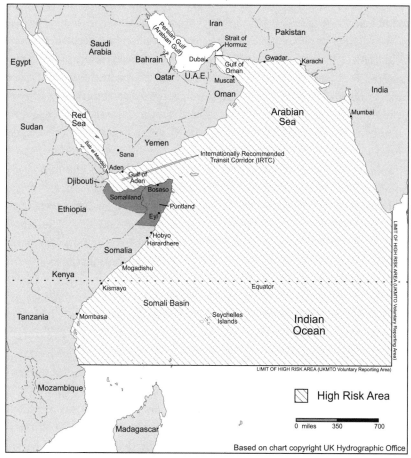

Based on chart copyright UK Hydrographic Office

This map, issued by UKMTO, the British Maritime Trade Operations antipiracy office in Dubai, designates the high-risk area for Somali piracy, which now includes much of the Indian Ocean. Over three years, the high-risk area has expanded from less than three times the size of the Gulf of Mexico to an area roughly equivalent to the size of the entire continental United States. The U.S. Navy Office of Naval Intelligence issues a weekly report on pirate activity, including a specialized weather and Sea State forecast that suggests what areas will likely be more vulnerable to attack from pirate skiffs. It also provides information about vessels currently being held for ransom. Readers interested in tracking pirate activity may check the site at www.oni.navy.mil/Intelligence_Community/piracy.htm.

Five months later, on 28 October 2007, those niceties still hadn't been worked out, but our playbook changed. Somali pirates hijacked the Japanese-owned tanker MV *Golden Nori* traveling from Singapore to the southern Israeli port of Eilat with a cargo that included 40,000 tons of highly explosive industrial benzene. War rooms at the Pentagon, U.S. Central Command (CENTCOM), Naval Forces Central Command (NAVCENT), and I'm guessing in the Situation Room at the White House quickly began thinking "*BOOM!*—we've got a 400-foot-long self-propelled floating bomb potentially headed to the Bab el-Mandeb choke point between the Gulf of Aden and the Red Sea, or to the southern end of the Suez Canal."

Someone called an audible, and when the pirates took the ship inside Somali territorial waters, they had company. Both the USS *Arleigh Burke* and the USS *Porter* shadowed *Golden Nori*. News media at the time speculated that the hijacking was a terrorist event in the making. The *Times* (U.K.) online provided this breathless update: "Laden with its highly flammable cargo of benzene, the *Golden Nori* floats like a ticking bomb off the coast of Somalia. The pirates who have hijacked her are threatening to kill the crew if their $1 million (£490,000) ransom demand is not met, while two U.S. warships train their cannons on the vessel."

The strategy adopted in that case was to target the skiffs that were bringing supplies out to the pirates aboard the captive ship. The Puntland government sent militia to the pirate-friendly port of Bosaso while negotiations were being conducted.

What no one said in that case—at least not aloud—is that we didn't have the legal authority to pursue *Golden Nori* into Somali territorial waters. It would be another thirteen months, 2 December 2008, before the UN Security Council adopted Resolution 1846, which acknowledged receipt of consent from the so-called Transitional Federal Government to "enter into the territorial waters of Somalia for the purpose of repressing acts of piracy and armed robbery at sea, in a manner consistent with such action permitted on the high seas with respect to piracy under relevant international law; and use . . . all necessary means to repress acts of piracy and armed robbery at sea."

Three weeks after Resolution 1846 was unanimously adopted, I received orders from the chief of naval operations to stand up Combined Task Force 151. The fight was on. It was going to be Terry and the Pirates.

CHAPTER 1

Rules of Engagement

They must have known I was coming. On 8 January 2009 the Commander U.S. Fifth Fleet, Vice Adm. William Gortney, announced the formation of Combined Task Force 151 (CTF 151) in the Gulf of Aden to combat piracy. A day later, apparently not wanting to mess with the old swashbuckler McKnight, the pirates accepted a payment of $3 million and released the largest ship they've ever held for ransom, the 1,090-foot very large crude carrier MV *Sirius Star*. The behemoth had been captured 450 miles southeast of the Kenyan coast on 15 November 2008. She carried a crew of twenty-five, and in her tanks were 2.2 million barrels of U.S.-bound Saudi Arabian oil worth $100 million. The hijacking caused a one-dollar jump in the spot price of crude on the world's markets. But it also signaled to me that the pirates were no longer confining their activities to the Somali coastline and the Gulf of Aden.

It's been suggested to me that I got the assignment because some wag in the Bureau of Naval Personnel was familiar with the long-lived "Terry and the Pirates" comic strip by Milton Caniff. In my experience, that kind of creativity doesn't play a role in the Flag Matters process, but the reference did serve as a starting point for many conversations at NAVCENT, especially the one in which Vice Admiral Gortney ordered me to "go catch some pirates."

The assignment was unique—and a dream—because there was no book or hard drive sitting on anyone's shelf with the rules and regs for doing the job. But my thirty-year career had prepared me to figure things out. I was commissioned in 1978 after earning my degree in history from Virginia Military Institute (VMI), and I served aboard six warships, including tours as commanding officer of USS *Whidbey*

Island (LSD 41) and USS *Kearsarge* (LHD3), before becoming executive assistant to the undersecretary of the navy.

Shortly after I was informed by Secretary of the Navy Gordon England that I had been selected for flag officer (officially announced April Fools Day 2005), I was notified that my first assignment as rear admiral would be as the commandant of Naval District Washington. Most aspiring flag officers would view this assignment as a step off the fast track to bigger and better leadership positions. As a VMI graduate with a history degree, I really looked forward to the assignment because of its deep roots in naval history.

The Washington Navy Yard is the oldest naval installation in the Navy and in the early days of our nation was the Navy's largest shipyard. During the Civil War, President Abraham Lincoln would visit the Yard to confer with Comdt. John Dahlgren on the latest developments in naval gunnery. The Yard is also famous for receiving the dignified remains of the Unknown Soldier from World War I, and after his famous transatlantic flight, Charles A. Lindbergh returned to America aboard USS *Memphis* and disembarked at the Yard to a tumultuous welcome. Still rich in naval history, the Yard today serves as a major office complex for the Navy.

During my tour as commandant, the Chinese chief of naval operations, Vice Admiral Wu Shengli, visited Washington. Part of the staff that accompanied the admiral on his visit was the naval attaché from China's embassy, Senior Captain Liu Hongwei. As a result of the numerous social functions that we were required to attend, my wife, Lisa, and I had become very good friends with Captain Liu and his wife, Yun. I had no idea that that relationship would pay big dividends a few years later, when I was aboard my flagship in the Gulf of Aden chasing pirates.

Lisa and I made some lifelong friends during our tour in the Navy Yard, and even to this day many people come up to me and say how warm and friendly she made the "Quarterdeck of the Navy" to our guests. We understood the importance of working as coalition partners, and these lessons played a major part in my daily interaction with the members of Task Force 151 and other navies in the Gulf of Aden.

When I stood up CTF 151, the pirates had the upper hand, and the combined forces based in Bahrain needed a task force designated specifically to fight piracy. The existing CTF 150 was formed as a counterterrorism unit, and it complicated the situation to have 150 try to go after pirates when certain countries in that task force didn't even have laws against piracy.

Retired Royal Navy captain David Bancroft, who was the first officer in charge at United Kingdom Maritime Trade Operations (UKMTO) in Dubai—the office that is first point of contact for civilian vessels under pirate attack—said that the coalition forces missed an opportunity just a few months before I arrived. He recently told me, "If the politicians had allowed the Navy, both U.K. and U.S., to be more robust after the 21st of August 2008—we lost five ships in just over twenty-four hours; *Yenagoa Ocean* being used as the mother ship to launch multiple attacks—then I honestly believe we could have knocked this problem on the head early. However, the kid-gloves approach that was taken gave rise to the pirates' brazen acts, as they knew very little action would be taken."

Interestingly enough, Vice Admiral Gortney, a jet jockey with more carrier landings than the Pentagon has field grade officers, acknowledged that this kid-gloves approach had permitted the pirates to come up with a pretty good business model. In a voice that sounds as though he's pounding on his desk even when he's just saying "good morning," he said the pirate mantra goes like this: "They will not shoot at me. I will get their money. And no one will arrest me. It's a good job."

Now it was my job to try to change all that. Two days after arriving in Bahrain I caught a flight to Djibouti, and then a helo out to the first of what would be four flagships, USS *San Antonio*, an amphibious transport dock ship. It was great to be back at sea with a mission that my staff and I could plan from scratch. Unfortunately, half of my staff of fifty had to remain behind at NAVCENT, because although *San Antonio* had room to spare while the Marines she normally carried were deployed in Iraq, we wouldn't be aboard her for very long, and things would be getting much, much tighter when we changed flagships.

Let's talk a bit about building a staff. In World War II, it was all about fighters who know how to win a battle. Today, my two most important people are my judge advocate general (JAG) officer—my lawyer—and my public affairs officer (PAO). Those are the people who may not help you win the battle, but they're going to keep your backside out of trouble.

Right after our team got our mission assignment, we were given our public affairs guidance. It was beaten into us that the barefoot Somalis with AK-47s that we plucked out of skiffs were "suspected pirates." Even though they were captured two hundred miles offshore with weapons, a boarding ladder, and absolutely no fishing gear, they were suspected pirates. Now I suppose you're asking, what's the difference between a suspected pirate and a pirate? An excellent question. I used to drive my PAO crazy with it. "When does he get his pirate merit badge?" Never got an answer. Just got more reminders not to call them pirates or terrorists. I guess if they were convicted—and you'll be reading an entire chapter about the likelihood of that happening—then they would be official pirates. But that's the type of thing war fighters are faced with out there.

At one point, we caught so many suspected pirates that we had no place to put them. So NAVCENT sent us USNS *Lewis and Clark*, a supply ship, and the crew members built facilities on her to hold the suspects until we could make other arrangements. In fact, the primary reason *Lewis and Clark* was there was to keep suspected pirates behind bars. Our public affairs guidance was to never—under pain of being keelhauled or something worse—ever refer to *Lewis and Clark* as a prison ship. It was beaten into us: "This is not a prison ship out in the middle of the ocean. They're only holding suspected pirates for a short period of time." I was given pages and pages of public affairs guidance rather than extensive operating plans on how to capture pirates.

One of the great things working in our favor when I got out there was that we actually had UN approval to go inside Somali territorial waters. And we could send our unmanned aerial vehicle (UAV), a ScanEagle, over the pirate villages and even farther inland. We had USS *Mahan* with us, and her crew could put a UAV into the air and keep it up there for eight to ten hours. They're tremendous assets—real force multipliers, doing things like pattern-of-life flights over fishing villages. We also had access to AFRICOM P-3s flying out of Djibouti, plus the helicopters that we had on board most of the ships. So we had a lot of air assets to work with.

While we were actively searching for pirates, the task force staff back in Bahrain was working on plans—how to conduct antipirate operations; what to do with prisoners; how to communicate, especially to deconflict air space when we've got several coalition navies flying helos in the same neighborhood; and the ever-changing rules of engagement (ROE). The problem was that we didn't have six months' lead time; we needed plans for the mission we were already working.

My first day out on *San Antonio* was beautiful. In fact, the entire time I was out there, I don't think the seas ever got over six inches, and it wasn't even terribly hot except for the middle of the day. Just a light sea breeze and no rain. The monsoon season that year was tame, which made it great pirate weather. It's why I say that piracy is a seasonal sport. During the monsoons that usually occur in June through August and December through February, the pirates stay home. That's precisely why I believe we could really work a plan that brought in heavy naval assets during pirate season and leave a limited show of force during the monsoon season.

Despite the fact that the task force had at various times ships from almost two dozen countries working this antipiracy mission, there were only three countries whose ships were actually permitted to capture pirates: the United States, United Kingdom, and Denmark. Everyone else was only permitted to deter piracy. The problem had to do with what would happen to any suspected pirates we picked up. We had a working memorandum of understanding (MOU) with Kenya, as did the Brits and Danes. But if, for example, the Turks snatched up some pirate suspects, they had to let them go. I asked if they could be transferred to one of our ships and then delivered to Kenya and was told, "No, that ain't gonna happen."

We had a great example of this problem when the German replenishment tanker FGS *Spessart* was attacked by pirates. They were repelled by the onboard security team, and several coalition warships gave chase. Fairly soon, we had them surrounded. But my JAG officer said we couldn't capture the pirates because they'd attacked a German ship and the Germans wanted them. So we had to keep them encircled until a German navy frigate arrived, picked up the pirates, and then waited for their government to decide whether to prosecute. The Germans were afraid that if we took them on board *Boxer*, then we (the Americans) would get to decide. It was nuts. I can't count the times I said to Lt. Cdr. Pete Koebler, my JAG officer, "You're kidding me!" But he never was.

A lot of it was fallout from Iraq, from Abu Ghraib. Koebler and my PAO, Lt. Cdr. John Fage, were the key folks making certain that we never ran afoul of the rules about treatment of detainees, which meant there'd never be any bad press about their treatment at our hands. And their task was no slam dunk, because the rules of engagement were rubbery—they would bend this way and that, depending on who was sitting in the chair back in Bahrain. So crazy things would happen.

We didn't bag any pirates during my three weeks on *San Antonio*. That's not to say that we didn't catch any—we just had to throw them back. Okay, so officially, they weren't pirates. Let's call them a group of mariners who said they were from Somalia, who just happened to be drifting at sea in a skiff. There was no doubt in my mind or anyone else's that they were engaged in illegal activity that was close to piracy. But we hadn't caught them in the act. Maybe they were amateur astronomers and were out there stargazing, or naval gazing. Who knows?

In one particular instance, our lookout spotted a boat with five or six young guys in it. It had no motor and wasn't terribly seaworthy. Our interpreter tried to piece together their story but couldn't nail it down. Ultimately, we figured that they must have annoyed the pirate leader on a mother ship, and he took their motor and just set them adrift to die. No question in my mind that these guys were pirates—or pirate wannabes. Our obligation at that point, however, was to treat them as mariners in distress and rescue them.

After much back and forth between my JAG and the lawyers in Bahrain, we were told to take them to the Yemeni port of Aden, where USS *Cole* had been attacked. We began a sprint in that direction and then got new instructions. Yemen wouldn't take them. NAVCENT had a new plan: they would have to be taken back to Somalia. We ended up transferring them to *Mahan*, which would undertake a pattern-of-life mission while down there and eventually hand off the forlorn mariners to the Puntland Coast Guard. I had every expectation that, sooner or later, one of our ships would be picking up these same folks again. All I could hope was that when it happened, we'd catch them red-handed.

CHAPTER 2

Finally, Terry Meets the Pirates

Things were tighter when my staff and I moved to USS *Vella Gulf* (CG-72), making her the second of four flagships during my command of CTF 151. When you see the numbers, it's easy to understand what I mean. *San Antonio* was built to carry a compliment of 669 sailors and Marines, including 66 officers. *Vella Gulf*, commissioned in 1993, was a much older ship, a *Ticonderoga*-class Aegis guided-missile cruiser designed for a crew of 360 with accommodations for only 33 officers. Even with my staff trimmed way down for sea duty, we were going to displace a lot of folks, and while we all knew that the mission comes first, it was still on my mind when we made the transfer.

The skipper of *Vella Gulf*, Capt. Mark D. Genung, was seeing the flip side of that equation. He knew we were coming off *San Antonio*, a relatively spacious, almost-new ship that not only had accommodations for a flag staff but had lots of room in which planning and ops staff could work, and it was going to be a tight squeeze to make things function smoothly on his much smaller cruiser.

Even so, there was a tangible change in mood when we got to the *Vella Gulf*. Unlike *San Antonio*, this ship had been fighting pirates for a while. So their heads were in the game from day one. The commanding officer (CO) said to me, "Okay, this is how we've trained; this is how we do it." He was essentially in Condition 3 counterpiracy operations. A quick explanation: Condition 1 is general quarters—you're under attack, you're taking shots. Condition 2 is a modified state; you're in a stressful situation, you may even be under attack, but you can't have the whole crew constantly in a high state of readiness, so you're kind of 50/50. Condition 3 is what you'd call wartime steaming—when you're in an environment going after somebody. This is your mission and this is what you can do. Condition 4 is steaming from Norfolk to Fort Lauderdale—no stress, maybe doing some training. *Vella Gulf* was in Condition 3, fully engaged, weapons systems manned, and helicopters flying almost every day. It was a true Condition 3 counterpiracy operation, and I loved it.

It's worth taking the time to tell the story of how the *Vella Gulf* prepared for the antipiracy mission because it's a great example of how a superb commander anticipates things to come. On the ship's previous deployment to the eastern Pacific, Genung was satisfied with the work his crew had done capturing drug smugglers. He had a great air detachment from the "Proud Warriors" of HSL-42 under the direction of its officer in charge (OIC), Lt. Cdr. Matt Bradshaw, as well as a very strong visit, board, search, and seizure (VBSS) team, but he was concerned that their skills would atrophy between the time they left the United States and began patrolling Pirate Alley several months later.

Since there were limited formal instructions for capturing pirates and embarking them on the ship, Genung's crew began coming up with its own techniques and procedures. Genung described the problem this way. "How do I capture a bunch of pissed off, probably narced-up, and probably heavily armed suspected pirates and get them off by small boat where you can't segregate them from each other, and then bring them back to the ship, all the while not getting any of my sailors hurt?"

It's well known that the pirates are young, often stoned on khat— a narcotic leaf they chew to get high and ward off seasickness—and armed with automatic weapons. Not a great combination. So Genung's plan involved not only the logistics of capturing the pirates and getting them onto his ship but also figuring out what happens if there's a firefight. Who does triage? Where? Just getting the wounded aboard from a small boat presents a challenge. If the pirates (or crew, for that matter) were injured and unable to climb a ladder, they would have to be put in one of the ship's rigid-hulled inflatable boats (RHIB) and brought up in the RHIB using davits. That can be challenging enough; doing it while the injured person is screaming in pain, bleeding, or going into shock adds another element of stress. To prepare for the eventuality of a firefight, Genung said, "We ran this as an exercise on ourselves, where I had sailors who volunteered to be pirates, and used all the techniques [necessary] to capture these pirates and bring them aboard."

You may be wondering why every Navy ship out there doesn't have personnel trained to handle hostile situations. It comes back to a policy decision that has been debated for years. Nearly every ship has what is called a Level II boarding team. This is the standard team that does routine, compliant boardings, where the master agrees, "Okay, you can come inspect my ship." The issue has been whether all ships should have what are called Level III boarding teams, that is, teams that can do noncompliant boardings. They can go in and put guns to foreheads if that's what is required. The Navy made a conscious decision not to train and fund ships to have the capability for a Level III boarding team, which has now become a problem for the antipiracy mission. When you're going after pirates, if it's an aggressive situation and you don't have a Level III team that's trained to take these guys under fire, you have to back off. Level IV teams, by the way, are special operation forces; in my opinion, there are not enough of those out there either. The only time CTF-151 has a Level III capability is when there is an amphibious ship with embarked Marines assigned to the task force. The Marines made the decision to have a trained Level III boarding team as part of their deployable forces. This has proved to be beneficial on several occasions, including the rescue of the crew members of MV *Magellan Star* in September 2010.

Although there is an antiterrorism element to fighting piracy, it plays out primarily on land. At sea, CTF 151 is engaged in a law enforcement activity, and suddenly *Vella Gulf*'s sailors were going to be cops and jailers, certainly missions for which most of them had not been trained. Genung's good luck was having a couple of crew members aboard who had been stationed at Guantánamo, and they were able to take the lead in offering suggestions on handling prisoners in a manner that kept everyone—good guys and bad guys—safe.

As I've mentioned, *Vella Gulf* had been deployed on anti-drug-running missions in the eastern Pacific, so there was some experience in law enforcement but with Coast Guard law enforcement detachment (LEDET) teams taking the lead. Drug runners are much less inclined to use their weapons than are young Somali pirates who've been taught that firing an AK-47 and rocket-propelled grenades at big ships is a way to scare them into submission. Genung was also conscious of the potential dark side of turning volunteer sailors into prison guards. There would be no Abu Ghraib incidents under his command.

Long before I came aboard and *Vella Gulf* became flagship for CTF 151, Genung had worked with Vice Admiral Gortney at Fifth Fleet to come up with an acceptable way to confine pirate suspects. His initial assignment had been to provide safe accommodations for as many as fifty prisoners, but that proved to be unrealistic for many reasons. Gortney finally settled on a plan for embarking twelve suspects inside the skin of the ship. It involved "pirate proofing" (think "baby proofing," but for people who hate you) a passageway in the area where sailors returning from a chemical-biological-nuclear warfare environment outside the ship are decontaminated. The area is immediately aft of sick bay, which made it ideal for getting the pirates processed through a medical evaluation, getting them cleaned up and showered, and clothing them in disposable coveralls—the so-called poopie suits that sailors wear to protect their uniforms when they're emptying sewage tanks. The combination of constant training coupled with preparation of physical facilities, all supervised by a skipper who had totally bought into the antipiracy mission, made *Vella Gulf* ready long before I came aboard.

But there's another chapter in the story of *Vella Gulf* that needs to be told before I get on with my CTF 151 pirate-catching saga, and that's the amazing job Captain Genung and his crew did with the hijacked Ukrainian-operated RO/RO (roll-on/roll-off) MV *Faina* just prior to the cruiser being assigned as my flagship. On 25 September 2008 (my birthday), the 500-foot, 13,870-ton Belize-flagged ship and her crew of twenty-one were hijacked by as many as fifty Somali pirates who identified themselves as the Central Regional Coast Guard. The vessel was heading to Mombasa, Kenya, with thirty-three Soviet-made T-72 tanks, antiaircraft guns mounted on four-wheel carriages, heavy trucks mounted with a multiple-launch rocket system, rocket-propelled grenades, and 812 tons of ammunition. The pirates claimed that documents found on board indicated that the cargo was destined for Juba, Southern Sudan, rather than for the Kenyan military, and there were press reports saying that the U.S. Office of Naval Intelligence (ONI), as well as other intelligence groups, had confirmed that claim, even though the Kenyan military denied it and said the arms were to be deployed only within Kenya.

The pirates initially set the ship on a course toward their stronghold near the city of Eyl in the northern Puntland region of Somalia but changed direction slightly when USS *Howard* caught up with them.

The orders to the Americans were clear: under no circumstances does *Faina*'s cargo reach land. The ship ended up anchored in more than forty fathoms of water about eight miles off the village of Hinbarwaqo, between the pirate-friendly ports of Harardhere and Hobyo, and there it stayed under pirate control for 133 days, blockaded by warships from the United States the entire time, and occasionally by at least one Russian ship, the missile frigate *Neustrashimy*, while negotiations took place over a ransom demand that began at $35 million and eventually declined to the $3.2 million that was reportedly paid by the ship's owners. Additionally, NAVCENT stationed the fleet tug USNS *Catawba* (T-ATF-168) to provide logistical support to *Faina*.

Puntland's minister of fisheries, Ahmed Said Aw-nur, was quoted by multiple news outlets, including the *New York Times*, urging a commando military operation, presumably by U.S. forces, to regain control of the ship. "If the Islamists get the arms, they will cause problems for all of Somalia." U.S. intelligence agencies apparently had drawn similar conclusions, but storming the ship had been ruled out. I'm guessing that there was real concern that the pirates would carry through on their threat to blow up the ship and the hostages—and everyone knew they had the wherewithal to do it.

So it became a waiting game, and the mission of playing man-to-man defense—making certain that nothing on board *Faina* made it to shore—fell to *Vella Gulf* for more than one hundred of those days. Nothing I've experienced or read during my time fighting and later studying piracy comes close to explaining the human agony caused by these pirates as does the experience that Captain Genung had during that assignment. For a couple of reasons, I've asked him to tell me precisely and completely how it played out for himself and for the hostages: first, because the question of whether fighting piracy is a valid mission for our Navy keeps popping up, and second, because many dozen merchant and fishing ships and crews have been held for ransom off the Somali coast—some for more than a year. Only in the case of *Faina* do we have an almost day-by-day account of the hell that those ill-fated hostages have been put through.

It began on 29 September, when, as captain of *Vella Gulf*, Mark Genung assumed duties as the on-scene commander from the departing USS *Howard*. The deal *Howard*'s skipper had made through his Somali interpreter was that the Americans would permit the pirates to resupply themselves aboard *Faina* in exchange for the right to speak with the master on a daily basis or as often as desired. Genung believes the pirates saw the agreement as positive because it allowed them to be confident that some level of negotiations would continue for the release of the ship. *Faina* was also the only hijacked ship anchored off the coast of Somalia that had a warship nearby, causing him to also believe that in the Somalis' minds, if they made that concession, the Americans would be unlikely to undertake a more kinetic response.

By the time *Vella Gulf* arrived, the Russian master of *Faina*, Vladimir Kolobkov, had died, probably from heat stress or a heart attack, and the only other Russian aboard (most of the crew was Ukrainian), first mate or chief officer Viktor Nikolsky, had assumed command. He, along with another officer, manned the bridge 24/7 at the direction of the pirates. Initially, Genung and Nikolsky spoke via bridge-to-bridge radio three times a day, but eventually they settled into a twice-a-day routine, typically at one in the afternoon and then again in the evening, and they did it every day that *Vella Gulf* was on station.

"My assignment was multiple," Captain Genung recalled in a lengthy conversation. "It was to ensure that none of the munitions on that ship left; to ensure that *Faina* did not get under way; to enable the safe release of the hostages; and finally—and I'm sure the admiral will probably laugh at this—to ensure it didn't get any worse."

Genung was right. I did laugh. Our Navy often gives its skippers missions where they're required to be successful, but higher command knows there's no way in hell that success is solely in the hands of that captain. You'll read about a few more missions like this in later chapters. Our intel on the *Faina* had been pretty good. Although ONI was certain that the vessel had not been targeted because the pirates knew what it was carrying, now that the bad guys had a chance to read the manifest and examine the cargo, they knew what they had stumbled upon. Somali experts interviewed for this book tended to downplay the importance of the capture of *Faina* because, they said, it's a RO/RO ship, and there's no Somali port at which those Russian tanks could be driven off, adding that even if the ship were run aground near the beach, unless they cut a massive hole in the side of the ship the tanks wouldn't make it to shore. But that doesn't mean that the pirates might not try to get some of the volatile cargo ashore. Genung explained it in detail:

I don't know how familiar you are with Soviet armor, especially the older armor. They're relatively thin skinned, so one way to defeat an antitank round the Soviets developed was something called reactive armor. And the way it works on the outside of the tank, when a round hits it, this reactive armor actually explodes. It dissipates the force of the round, making it less likely that it'll actually penetrate the thin armor of the tank and take it out of commission. Well, think of what we've been dealing with for years and years in Iraq and Afghanistan and potentially in other places around the world with IEDs [improvised explosive devices]. Reactive armor—I suspect, I'm no expert—would probably be some of the finest IED-making material in the world.

So while it was true that there was no way those tanks were going to be driven off *Faina*, there was a possibility that the explosive armor, the small arms, and tons of ammunition could be offloaded into small boats and ferried ashore. That could not be allowed to happen.

Included in *Vella Gulf*'s mission of not letting things get any worse was the concern that terrorists would try to either capture or damage the cargo on *Faina*. "Think about what's going on in Somalia at the time," Genung said to me.

You've got this low-grade civil war ongoing; you got al-Shabaab now getting involved in this civil war, and arguably, they were not necessarily in favor of piracy. But the pirates had reported that the manifest showed that these weapons were going to the government of South Sudan—it said "GOSS." There were significant signs that al-Shabaab would either (a) want that cargo for themselves for the IED-making material that we described, or (b) would not want those munitions to go to the government of South Sudan because that's a predominantly Christian group as opposed to the Muslim north. So there's a bunch of reasons why al-Shabaab would not want that ship to be able to either send the cargo forward or even to leave Somali waters.

So, again, I had multiple responsibilities. I had to be able to defend the ship against an external attack. I had to ensure none of the cargo left. I was there to ensure the negotiations would culminate in the safe release of hostages, and then, whatever the heck else, don't let the situation get any worse than it already is.

In addition to Genung's regular crew, he had a five-man sniper detachment of Marines off the amphibious assault ship USS *Iwo Jima* that would man stations in case a firefight erupted.

We periodically did health and comfort imagery, where we would work with the pirates and ask for all the hostages to be put on the bridge. The more we did this, in my opinion it became more and more likely that one of the hostages who clearly were psychologically [troubled]—it was a very tough situation for them—[would do something]. I became aware that we could have a Berlin Wall situation where one or more of the hostages could attempt to jump in the water and try to get rescued, and I might find myself in a firefight. The Marines were part of our ability to be able to respond to that.

Captain Genung's assignment to guard *Faina* and, in essence, give hope to her imprisoned crew was personally transformative in ways that military assignments rarely are. I asked him how having those twice-a-day conversations with Nikolsky affected him.

As time went on, I found myself being a mentor to him. When I'm talking to Viktor and saying, "Viktor, how're you doing?" He says, "I'm not sure we're gonna get outta here. I don't think we're gonna get out of this alive." And so, I'm finding myself on a bridge-to-bridge radio mentoring somebody who was not the captain when this whole thing started, who is now the acting master, and as a commanding officer of a navy warship, talking to another commanding officer of his ship, saying, "Captain, you have to be strong for your crew because they are looking to you for strength. I assure you that you will be home with your son again. I, or another United States ship, will always be here until you're released by the pirates. This will end, and you will come home." But keep in mind, it was a very, very tough situation. The pirates had taken most of their clothes, a lot of their personal effects. They're only eating one meal a day. The crew, compared to the master and the first mate who was up on the bridge with him, had it far worse because they were in a relatively small space about twenty-three hours out of the day. I had negotiated with the pirates to at least give the crew an opportunity to get out and get some fresh air about an hour a day, and we would routinely watch that happen, and I would note it when it didn't happen. And I would remind Viktor. And also keep in mind that relative to earlier in the process, the ship ran out of fuel for operating their main electric plant, which meant that about twelve hours of the day they had no lights, no ventilation, no pumps that provided water. We were very near the Equator and, although it was September through January, when the sun shines on a steel ship that's a dark blue with a white superstructure, it's gonna get warm inside, especially with twenty people inside a small space. So it was hell on earth.

On a personal level, Viktor would share with us the telephone number of his son, and we would call and talk to his son and let him know that he was alive. When we took those pictures, they were very important to me for a number of reasons. They allowed us to understand the health of the hostages. It was a means for me, as a naval officer, to ensure that their families knew that their sons were okay, because one of my best means of intelligence was Google alerts. We could see what would pop up regarding *Faina*. And oftentimes, within a day or so of the pictures that we would generate and they would get released by Fifth Fleet, they'd be reproduced in the Ukrainian and Russian newspapers, so we could have a great deal of confidence that their families could see them. So [it affected me] on a lot of levels, as a human being, as a naval officer, as a commanding officer of my ship, as a brother captain. A lot of levels.

I asked Genung if he had been provided assistance from any psychologists who might suggest ways to sustain Nikolsky and his crew. "No, this was based on almost thirty years of [on-the-job training], it was based on experience. I guess the sea story—it takes sixteen or seventeen years to grow to be a commander of a ship. I took command of *Vella Gulf* around the twenty-two-year point of my naval service. But nothing in my training had ever prepared me for this. Just the medical assistance team and discussing things with my senior leadership, my XO, and other folks as we talked through the situation."

Only twice during *Vella Gulf*'s more than three months of guard duty did she go off station. The first occurred when a petty officer was diagnosed with acute appendicitis. Genung left a command element and all his Marines aboard the fleet tug *Catawba* and raced south at maximum speed. Then he put the sailor and a corpsman on a helicopter at maximum range and launched the helo to another Navy ship that was farther south. That ship raced south and at its maximum range launched the helo and brought the sailor to Mombasa, Kenya, where he was transferred to a fixed-wing aircraft and flown to Nairobi, where he was successfully operated on. That took *Vella Gulf* off station for about a day. Then, in December 2009, after some seventy days keeping watch over the hijacked ship, *Vella Gulf* was relieved by USS *Mason* in order to do a four-day port visit to the Seychelles, which Genung describes as "one of the nicest liberty ports in that neck of the woods."

The logistical support this particular group of Somali pirates had was extensive. Genung said that every day, or at least two out of every three days, a skiff would make the eight-mile trip from the pirate village with provisions. If it brought meat, it would take the form of a couple of live goats that would be slaughtered on board as needed. About every five days the pirates guarding the hostages would be brought a supply of khat. And periodically the guards would be changed, with the pirate commanders rotating every two or three weeks. Genung was able to keep track of those changes because he'd realized that the voice he was hearing on the radio had changed. "They would say something to the effect, 'He wasn't feeling well because he's got malaria, so he's at the hospital.' But my sense probably was that he was home for a conjugal visit and after his two weeks off, he was gonna come back and relieve the other guy again. And they would just trade off, back and forth."

I was curious about his negotiations with the pirates to allow the hostages time each day on an open deck. I asked what he had to offer to get that concession. "Keep in mind," he told me,

> it's bad for business for the hostages to get hurt or die, because then from [the pirates'] perspective, governments would consider potentially more extraordinary measures to get those hostages back, versus paying a ransom. The pirates were very reluctant to even admit the death of the master. We only figured it out because there was some confusion on the issue once I got a whole copy of the manifest from the shipping company and compared it to the name of the guy I was talking to— hey, that's not Vladimir, that's Viktor. And then they finally admitted it.
>
> So my sense was that we appealed to the pirates' desire that the hostages remain in good health and that we are assured of that. Then it was more likely that everybody would negotiate in good faith. Keep in mind as this was going down, this was about the same time that the Russians deployed some ships down into the Gulf of Oman, and there was a lot of thought on our part whether or not the Russians were actually going to turn south and come down to my neck of the woods, which would've made things interesting. The Russians had indicated that they were pretty unhappy about this; it was a Russian master who had died, a Russian acting master, a Ukrainian ship, so they have some relationships with the Ukrainian government. So I could see the pirates potentially [making a deal with us] for a bunch of reasons, and maybe most of all, because it's good business.

There actually were other tactics we had tried in the past to gain an advantage over the pirates when we found ourselves in a situation like the one *Vella Gulf* was in. This goes back to my first trip to NAVCENT in Bahrain, when we were experimenting with tactics. One of the simplest things we could do was keep the pirates from communicating with their bosses on shore by interfering with their comms, whether they were using bridge-to-bridge radio or satellite phones. We could actually cut them off.

We also tried placing a destroyer out there near the pirate camps along the Somali coastline, and they would radiate active sonar into the near-shore shallow water, and all anyone could hear was a "BBBAAAAAAAARRRRRR" sound in the water that was just sound vibration. What we found out, however, was that it was more annoying to the hostage crews aboard their ships than it was to the pirates on the ship.

And then there was the BMT. The Barry Manilow treatment. In the middle of the night we'd turn on the loudspeakers playing Manilow's music, just to try and keep the pirates from getting any sleep. Okay, maybe it wasn't always Manilow, but it didn't matter because it didn't really work. We found that the only thing that really scared the pirates was when we would fire illumination shells at night. Because then they thought we were coming after them. I'm going to guess that none of the other stuff bothered them that much because they were all drugged up on khat.

After nearly four months alongside *Faina*, *Vella Gulf* was given her next assignment, which was to move north to the Gulf of Oman and embark me and my staff, becoming flagship for CTF 151 on 4 February 2009. Coincidentally, that same day a ransom of $3.2 million was paid for the release of *Faina* and her crew. Early the next day the pirates left the ship, and *Faina* arrived at the Port of Mombasa on 12 February, where the cargo was unloaded and turned over to the Kenyan military.

Now it was my turn to get directly into the pirate-catching business. Early one afternoon a week after my team and I embarked on *Vella Gulf*, we got a distress call from MV *Polaris* in the Gulf of Oman saying it was under attack. This was a 420-foot Greek-owned chemical and product tanker registered in the Marshall Islands with eighteen crew members aboard. *Vella Gulf's* response was balls to the wall. I had drilled it into the commanders of coalition ships that the first thirty minutes of an attack are critical in terms of response. The attack was happening about thirty miles away, and it was clearly going to be a race to get there, first with a helo and then with our ship and *Mahan* (with ScanEagle), which was also in the area. We knew that the pirates weren't attacking ships within sight of warships for the same reason that nobody robs a bank with a squad car parked in front of it.

Mark Genung has great recall on what happened.

We confirmed their location, we directed the ship if they weren't already doing it, to go to their maximum speed and start erratic maneuvering. They said they were, but keep in mind this is a ship whose maximum speed was like 11, maybe 13 knots. Relatively slow compared to the pirate skiff that was attacking them. Let me try to put it in perspective. On a Navy ship, let's say I'm going to launch a boat on the right side of the ship. I maneuver so the seas and the winds are off my port beam. What that does is, I've got the nice smooth water on the starboard side. I slow down to probably somewhere [that] I've got good rudder control but not too fast, maybe three to four knots. And then I launch my RHIB. We do this and practice this in relatively higher sea states as well, but the whole point of the story is, it's really, really dangerous under the best of circumstances. So, by *Polaris* operating at eleven or twelve knots, she's going relatively fast to do small-boat operations, and further, she's basically putting her rudder over left and then right. She's just basically slaloming.

Fortunately, when the pirates attacked her, they approached her from forward of her bow, and the pirates passed on her port side, cut under her stern, and then made the approach alongside the starboard side. And the reason they did that is because when they overtake from behind, it's a lower relative speed and easier for them to do the next thing they want to do, which was to throw an aluminum ladder with a hook on the end and attach that to the top, and then start climbing up the ladder and get on board.

Now when they came alongside, they were able to get a ladder thrown on and attached, but because *Polaris* maneuvered—that slalom maneuver—the skiff was unable to maintain position alongside for a couple seconds. So they had to rapidly try again to regain position. A very brave crewmember on board the *Polaris* ran over to the ladder and threw it into the ocean.

Genung surmises at that point the pirates were thinking that there were other targets in the sea; they would try another day.

Even doing 30 knots, *Vella Gulf* was almost two hours from *Polaris*. But Genung launched a helicopter that can do 180 knots and get to the vessel under attack in about ten minutes. The helo, armed with a machine gun, can send back video imagery. Before it got to *Polaris*, the vessel radioed that the pirates had given up the attack after their ladder was knocked into the water.

After telling *Polaris* to continue at maximum speed with evasive maneuvers, Genung asked them which way the pirates went. The response wasn't helpful: "I don't know."

"Okay, let's try this again," Genung said. "Did the pirates go north, south, east, or west?" The answer comes back, "They went east."

Now the chase required a little bit of navigational math. *Vella Gulf* was about thirty miles northeast of the scene. Genung decided to search for the pirates.

> I turn my ship south with the intent to get into the wake of the *Polaris*, which is actually a relatively standard technique that you'd use if you had a ship or a convoy attacked by a submarine, and now the sub tries to break contact with the convoy. If you were to maneuver in that manner, you're pretty likely to find the submarine back there in the wake somewhere. This is twenty-some years of experience and applying it to this case.
>
> I sent my helo directly to *Polaris*, and by the time they got there, they reported, "Okay, we can't see the pirates anymore," because I was concerned that maybe others could attack [from the same mother ship], and I wanted to assure myself that *Polaris* was still safe.
>
> I then directed my helo to proceed east and commence a search pattern to look for the skiff. Meanwhile, a young sailor—probably eighteen, nineteen years old, God bless him, says, "Sir, I see a skiff on the horizon." I could barely see it with the binoculars. He did a great job. And what we could see was a skiff that was white, and as we got closer, we could see it had multiple engines. So we called *Polaris*. "Hey, *Polaris*, what's the color of the skiff that attacked you?" "White." "Good. How many engines did it have?" "Two." We see two. "How many pirates did it

have?" "We saw seven." We start counting heads. We see seven. Okay, I got a white skiff, two engines, seven suspected pirates. I think this is our skiff.

Vella Gulf was still closing in on the skiff at thirty knots, and as she approached it, Genung had his helo come in close. His Somali interpreter got on the long-range acoustical device (LRAD)—used here not as a defensive weapon but as a very loud loudspeaker—and told the pirates to stop and put their hands in the air. Then Genung turned to me and said, "Sir, I recommend we capture these pirates."

I went down to my command information center and called Vice Admiral Gortney and Commodore Tim Lowe, the Combined Maritime Forces deputy commander. They concurred with capturing the pirates. It was all, "Great job! Success . . . let's get the SOBs!" They could not have been happier.

Vella Gulf launched two RHIBs. The helo was overhead providing cover. And all the 50-cal machine guns aboard were manned. It was going down exactly the way Genung's crew had practiced it while they were guarding *Faina*. The cover RHIB was manned with a VBSS team, a half-dozen members in body armor, automatic weapons, pistols, and video equipment. The approach RHIB carried the OIC, a corpsman, and the Somali interpreter, who had stayed on the bridge until the last possible moment. Captain Genung's concern at that point was that nothing untoward happen.

> The key thing I was worried about as we maneuvered was to ensure I'd make it very unlikely that any kind of fratricide could occur, so I was always careful about how I'm going to maneuver my ship or my two RHIBs, where the helo was, so if the pirates decided that this was not a good idea, that we would minimize the likelihood as we circled the pirates that we would have any fratricide.
>
> We put the interpreter in body armor and put him down in the RHIB because I wanted to have somebody to be able to tell the pirates, "Okay, one at a time, one thing, one thing only," and "keep your hands in the air."

He wanted his corpsman in the RHIB to be able to take charge if a firefight broke out, deciding who would get triaged first. Fortunately, that never became an issue. What was of some concern was the priority for bringing the pirates on board the ship. Genung explains:

> What we agreed to among ourselves is that we wanted to bring back first whoever was the leader. So we monitored what we thought we saw with the communications going on back and forth, and who seemed to be talking to them. The Somali interpreter helps us kind of figure out who we thought was likely to be the pirate leader because we figured if we got him off first, then the other guys would be more likely to come along willingly. But if we accidentally left the pirate leader on, and he sees more and more of his friends are leaving, he may say, "The heck with this, I'm gonna fight my way out of here or try to escape."

All of the pirates were patted down for weapons. Then they were given life vests and taken off the skiff two at a time and brought to the appropriately named pirate's ladder where they would climb aboard the ship. From there, the processing was done just the way it had been practiced: take pictures, do a medical evaluation, get them out of their clothes, and make sure they hadn't smuggled a grenade or small weapon aboard. Then wash them down, put them in a poopie suit, and escort them to the holding area just aft of sickbay.

When I had embarked on *Vella Gulf*, Coast Guard LEDET 405 had come with my staff. The group was commanded by Lt. (jg) Greg Ponzi. He was an expert on law enforcement at sea. Their job was to make sure that evidence was properly collected. Captain Genung said,

> I was keenly aware of the fact that I was not capturing prisoners of war, but, in fact, I was capturing criminals [for whom] I wanted to eventually ensure that we had an extraordinarily solid chain of custody. And be able to convince a jury that these guys were engaged in piracy. One or two of the LEDET members were in the skiff, but mostly where they really helped us out was as we catalogued all the evidence we found, and statements and imagery to build a solid case—dotted the i's and crossed the t's— because, again, we're not trained in that. We don't do posse comitatus kinds of things very often. Plus, we had

a[n] NCIS agent that was part of the admiral's staff, and that really paid off for us.

In short order, the *Vella Gulf* crew had seven suspected pirates on board. Genung sent his teams back to the pirate skiff to look for weapons, which are usually thrown overboard before pirates surrender. In this case that didn't happen. They found rocket-propelled grenades (RPG), AK-47s, grappling hooks, and a whole bunch of spark plugs, probably because they run lousy fuel. Everything came off the skiff and was catalogued. Then they took the outboard motors off the skiff and brought them up, followed by the skiff itself. Genung told me, "I wanted a very ironclad custody chain to support what I envisioned was someday a trial for these guys."

We convinced the master of *Polaris* to slow his ship down so we could send a RHIB over and bring some of his crew members back to *Vella Gulf* in order for us to conduct a lineup and have them try to identify the pirates we'd caught as the ones they'd seen in the attacking skiff. That worked well. But we knew that a major problem for any prosecution was that the next port of call for *Polaris* was Singapore. Later I learned that the master was interviewed there by an NCIS investigator.

By about midnight, it was all wrapped up. As I toured the mess decks that night for mid-rats, I can still remember the smiling faces of the boarding team members telling the story of the day's capture. One sailor said, "Admiral, this is why I joined the Navy."

I was asleep in my rack several hours later when I sensed the ship turning at high speed. It was 0325 when the phone rang and a voice said, "We got another one." I'll let Genung describe what happened next.

Ens. Ian Townsend, standing watch as officer of the deck, heard the urgent call from a merchant vessel over the bridge-to-bridge VHF radio. The motor vessel *Prem Divya* says, "Hey, we're being attacked by a skiff." This is night. "We're seeing shots fired." Same kind of thing. I get the call, we go to emergency flight quarters [for my helo], we're going thirty knots. It's dark. It's long before sunrise. We're closing the scene, we're telling *Prem Divya*, "If you're not already doing it, maneuver at your maximum speed."

Prem Divya is an Indian-flagged, 58,000-ton crude oil tanker, and her top speed is about fifteen knots. She radioed back that she was maneuvering but then said that the pirates had broken off their attack and that the skiff had left the scene and headed south toward Somalia.

When *Vella Gulf*'s helo got to the scene, it used FLIR (forward-looking infrared cameras) to search the area and confirmed that the skiff was gone. At the same time, another ship in CTF 151, USS *Mahan*, launched her unmanned aerial vehicle. Just after sunrise, at 0609, the helicopter found a skiff with a long ladder and two people aboard, heading south at high speed toward Somalia. Genung did the calculations.

> I was about twenty miles behind him, I'm going thirty knots, so I've only got about a ten-knot closure rate on this guy. It's going to take me a couple hours. Meanwhile, in that time period he would be in Somali waters. In other words, my ship couldn't intercept him unless I could slow him down. I requested from Admiral McKnight permission to do warning shots on the skiff.
>
> Before we did the warning shots, the helicopter did a number of things that are standard operating procedures in these circumstances. The helo went into a hover in front of the skiff, and the skiff just basically kept driving right past him, went around him. Clearly would not stop just from the helicopter hovering in front of him. So, based upon what we had and the fact that he was leaving the scene of a crime at a high rate of speed and had pirate paraphernalia, we asked permission to do warning shots, which was granted. We fired one set from the helicopter's machinegun, which did not stop the skiff. [The helo] asked for permission and we concurred with doing a second set of warning shots—again, they were firing these fore to the bow of the skiff. The skiff now stops. The helo stays on the scene circling around, and we steam up over the horizon. After they slowed down, a whole bunch of people came out from underneath tarps, and all of a sudden, you see there are nine suspected pirates on this skiff.

Lt. Cdr. Matt Bradshaw described the capture as quite hectic compared to the normal helicopter maneuver. He said that under a normal approach from a helicopter to a fishing boat, the boat would stop when directed. But in this case the pirates knew it would mean capture, so they started making S-turns, trying to outflank the helicopter. In the end, the skiff will always lose.

About the same time, *Mahan* arrived and put a RHIB in the water assigned to maintain oversight. Genung said, "Then, because my guys [on *Vella Gulf*] were the most proficient pirate-capturers in the world at the time, we used my RHIB to then do the approach and capture the suspected pirates."

That's how Capt. Mark Genung and his crew got me in trouble with Vice Admiral Gortney. We were authorized to catch and hold a dozen pirates. Suddenly, due to his efficiency as pirate-grabber extraordinaire, we were now over our bag limit. I might as well let him finish the story: "We got those guys aboard and we put them on the fantail because I already had seven inside, and I had nine there. I knew at this point in time, the same day, we were going to be doing a transfer of suspected pirates to another ship, the *Lewis and Clark*. This had already been prearranged for the first set of pirates."

Okay, I need to interrupt. USNS *Lewis and Clark* is a T-AKE, a dry cargo/ammunition ship operated by the Navy's Military Sealift Command to provide multiproduct combat logistics support to the Navy fleet. *Lewis and Clark* is the lead ship in a new class of so-called underway replenishment vessels. She can deliver cargo, provide fuel in limited quantities, and repair parts. While steaming around the high-risk area of the Gulf of Aden and Indian Ocean, she had also been given a new role as a prison ship. Yes, I said prison ship. I always felt like little Ralphie in the movie *A Christmas Story* saying the "F" word when I briefed the press on *Lewis and Clark*. If I ever said the words "prison ship," it was all over; I was dead. What would it be? The guillotine? Hanging? The chair? The rack? The Chinese water torture? Hmmm. Mere child's play compared with what surely awaited me. That was a term that my public affairs team declined to let those of us catching pirates use—but that's what she was. She'd been outfitted with facilities appropriate for holding criminals, and a detachment of Marines were there to guard them until they could be transferred ashore.

Now back to Captain Genung.

> We did the same thing [for the *Prem Divya* pirate sus-
> pects] that we did the day before. We go aboard this skiff,

we find RPGs, assault rifles, and also in the bilge was a whole bunch of spent cartridges from firing AK-47s. And remember how I started this sea story was, hey, *Prem Divya*'s reporting they're taking shots from a skiff. So, based upon the cartridges in the bottom of the skiff and all the weapons and the pirate paraphernalia, I was utterly and remain utterly certain we caught the skiff that attacked *Prem Divya* that night.

We got them embarked, and my boarding officer reported the skiff had some damage, it had some cracking in it, and it was taking on some water. There's a lot of fuel spilled in the bilge, and it was his professional assessment that this skiff was not seaworthy and it was not safe for us to try to take any of the fuel or the skiff aboard like the other one we did. We reported this to the chain of command, and then our intention was to sink it at sea, which we ultimately did. And I don't know if that's the part that got the admiral in trouble.

Yeah, Mark, that's the part. Here's the way I recall it went down. I had the sense that we were going to get orders to release the second batch of pirates, just put them back in their skiff and let them go on their merry way back to Somalia where they could replenish and do it all over again. So as I was boarding a helo to go pay a visit to *Absalon*, the Danish ship that was part of CTF 151, I said to Captain Genung, "Make that skiff go away." Or something similar. It didn't take him very long to carry out that order. Before I even landed on *Absalon* we could see black smoke coming from the burning skiff. I asked Genung what they shot it with. I thought it might have been the 5-inch 54. Not the case, he said.

No, it was far more satisfying for my sailors to fire 50-cals. And it gave some of them a great deal of satisfaction when the suspected pirates on the fantail could look on the right side of the ship and see us sinking their skiff. It burned very, very nicely and made for great Christmas card pictures.

There was a discussion between the lawyers at Fifth Fleet JAG and the admiral about releasing the second set of pirates, and we felt that was inappropriate because even though it was inherently self-buoyant, [their skiff] wasn't seaworthy, and I wasn't going to put nine souls back in that boat. I have responsibility by international law to rescue people under those circumstances. I discussed it with the JAGs, and I was not willing to put pirates back in either skiff.

I think that is a perfectly reasonable and defensible position for the skipper of a U.S. Navy ship to take. Approaching this not just as a rear admiral in the U.S. Navy but as a citizen with good common sense, I couldn't understand how the U.S. Navy could spend all this time, effort, and money to capture these people, and then NAVCENT wanted us to turn them loose. Both Genung and I fought that battle with NAVCENT/Fifth Fleet. Their lawyers were 1,400 miles away and they had all the answers. They were saying we didn't have enough evidence, but my lawyer, Pete Koebler, was out there with me and said that we did; an NCIS agent sat there and said we did; Coast Guard people sat there—all the smart people that I had out there that know how to collect evidence—and said both cases were just as sound.

I had a conversation with the lawyers that went something like this:

> I'm worried that we're having a legal emergency here. Why are we in such a rush to release these guys? Well, *Prem Divya* said they didn't see anything? Well, who's gotten a statement from the crew of the *Prem Divya*? Who has gotten the statements from these guys? We know the next port of call; we can send an NCIS agent to go interview these guys. Meanwhile, I've got a skiff that's got all these weapons, spent cartridges, their equipment, and these guys were racing home, leaving the scene of a crime. My sense is (a) I can't safely put them back out on a boat, and (b) there's no legal necessity to do so.

And so, at that point in time, the JAGs agreed with my brilliant legal analysis, and we agreed I was not going to do that. It just bugged the hell out of me because what I kept hearing from the other end was "catch and release, catch and release, catch and release," as if this was some sort of tarpon tournament down in southwest Florida. They even asked me if we could take the pirates from the second hijacking attempt and set them free in the skiff that belonged to the pirates who were being held for attacking *Polaris*. It was like Avis Rent-A-Skiff. I told them no, because we had to keep the other skiff as evidence, and it wasn't in great shape either.

We were going back and forth with the big, unanswerable question—who's going to take the pirates? Koebler handled it on a day-to-day basis. My attitude was, "I've done my job, now your job is to figure out how to get rid of them." And then I called Gortney's chief of staff. He yelled at me, "Well Gortney's saying no." And I yelled at him, "But we still have them. We've gotta get rid of them."

Ultimately, both groups of pirates were transferred to *Lewis and Clark* by helicopter. But before I go into what happened to them, you need to hear how it all ended for Mark Genung's crew on *Vella Gulf*. It's his story to tell.

> Now we've captured the second set of pirates, and I get an e-mail from the commanding officer of the *Mason*. The *Mason* is the ship that relieved me on station for *Faina*. And he forwarded on to me a letter from the master of the *Faina*, Viktor Nikolsky. I got on the 1-MC, and the first thing I say to the crew is, "Okay, congratulations to the most famous pirate catchers in the world right now," and two, "I've got something I want to read to you," and I read it verbatim, and I was choking up at the end. This was the letter I got from Viktor:

Dear Captain Mark and the crew of the *Vella Gulf*: On behalf of myself and the crew, I wish to show my sincerest appreciation for all the support *Vella Gulf* has shown us during our four months of captivity under Somali pirates. Our liberation would not have been possible without your constant presence. It is difficult for me to express my feelings towards you and your crew. Our lives were spared because you were here to protect us. You gave us the strength to endure the hardest of times. We will keep *Vella Gulf* and her crew in our hearts and in our prayers forever. We wish you a safe journey home and good health for all of your days. Thank you for everything you have done. Your friend, Viktor Nikolsky, captain of the vessel *Faina.*

And it was also signed by a number of his crew from the *Faina.* So, right after we captured these two sets of pirates, I was able to read that letter. And keep in mind where my crew was coming from at the time. We spent 100-some-odd days on station, playing man-to-man defense on *Faina.* And the crew, like anybody else, was saying, "Gosh, why can't we stop allowing the pirates to resupply themselves? Why can't we do something more positive to get the hostages rescued?" And I reminded the crew of our mission, including the one, "don't make things any worse." What if we did that and the pirates now started shooting the hostages? Now what're we gonna do? So, when the whole thing came down to, hey, we're now gonna become the flagship for Task Force 151, the crew was very excited, because they would come to me and say, "Captain, does this mean we're now gonna be able to go on the offensive and capture pirates?" And I was able to say, "Yes, as soon as we figure out how to do it."

Mark Genung was locked and loaded, well prepared, into the mission. He wanted to accomplish something. If he had stayed out there for six months, he and his team would have caught all the pirates.

Now I've got to talk about what happened to the sixteen captured pirates once they were on board *Lewis and Clark.* They were only there for a couple of days when I got an emergency call from the master of *Lewis and Clark* saying he had all his crew members running around wearing surgical masks because all the pirates had tested positive for tuberculosis. It turned out that just about everyone in Somalia seems to test positive for TB because they've been exposed to the disease. Fortunately, we learned that it doesn't mean they have it, and that they're not contagious.

While this was all playing out, I was still flying around to visit the ships that were part of my coalition. I got over to visit HDMS *Absalon,* which is a beautiful two-year-old, 451-foot flexible support ship that will ultimately be credited with capturing eighty-eight pirates, including one group that was sent to the Netherlands for trial. I told her skipper, Capt. Dan Termason, my problem, and he said, "Hey, we've dealt with this before."

He said that he had a detachment of Special Operations Forces (SOF) aboard—very capable guys. He told me he puts suspected pirates in a rigid assault craft—it's a little bit more upscale than our RHIB—with his SOF. They launch it through their stern gate. Then, at midnight or two in the morning on a night when there's no moon, they take them into shore—not right to Bosaso where the pirates operate from, but somewhere on the Somali coast where they can put them in the water and make sure the pirates can walk to shore. They just say "Don't do it again" and turn them loose.

I was listening to him tell me this and said, "Wow, that's great. Do you think you could help me?" And he said he would make a call. He walked over to his Inmarsat phone, called his boss back in Denmark, and his boss said, "I don't think there's any problem. We've done this before, but let me check with higher authority." The boss called his boss, and about half an hour later, he had approval.

I said "fine" and went back to work it with my staff. Frankly, I was astonished that it took him less than two hours to get an okay. In my world, it would take two months, because we would have to brief everybody, emphasis on *every*. With PowerPoint. And *every*body's going to change the PowerPoint.

I went back to *Vella Gulf*, and that was the beginning of what we called Operation Midnight Express. (If you haven't seen the original movie—it's worth the time. Has nothing to do with pirates, though.) I was excited when I got back. I called Vice Admiral Gortney, and he said, "That's a great idea. Sounds good. I think we'll support it." Then he said, "Build me a PowerPoint brief." No surprise there.

I sent some of my guys back over to *Absalon* the next day, and they worked on the particulars. They built the brief, I touched it up, and we sent it forward. And you know the plan never got any support from the NAVCENT "council of captains," and the further it went up the chain of command, the stupider the plan got.

There were two big objections. Number one, they said we never trained for it. We were just going to go in there and do it. And Dan had wanted some Americans—they didn't have to be SOF—with his guys when they went into the beach, so there would be an American presence; if something happened, he could say, "Well they drowned, too. They went down with the ship, too." He wanted it to clearly be a joint operation. So the objection was that we never planned it. It was an "Execute! Just Go!" But this is the U.S. military. We gotta have plans, we've gotta have a beach survey. It's a long, drawn-out thing.

What happens if there are three squadrons of bad guys with guns on the beach waiting for us? The chain of command found everything that was bad with the plan. The water depth. The country. Blackhawk Down! This could never happen. Say the boat goes ashore, gets caught in the surf, and then the next morning you wake up and there are Americans sitting on the beach cooking hot dogs because their craft is upside down. All that kind of stuff. It's on the front page of the *Washington Post*. The Danes are standing there too. Now we got the Danish press excited. The State Department and the Joint Staff had no desire to support the operation. It would have basically been a Danish-led operation, and I don't think they were comfortable with that. If they were pirates captured by the United States, then the United States should have the responsibility to get rid of them, not the Danes.

At one point I thought, it's a good thing I didn't brief my chain of command on the Russian solution. We were all aware that when the Russian Navy caught a bunch of pirates one afternoon, by the next morning the pirates would be gone. "It's a very big ocean out here, gets very dark at night." That became known as the Russian solution.

But this was still "Terry and the Pirates." Or more correctly, "Terry Still Has the Pirates." The lawyers continued going back and forth, so we said, "Let's try what we did the last time, when we talked to the head of the Coast Guard in Puntland and see if that will work."

A brief lecture on politics and geography is in order. The Puntland State of Somalia was declared an autonomous state in 1998. It is in the northeastern part of the county, and, according to its Ministry of Planning and Statistics, about a third of Somalia's population lives in the territory, which contains about a third of the nation's geographical area. While Puntland has its own government, it has not sought independence from Somalia.

We had some experience working with the Puntland government, or at least with the head of its coast guard, such as it is. So we got in touch with Puntland authorities again. Pete Koebler handled most of the negotiations with the coast guard and minister of defense. However, they explained to him that only the president of Puntland could approve the transfer. Sensing the only way he could return our captured pirates to Somalia, Pete came to my stateroom and said that the president of Puntland would like to talk with me about the transfer of the pirates. That afternoon we called President Abdirahman Mohamed Mohamud, and I explained our dilemma to him. Speaking in a formal, very presidential voice, he said, "Admiral, it is a real pleasure to work with you and stop the spread of piracy." He stated that piracy was hurting the reputation of his country, and he would make sure these individuals would be taken care of when they returned. I thanked him for his support, and I later learned that this batch of pirates was actually headed to prison. He also said, "This is our last favor." I translated that to mean, "This is the last time we're going to do this for free. The next time, make sure you bring a suitcase full of cash."

So at the appointed hour, *Lewis and Clark* and USS *Monterey*, which my staff and I had moved to as the third of four flagships I would have during this tour, slipped into Somali coastal waters and met up with the Puntland coast guard vessel. It was a former fishing boat, about 75 feet long, and in need of considerable work before I would rate it as not-quite unseaworthy. The crew had no lifejackets. The boat was in shambles. Probably gets under way about twice a year. They actually said to us, "Look, we can't even afford lifejackets. You give us some of these things, we can patrol the coast." This is a suggestion that has actually been made and seriously discussed among the international experts trying to figure out how to fix Somalia, but nothing has yet come of it.

After we handed off the pirates, we asked the head of the coast guard who was on the boat what would happen to the pirates. He said something to the effect that they were going into the slammer. We moved off shore, and my staff prepared an after-action report that said we had off-loaded the pirates, everything was very cordial, here is what we saw, and the Puntland officials said the pirates were going to prison in Somalia.

Well, that report made its way to the State Department, and if I recall correctly, the unofficial report of State's reaction began with, "Tell me that's not true." And it went downhill from there. State Department officials finally said, in essence, "It's over with. There's nothing you can do now, but you've got to stop doing that, stop turning them over to Puntland, because if they're going to go to prison, they're going to live with rats or alligators or some other horrors." My takeaway was that State did not want the pirates that were captured by the Americans to serve their time in a Somali prison.

Now back to the first group of pirates, the ones who attacked *Polaris*. They remained in residence in the specially built prisoner accommodations aboard *Lewis and Clark* for several weeks. You need to understand that this was the first time in their lives that they had been seen by a doctor, eaten three meals a day, and had toilet paper to use. In fact, they all gained weight in our custody. Then they were transferred to USS *Leyte Gulf*, which was bound for Mombasa on a goodwill mission from Naval Forces African Command. On 5 March 2009, pursuant to the MOU, the pirates were turned over to the Kenyans to stand trial. This happened at a time when the Kenyans were still willing to accept pirates for trial in their courts.

A postscript to their story comes via a nontraditional source: WikiLeaks. While searching the Web to determine what disposition the Kenyans were making of piracy suspects, an unclassified cable dated 16 July 2009 from the American Embassy in Nairobi popped up. The summary of the cable said that there were one hundred Somali piracy suspects being held at that time in Kenya, adding, "The manner and delivery of quality of evidence, as much as the number of transfers, has dampened Kenya's enthusiasm for piracy cases." A bit further down the cable was this:

> 3. On June 30, 11 U.S. Navy and Coast Guard personnel (accompanied by Navy and Coast Guard JAG officers) and two Filipino seamen were assembled in Mombasa to testify in the trial of seven Somalis accused of piracy. The suspects were captured by the USS Vella Gulf on February 11, 2009 after they attempted to seize the MV Polaris, a Marshall Islands-flagged vessel. They were turned over to the Kenyan authorities on March 8. Trial was scheduled for July 1–2 and July 7. However, only one U.S. witness testified before the magistrate suspended proceedings to consider a defense motion challenging Kenya's jurisdiction. The magistrate is expected to deny the motion when he rules on July 16. (Note: The High Court of Kenya has rejected the same jurisdictional challenge made earlier on

appeal by defendants captured by the U.S. Navy and convicted in 2006. This ruling is generally viewed as binding on this issue.) However, the case is likely to be continued until September due to lack of courtroom availability, so the witnesses were sent home with the hope that they may be able to return when trial resumes. Logistics and expenses for the Filipino crewmembers' participation in the trial were arranged by the Marshall Islands maritime organization and the private shipping company that employed them. (Note: A similar motion challenging jurisdiction was also made during the week of June 29 during the piracy trial of nine Somalis caught by the German Navy and handed over to Kenya on March 11, and it also resulted in a delay of that trial.) Post's Department of Justice Resident Legal Advisor and Bernadette Mendoza, the Deputy Chief of Mission from the Embassy of the Philippines in Nairobi, traveled to Mombasa to meet and assist the witnesses and participated in pretrial conferences with prosecutors. Ms. Mendoza indicated that her government remains very concerned about the impact of piracy on its seafarers, and noted that there are currently 46 Filipino seamen being held hostage for ransom in Somalia, the largest number from a single country.

CHAPTER 3

Piracy 101

At the outset of this project, my goal was to learn everything I could about Somali piracy. My professional vantage point had been from the sea. I saw pirates up close, saw the havoc they raised and the economic, emotional, and physical toll they took. But saying you understand pirates and piracy because you've captured a handful is like saying you understand how the U.S. Navy works because you've eaten dinner in the captain's wardroom on a carrier. Studying our Navy is probably easier than studying Somali piracy. There are thousands of books and academic papers to read, thousands more experts on subjects wide and narrow to interview.

Not so with the Somali pirates and piracy. There's been relatively little of depth written about them, and a convention of experts in the field could have easily been held in my cabin on *Boxer* with room left over for a squad of off-duty SEALs. It was essential for me to gain an understanding of who the pirates are, what really motivates them, and how their operation works. To do that, I turned to the "A-Team of Piracy," two well-known, long-time experts in the field and one young man—a very brave man, as you will find out shortly, because he actually walked the streets of Somalia with the pirates—who is well on his way to joining that exclusive "convention of experts."

Martin M. Murphy is a witty Brit who is currently serving as a senior fellow at the Atlantic Council of the United States, one of those think tanks in Washington that the media occasionally mention. His most recent book is *Somalia, the New Barbary? Piracy and Islam in the Horn of Africa*. It includes a definitive examination of each of the hijackings in the 2007 to 2009 piracy heyday. He'd previously written *Small*

Boats, Weak States, Dirty Money: Piracy and Maritime Terrorism in the Modern World.

J. Peter Pham is director of the Michael S. Ansari Africa Center at the Atlantic Council. He's a frequent guest lecturer at the Foreign Service Institute, the U.S. Army War College, and the Joint Special Operations University, as well as an advisor to the chief of naval operations and AFRICOM combatant commanders. Dr. Pham served on election observation delegations to Nigeria in 2007 and 2012, and to Somaliland in 2010. He maintains close contact with multiple sources in Somalia and Kenya, and is able to provide unique insight into the piracy situation.

Jatin Dua is a doctoral candidate in the Department of Cultural Anthropology at Duke University. He has used the fact that he's young, ethnically Indian, Muslim, and fluent in Arabic to gain access in Somalia to the people he wanted to meet and interview, and to put them at ease. He was in Kenya for the last six months of 2010 and spent the first three months of 2011 traveling between villages in Somalia, Somaliland, and Puntland, where he told them truthfully that he was a college student doing field research for a doctoral dissertation yet managed never to mention that he is an American. Fortunately for him and for us, no one ever asked.

I asked Dua if he was concerned for his own safety, and he said that when he was in Somalia, the pirates were having a very good year. There was a lot of money around, and he never felt threatened. He felt the recent kidnappings, including the two that led to the SEAL raid as well as the capture of an American journalist, were happening because the pirates were feeling pressure to do something that could generate income—successes at sea continue to be way down. Dua isn't talking about returning to Somalia anytime soon.

Dua spent considerable time in Bosaso, Puntland, a northern port city on the Gulf of Aden. There he was able to interview people involved in all facets of the piracy operation: the men who actually went out in boats; those who were financing specific attack groups; others who were providing services, such as food and water for the hostages and for guards on the captured ships; and the men who were involved in ransom negotiations.

Bosaso is one of the largest ports in Somalia. There is no doubt that it could be labeled "the capital of piracy." A large majority of all the pirates who take to the sea leave from Bosaso. If you live in Somalia and want to earn your pirate merit badge, Bosaso is the place to locate.

Many of the contacts Dua made were by sheer chance, just being in the right place long enough. He had offers from people who wanted him to hire them as so-called fixers—this is what journalists working for companies with big budgets do in order to get to the right people quickly. But he made it clear that he wasn't a journalist, that he couldn't pay anyone for access or interviews. He also told people that he was neutral, not supporting any side; he was just an academic writing a dissertation. He discovered that a lot of the people involved in piracy loved talking about their exploits. They were in a growing business, ransoms were going up, and it seemed as though the danger factor had actually gone down. This was before a significant number of high-end ships began carrying armed guards who had no hesitation to open fire when approached by pirate skiffs.

When we spoke, he offered to run through a typical piracy operation of the kind represented by the people he spoke with in Bosaso, people who were increasingly moving their operations south toward Hobyo, which is on the eastern coast of Puntland, adjacent to the Indian Ocean rather than the Gulf of Aden—traditionally, Pirate Alley.

Their modus operandi was far from sophisticated. "They go up to the international shipping lanes and just hope and wait to pick the first slow-moving boat that comes along. In one case, this group did not have much maritime experience. They'd get lost; they'd have no idea where they are. They found a dhow, a sailing vessel, and they slide down the bow, raided it for food and water. They didn't actually turn it into a mother ship because it was not what they were looking for, but they did get one of the crew to navigate them toward the shipping lanes."

And then they were successful. It was February of 2011, and the pirates hijacked what he recalls was a Panamanian-flagged ship. "I was on the ground in Bosaso at this point, so I heard from one of my contacts that 'the guys you had interviewed—they've gotten a ship!' And there was this sort of buzz around the area." Dua said this particular group was small, not part of one of the larger crime networks run from Bosaso. He also said that, with only one exception, this group of pirates had never actually been out on the ocean before, and they weren't from any of the local clans. That would change; in order to negotiate for ransom, they ended up nested in one of the larger groups.

The Puntland government had made it clear that it did not want pirate bases and captured ships near Bosaso. So the pirates forced the captured crew to navigate the ship south, to a coastal area that was more receptive. "And as you're going down, there are people calling from Bosaso, wiring money, and saying, 'I'm paying for the food and water for everyone on board, and in return, I want a certain percentage.' And someone else says, 'I'm a negotiator. I will negotiate up front. If it's successful, I want my cut.' People sort of jump on and say, 'I have this technical skill,' or 'I will pay' for certain things."

One of Dua's primary informants was a car dealer who was doing very well, thank you, because piracy was booming. "It was strange because I thought I would go talk to pirates, and for the first month, I was talking to businessmen who, in some ways, gave me much more of an insight into the piracy operations." He learned that as soon as pirates became successful, the first thing they did was buy a Land Cruiser. "Now, this businessman most of his life has been bringing Land Cruisers from Dubai, but he realized that they'd become status symbols for the pirates. So he contacts them [on the hijacked ship] and says, 'Okay, you're a pirate now. Don't you want a Land Cruiser? I'll send you four or five, and you don't have to pay me until you get the ransom.'"

When I was out there on *San Antonio* and *Vella Gulf* and pirates were questioned, they always said there was what amounted to a pirate code not to harm or kill the hostages. They said it was very important to keep them safe. But hostages have died. I wondered if there was any acknowledgment among the pirates that they might have to kill people to accomplish their mission.

> In 2011 there wasn't, which was surprising to me, given that I actually was in Puntland when the four Americans [on the hijacked sailing yacht *Quest*] were killed, and everyone would sort of distance themselves from it and say that it wasn't the typical way of doing business. When I was on the ground in Somalia, there were conspiracy theories. There are always various sorts of theories to explain what happens, and there's a fascinating way in which Somalis relate to each other through these conspiracy theories. There was a big theory that this had nothing to do with pirates; this had actually been French or Russian [military] or someone else had killed them, and it was being blamed on the pirates because, that way, people would be less sym-

pathetic to their cause. But everyone said, "There's no way a pirate would do this—or at least a proper pirate."

Pirates recognize that the safety of the hostages is what gives them ransom, so there is a risk calculation which recognizes that you have to keep hostages safe, especially if they're Western hostages. The pirates would always joke about the fact that I am ethnically Indian, and they had a whole sort of calculus, you know, someone European, white, we would actually give you very good treatment. But with you, it doesn't matter, actually, because you're Indian, so your government won't care. I said, "Well, I'm a mix," but there was always this sort of classification of hostages, where Indians/Filipinos, you didn't have to give them the best food and water, and if some of them died, that was okay. But as soon as you got up to Danes, Brits, or Americans—white Americans—those groups you actually took special care of, because those returns were the highest. So not only was there a decision not to harm us, there's a whole typology on how different kinds of hostages are to be treated.

My conversation with Jatin Dua took place before Navy SEALs rescued two hostages being held in an inland camp, killing nine pirates in the process. I had asked him if there was any concern that someday someone will get fed up, and there will be an attack on land—a kinetic effort to start knocking out pirate villages. He said he used to bring that up in conjunction with discussion about local Somali leaders who were in the process of deciding whether enough is enough, and ordering the pirates out of the area. But it's complicated because the tentacles of piracy were deep in the larger community. Dua said,

> What's significant is a lot of tension exists among various communities about whether or not to welcome pirates or to be part of this pirate venture. There are many people who debate it, and ask, "Is it lawful to not actually engage in piracy but provide food and water to hostages in return for money?" And there are a lot of people who are against the lifestyle that a lot of pirates have adopted. And it has impacted clan relations, so I would often bring that ques-

tion up in conjunction with, "What if you no longer have a land base?" And there's both the recognition, "Well, then we can move. There's a lot of space that we have," or that one pirate somewhat exaggeratedly said, "We have the upper hand because we can always go out and just start killing people or trying to blow up ships."

There's recognition that this is an important transit zone, and they would often claim, "we don't have any resources; what we have is the ability to extract a tax from people who are going through this transit zone." It was no longer the language of, "We're protecting our waters." In the time I was there, it became very much about the shift from that narrative to, it's about, "we have an advantageous position that we're trying to exploit by taxing ships that are going through the region."

Dua said one of the pirate groups that cooperated with him started off by calling itself the Puntland Environmental Protection Group, but by the time he left it had changed the name to Puntland Private Equity, saying essentially, "We're just businessmen; that's what we're doing. There's nothing else here."

One of the mysteries of the pirate world is what happens to the ransom money once it has been paid. I've discussed it with several experts, but Jatin Dua had an opportunity to observe the initial steps in that process, and I asked him to describe in detail what he saw and learned. Is everybody getting a share, from the lowliest pirate to the president of Puntland? Is it all about spreading the wealth, or is just a select group profiting?

I would have to say, in some ways, I have found evidence of all of the above. And found evidence that this is a very redistributionist system. There has been incredible inflation on the coast of Puntland, and part of that is because sellers find it profitable to sell goods at higher prices to pirates. So there is both money coming in, but there's also the converse, which is inflation. A lot of people would complain that they could no longer afford *posho*, which is their starch staple, because all the pirates took it, and it was too expensive to [buy it]. [Pirates] would come in and be willing to pay ten dollars for a bottle of water when before, you could get it for fifty cents.

But then there were also others who said, "I'm not a pirate, but I'm a shopkeeper, and business is booming right now." I'm basing this off sixteen instances where I tried to ask people, "Tell me where all the rest of the money goes." There's a 60/40 cut initially, so if there are big financiers involved, 60 percent of the money will go immediately to them. And then most of that 40 percent that's left is distributed among the crew and spent in Somalia itself. So there's a significant portion of the ransom money that is spent in Somalia. Which makes it also harder to convince people not to support them.

With big money to be made, even by people who had a very small piece of the pie, I wondered if pirates go back to sea a second time, or even multiple times. Dua said that some are very disciplined. They take their ransom money and use it to emigrate. Interestingly, he also said that the desire to leave Somalia is one reason that the international naval response is not scaring them off. "The threat of being incarcerated isn't a significant deterrent because that, too, becomes a form of exit. There's the sense that anything, especially prison in Europe, would be a great idea, 'because then I can get asylum.'"

So it's a toss-up for the pirates—arrest, conviction, and asylum in a Western nation, or success, money, and emigration. But Dua added his perception that there are also two classes of pirates: the ones who are doing or have done very well, or the majority,

who have to keep going back because they actually are in debt, even though they've been successful three or four times. They don't have enough money because they blow it on cars—they're young men, drunk and hanging out with prostitutes. It has upset the clan structure—Somalia's a fairly hierarchical system, so the elite clans no longer hold that much prestige because there are some young guys from lower clans coming up with a lot of money and saying, "I want to marry into your clan. And I have a million dollars." But then, all of a sudden, he has no money after that.

So there is a lot of indebtedness that I observed as a result
of piracy, which perpetuates the cycle.

It's clear that from the start of what I call the modern hijacking era,
in 2005, with the hijacking of the liquefied petroleum tanker MV *Feisty
Gas*, which was ransomed for $315,000 after being held for less than
two weeks, piracy has only gotten uglier and more profitable. In 2010
a ransom of $9.5 million was paid for the release of the supertanker
Samho Dream and its crew of twenty-four. They'd been held hostage for
seven months.

Ransom demands and payments have gone up exponentially, and
the pirates or their financiers have decided that they're willing to wait
as long as necessary to get high seven-figure payouts. They don't care
how long they keep people in captivity. If they keep the hostages another
month and it drives the price up by a million dollars, it's worth it. And
so on. Dua said,

> When it first started, it seemed like it was a self-financing
> operation. There was a financier who bought the boat,
> got the men. And then one or two financiers [paid] for
> everything. Now, the costs are spread out. So when every-
> one knows that there's a chance of getting $10 million or
> $13 million, more and more people are willing to invest in
> holding the hostages now. I've talked to a few negotiators,
> and they said that pirates are far more stubborn in their
> demands now. Usually, they would start at some exorbi-
> tant figure and very quickly end up at a million dollars, or
> $500,000. Now, they say, no. They ask $13 million and
> end up around $10 million. So everyone's sticking to that.

The negotiators are a group unto themselves. Some are Somalis
who speak multiple languages and use satellite phones to start negotiations. But they only do preliminary negotiations, get on the phone and
call the shipowner, are involved for a little bit, get their cut, and leave.
Dua said he has thus far been unsuccessful in contacting operatives in
South Africa and London who have been involved in multiple ransom
negotiations.

The pirates are all Muslims, as is Jatin Dua, and this was a focus of
his questioning.

A lot of them would start off by saying, "I know I'm a Muslim; this is not what I should be doing, but—" and they would tend to justify it. They recognize this is not just problematic. Oftentimes, they would say, "This is haram, you know, unlawful. We know it." But then they would say, "We'll do this for the short term, make some money, and then once I become a legitimate businessman, I'll marry and have a wife, and we can move to Europe or somewhere else, and then I will go on a to hajj to Mecca and atone for my sins and everything will work out." So in that sense [religion] is important because everyone that I talked to would have a narrative for that justification. But in terms of actually changing their actions, no, it didn't seem that it was very important. But it was important to a lot of community members in coastal villages, and most of these pirates aren't coastal, so in that sense [the community members] don't have a lot of control over them. A lot of coastal villages would say that "we're Muslim, this is not something a good Muslim would do, so we should not associate with pirates."

In one place [I visited], a few village elders had come to a negotiated agreement with the pirates that they could use the town, but they weren't allowed to be out after dark, they weren't allowed to drink in public. A code of conduct had been created. In Somalia, customary laws and those kinds of codes are far more important than going to Sharia law and saying, "Look, this is clearly a violation of Islamic law." At some level, for Somalis, that's secondary to working within the customary clan system.

And what about the future? Where will this all end up? Jatin Dua's sense is that there'll be a return to smaller-scale piracy, targeting dhows and fishing vessels rather than huge crude carriers and container ships that have armed guards and follow best management practices to deter piracy. He's spoken with small-boat operators who regularly sail from Mombasa up the coast to Mogadishu and Kismayo. They told him that in the past two years, no one would touch them; now, they're being attacked more and more.

Dua feels the situation is also trending toward more insecurity on land.

> You now have many groups of young men with weapons, and this, in Somalia, has never been a good thing. There've been more cases of kidnapping on land, and I think that definitely has become an established form of livelihood in Somalia. For a whole generation of people who've never seen any form of government, piracy or this kind of [criminality] is the way to work. And it becomes a government. If you'd asked me this question last year, I would say there's a move toward legitimate business, and a lot of the pirates were moving in that direction, moving to convert their money into other property in Kenya or other places, and moving out of piracy. I'm a little more skeptical of that, just having seen the way things have progressed in the last nine months [of 2011], and I think it's become more difficult to be a pirate, which will also make it more desperate, and there'll be an increase in violence. So, yes, I guess I'm more pessimistic now about the future—I think it'll lead to more criminality and more insecurity on land.
>
> There's more willingness by the pirates, at this point, to hire themselves out for any kind of work. A friend of mine who is based on Bosaso said that there's a lot more crime in Bosaso, and if the situation stays like this, there'll be a lot more risks taken, and maybe the rule not to harm hostages may change, and it may become about pilfering ships again. It remains to be seen. It's a fairly volatile situation.

Which raises the question, what do you call a pirate on land? A criminal? Doesn't sound nearly as romantic, but if you think about it, the job description hasn't changed, just the locale.

Peter Pham is the antithesis of the image of a deskbound think-tank academic. He's been in and out of the Horn of Africa, including Somalia, several times a year since 1993, lived on the continent from 2001 to 2003, and guesses that he's spent several years of his life doing fieldwork there. He plans to continue doing this work, despite the increasing danger for foreigners as evidenced by recent kidnappings. He has trips planned to Kenya and Somalia, but he said, laughing, "That's one place my wife doesn't go. She'll go with me on trips to Morocco and South Africa, but not there. But she knew what she was getting into when she married a guy who [studies] conflicts in Africa. So, inevitably, it's going to be war zones and other places like that."

Pham was born in Paris in 1970. His parents were South Vietnamese academics at the time. They came to the United States when he was five, and he was raised in the Midwest. He studied economics as an undergraduate at the University of Chicago and received his doctorate at the Gregorian University in Rome in social sciences. He also has a law degree.

As for his travel to dangerous parts of the world such as Somalia, Pham said he hasn't been in trouble since the late 1990s when he tangled with child soldiers in Liberia. He said,

> I can deal with warlords fairly well. I'm levelheaded enough. Warlords, generally, are rational. It's the eleven-year-old kid who is probably high, and even if he weren't high, he doesn't get the bigger picture that it's a very bad idea to shoot any American, anywhere, much less an American who's in a car with diplomatic plates. The warlord would appreciate that it's the one thing that will probably get a U.S. plane overhead, and other actors. You shoot the American and there's the *Iwo Jima* offshore; some bad things are going to start happening.

When I spoke with Pham in his Atlantic Council offices, the kidnapping of several tourists off Kenyan beaches had just taken place. And, of course, several hundred mariners were still being held hostage by the Somali pirates. How can he be assured of his safety there?

> Two things: a lot of it has to do with Somali society and culture—if you're welcomed, if you're a guest of a clan. If I go there, it's okay. It's a matter of serious loss of face to one of the major clans there [if something happened to me]. In the case of Puntland, the president himself, since I've eaten his bread, he personally and his whole clan would be obligated—unless they wanted to lose more face—to get me out. So anyone stupid enough to take on me—not that there wouldn't be people—would have to realize that. The key thing is your protector is powerful enough; then

you're fairly safe. You're adopted into—not adopted formally, but in the sense that they've extended their hospitality to you. You're there, and you're free to move about.

With that freedom, Pham was able to speak with people who held
leadership roles in pirate operations. I was especially interested in the
story that piracy had been formalized to the point that investors could
actually buy stock in particular ventures—before the boats went out
seeking a target. He said, "When you talk about pirates, you really are
talking about a broad range, from some guys who are running literal
businesses that you can actually go and buy shares in, to six kids who
found a motor and a boat and are out there thinking they're going to
strike it rich. And you've got everything in between." He said the well-
established operations had been developing ongoing relations with the
terrorist group al-Shabaab and actually worked deals where al-Shabaab
gave the pirates weapons training in exchange for being brought cargo
from hijacked ships. Sometimes, the cooperation went even further,
resulting in a more sophisticated piracy operation, including coordi-
nated command and control.

Pham said that the mechanism of shares being sold in a pirate venture was brought there by a U.S.-trained Somali named Ali Mohamed,
who "was stupid enough to have come back to America and is now in
federal custody." Mohamed was arrested on 20 April 2011 at Dulles
International Airport and was indicted for conspiracy to commit piracy,
piracy under the law of nations, attack to plunder a vessel, and aid-
ing and abetting in the crimes. Mohamed was the negotiator after the
Danish-owned MV *CEC Future* and crew of thirteen were hijacked in
November 2008 and held for seventy-one days until a ransom of $1.7
million was paid. Pham said Mohamed was the "backroom guy" who
organized things for a number of the major pirate groups. (While the *CEC
Future* was under attack, its captain was on VHF radio with a coalition
aircraft. The entire conversation can be heard at http://gcaptain.com/
cec-future-hijacking-vhf-recording/?7634.)

Pham got to know Mohamed—a U.S.-trained paralegal who spent
about fifteen years in the States—when he was helping a friend negotiate
the return of a boat that was being held by Mohamed and his associates.
Pham said they got into a conversation about the financial side of piracy,
and Mohamed explained that watching Wall Street was where he got the
idea of selling stock to the little people. Mohamed told him that

since the '80s, we're all in the stock market, whereas before it was a much smaller group of people. So now everyone has a stake in holding up the system. And the same thing with piracy. They don't need the widow's mite to finance their operations, but they let the widow have her little bit in it, and everyone else, so that there's a broader societal buy-in to what they're doing. It's a very sophisticated long-range plan, but it does buy them, in a conservative society—these guys are bringing drugs, loose women—all these things to communities that ordinarily wouldn't tolerate such behavior. But now that they're all shareholders in this enterprise, they're much more willing to put up with it than they would be otherwise.

It was, Peter tells me, "societal buy-in, or at least participation in piracy operations." He said piracy is primarily financed by established gangs, Afweyne, Barad, Boya.

Those guys are well-established. They can finance themselves. But for most, if you want to start piracy, you get a logistics guy. "What do you need? How many boats?" He prices it out. Just like any other small business startup, you put together a business plan, resumes—not formally, but in the oral culture—put a package together and then invite people to invest in it for a certain share of the take. And in Harardhere, Hobyo, Eyl, there are actually places, cafes, where people who do this [gather]. And just like Lloyd's started as a coffeehouse, you can go and there are people who've got piracy plans, and they're the middlemen, and you can bring your two hundred dollars, put it down [and buy in].

Pham estimates that there are, at most, two thousand to three thousand Somalis actively engaged in piracy, either offshore or directly involved in the operation. "Now, there are all sorts of people who got their one-hundred-dollar share in piracy, but those people can be weaned easily. They're not becoming wealthy off of it. They're making a nice little savings account—a few dollars added each month."

The big money goes to the bosses of the entire operations. These are the guys, Pham explains,

> who actually have the villas that you can see on Google Earth. The financiers abroad in the diaspora who put up the real money behind the big operations, who invest in them—the thousands, hundreds of thousands—and who take, probably, 30 percent of the take. They're the ones who're raking it in. What it works out to, though it's not labeled "A" and "B" shares, but there are, essentially, "A" and "B" class shares in piracy. And so, the big dollars buys you in not only big, but you get the big take of the ransom, and then the dividends paid are generous, in relative terms, as a return on capital. But since these [village] people are putting one hundred dollars in, if you get two hundred dollars back, you've doubled your money. Okay, so you live [on it] one month longer. But they're not raking it in.

The point he's making is that the situation in Somalia is considerably different from that of the farmers in Afghanistan who can make a fortune growing opium poppies, and who will undergo a radical lifestyle change if they have to forgo that operation and start growing basic agricultural crops.

With a systematic development on land, Pham believes that the little people investing in piracy could be weaned from it; they'd welcome the opportunity to not have the nuisance of a criminal element riding roughshod over them. That could happen, he said, because "most of the pirates don't come from the fishing villages that they've essentially taken over. Some of the big families that are engaged in piracy are actually up from the highlands, never lived by the sea. They're criminals, and this was the target, this was a business opportunity, and they came down to the shore and put themselves in business."

Pham laughs at the notion that pirates are just fishermen, outraged at other nations poaching their fish and despoiling their waters with illegal dumping. Despite the fact that Somalia has a coastline that lends itself to exploitation of huge fish stocks in adjacent waters, the Somalis actually disdain fish and fishing.

> Culturally, the sea was there, and they looked at it from a distance. The American dream is your house with a white

picket fence; the Somali dream is somewhere off in the land, with lots of camels. If Somalis had a choice, they would eat camel every day, but that's for the truly wealthy. So if you can't have camel, maybe goats and sheep. If you can't have that, maybe cattle. And if you're really poor, some chickens and maybe you can plant a few things. And then if you're truly down-and-out and living by the seashore like no good Somali should, then you can eat fish. You have a bigger chance of starting a fight if you call someone a "fish eater" than if you've insulted the virtues of their mother. Now, I wouldn't recommend either in Somalia.

So the whole idea that—and I'm not justifying fishing without a license or exploiting the economic zone of Somalia, but the idea that Somali [fishermen] went out of business because of foreign trawlers is laughable, because any Somali fisherman would've been out of business years ago for want of customers.

He said the intersection of fishing and piracy came at the very beginning, when the warlords sent their troops out in pirate vessels to extort the foreign fishing trawlers for protection money.

You have to admire the Somalis. They came up with a storyline that they saw would win. It fits exactly into our preconceived notions of environmental impact, and we buy it lock, stock, and barrel without knowing that Somalis wouldn't touch a fish. The funny thing is, the trawlers have been long gone for most of the decade precisely because of the piracy. No one's crazy enough to go fishing in the EZ [economic zone]; forget about the territorial waters. Now, it's just a nice justification to make us feel sorry for the poor pirate, when, in fact, it's purely criminal.

He adds that the irony of the fishing situation is that as a result of the foreign trawlers being driven off by the pirates, fishery stocks for commercial species like tuna are way up off the Somali coast.

I asked Peter Pham if he could help me understand the negotiations that take place between pirates and a shipping company once a vessel has been hijacked. Who calls whom if MV *McKnight* is pirated in the Gulf of Aden? He offered what he described as a concrete example: Andrew Mwangura, who heads the East African Seafarers union in Mombasa, a Kenyan citizen who is part Somali. Pham said, "Supposedly [Mwangura's] ministry is to help seafarers, and he does provide the Mombasa equivalent of a seaman's institute," which in his description sounds a lot like a USO center at Dulles International Airport.

> So if the MV *McKnight* gets taken and it's a Maersk ship, someone like Andrew will call up Maersk and say, "This is Andrew Mwangura and people are shooting, and I've got a lot of contacts here, and I've heard that the correct gang, Garaad, has your boat. And it's in Harardhere now. And I can help facilitate. . . ." And the fact is, he's the front man. But officially, he's just a well meaning [nongovernmental organization]. And he'll help. And if you're ingenuous enough to let him take you in, you expose your entire negotiating position to him, and he's in bed with them.

(When I asked Martin Murphy about Andrew Mwangura, Murphy took a different tack than did Pham. "I think he's got very good connections. How good they are into the piracy, I don't know. I don't think he's been paid money by the pirates. I'd be very surprised at that . . . half the constituency thinks Andrew's straight and the other part doesn't trust him an inch." He believes Mwangura is not distrusted because people think he's a pirate advocate or that he's on the pirate payroll; they just don't necessarily trust his information. "Nobody has ever suggested to me that he's on the take. I've spoken to him. I've met him once. He's a very engaging character—that doesn't demonstrate anything, but I think he's probably more straight than he is bent.")

Pham continued his description of the negotiation process between the pirates' representative and the shipowners, which he said is a game at this point.

> The game is—the pirate is running up costs from the moment he sailed, and a lot of his investors want their return now. He may have had to borrow money, in fact, from people who didn't want to be investors but simply lent money. They'd like their money back. So he's got a lot of people [to pay], and he's got bills coming in. He's got to

pay the caterer who's feeding the guards; you've got to pay the guards. They want to be paid daily; they don't trust you to hold their pay for two weeks. Somali pounds are going out the door, or in some cases, U.S. dollars, and it's eating into his capital. In fact, he's probably in debt at this point. He's got your boat—but he's also running up costs.

On the other hand, they've got an interesting cultural mindset. The longer they hold your boat, they'll raise the ransom to a certain extent, to pass on the costs to you of feeding your crew and all that. I've seen this on a number of occasions—they'll even give you itemized statements, you know, "slaughtered two sheep today." This was going back a couple years; I remember they were charging us about $130 for sheep slaughtered. Of course, when you're talking about ransom close to a million, who cares about $130. But very businesslike. They were tallying the costs. So you've got this clock going. You know the guy wants to get this over with and paid as soon as possible. On the other hand, your costs are running up, too, so you end up negotiating. Sometimes the dickering goes on for weeks. Sometimes the dickering is with your own insurance company, who's going to pay. At the end of the day, you settle on a number everyone is willing to live with. Unfortunately, that number keeps going up and up. We started with a $100,000 number, even less in the 1990s. Late '97 was the first million-dollar ransom, when the Taiwanese paid Abdullahi Yusuf, then the pirate warlord in Puntland, paid him a million dollars for the *Shen Kno II* and its crew. That million dollars made him president of Puntland, and then, in 2004, president of the Somali Transitional Federal Government, and the darling of the UN. He was the first million-dollar pirate. That's yet another one of my hobby horses—the fact that there is no consequence to being a pirate, and you can go from being a pirate to being a UN-recognized head of state.

Dr. Pham said Yusuf occupied the post until December 2008, when the international community—especially the Ethiopians—forced him to resign. He died in Dubai in March 2012 and was buried in his home-town of Gaalkacyo, whose landing strip has now been christened the Abdullahi Yusuf International Airport.

When I first came to Bahrain as commander of Expeditionary Strike Group 2, we were aware that some ransom payoffs were handled in Dubai. A guy would walk into a hotel room with a briefcase. He'd leave, a phone call would be made, and the hijacked ship would be released. But when I came back in 2009 as commander of CTF 151, the method had changed. They wanted to cut out the intermediary and increase the shares for the pirates. However, you still need to get the money to the pirates, and today in the world of capitalism, companies are doing airdrops from small planes usually flying from somewhere in Kenya. In fact, there are some great pictures of parachutes carrying bundles of hundred dollar bills floating down near captured ships.

Peter Pham told me the story of a friend whose company operated the *CEC Future*.

> My friend, Per Gullestrup, wanted his boat back as soon as possible, and his crew. And he knew [the pirates] were going to count [the ransom money] because we'd seen from other hijackings that they sat there and counted the bills. So we threw in a cash-counting machine for them in the drop, to hurry their counting, so we could get the ship and crew out as soon as possible. One of them had a heart condition and was ailing. We threw that in as a bonus because they can't count very well. I've watched videos of counts where it's painful to see. They can't keep the numbers straight and they start all over again. Even for the most seasoned pirate . . . it takes a long time to count five million dollars in one hundred dollar bill increments by hand.

I asked Pham to help me follow the money.

> What happens then with the money, the individual pirate crews disperse? Oftentimes, they operate like a pack of wolves. Garaad's crew seized the boat, but it can't sail it back and control it without calling for assistance. So you end up with one crew that took the boat but needed two

other operations to help bring it in. And then, so you've got all these parties, and none of them trust each other, so that's why they have to count the bills out openly. And then the various crews take their money and go back [to their base]. When they get back, they have to then account for it among their own, dividing it up. The investors get their cut; the government gets its cut—whatever governmental authority, local clan, the local shareholders get theirs—so everyone has to be paid out of this. Now, the biggest chunks—30 percent or more—that goes to the diaspora Somalis who put in the big bucks.

He said the distribution out of Somalia is actually made through the Islamic Hawala money transfer system, which is most simply described as the transfer of money without actually moving it. A succession of brokers make payments per the instructions they've received, and each broker takes a small commission. Hawala operates with a network of money brokers in the Middle East, North Africa, the Horn of Africa, and South Asia. There's also reason to believe that it reaches as far as the Somali diaspora community in Minnesota.

Pham said the U.S. hundred dollar bills may never actually leave Somalia. While he believes it's unlikely he can ever prove it, he's certain that if money is transferred by Hawala to Dubai, to Australia, and other places, it's also being transferred to the United States. "So Cousin Abdi is owed $50,000 on his $25,000 investment, so you walk into Hawala in Eyl and hand the man there $50,000, and he sends an email, and Abdi walks into the mall in Minneapolis and walks out with his money a day later." He said he knows that the FBI is interested in investigating the scheme.

Years of study have convinced Pham that, if nothing else, the pirates are adaptable. Whether they will continue to stay a step or two ahead of the coalitions fighting them is a question he can't answer. In late 2011 he went back to the Horn of Africa to investigate the latest wrinkle in piracy, one that developed after the pirates encountered problems using recognizable mother ships. These were pirated vessels that no one had bothered to ransom. Pham said, "What they're doing now is using Pakistani fishermen. And it's symbiotic: 'We'll let you fish in the EZ and won't molest you, and we float along with you, and we tell you when to drop us off.'"

He also said the pirates have drastically extended their range. There are reports from the Maritime Security Center HOA that Somali skiffs have been sighted thirty miles off the Gujarati coast of India, indicating that they're following fishermen all the way home to South Asia. As an indication of how piracy gets enmeshed in international politics, Pham said, "The Indians keep putting out information alleging that the Pakistanis are behind it in a governmental sense. Personally, I think the ISI [Pakistan's Inter-Services Intelligence agency] has bigger fish to fry than to engage in piracy. But certainly the Indians are spinning it that way." It should be noted that India is one nation that has very little tolerance for these swashbucklers from the sea. In March of 2011 the Indian navy battled a hijacked ship of pirates off their coast. The navy captured sixty-one pirates during the battle. The pirates were taken to Mumbai for trial. A self-appointed pirate leader named Bile Hussein threatened future "trouble" for Indian sailors and ships. "They better release them, considering their people traveling in the waters, or we shall jail their people like that," he said. "We are first sending a message to the Indian government of releasing our friends in their hands or else they have to be ready for their citizens to be mistreated in the near future."

To Martin Murphy, an internationally recognized expert on piracy and irregular conflict, the reasons that Somali-based piracy has flourished are obvious. He said, "Piracy, of course, has always been a crime of opportunity that is sustainable only in places that offer a combination of rewarding hunting grounds, acceptable levels of risk, and proximate safe havens." Check, check, and check. And now that the pirates have had a taste of the good life, Martin believes they see no reason to give it up.

The circumstance of the Somali pirates is, perhaps, quaintly reflected in the title to a song about the troops coming home from World War I battlefields in Europe: "How 'Ya Gonna Keep 'Em Down on the Farm (After They've Seen Paree)?" Just as it has been impossible to get the Afghan farmers to revert to growing staples instead of opium, it has been equally difficult to ask a Somali pirate to give up the potential for unbelievable riches in exchange for—what? There is nothing else. There are no other viable options to generate income. And Murphy is not just speaking of the skinny teenage pirate; he's talking about government officials and clan leaders. But he has some optimism.

> I think it's possible to get them out of the business. I think that they are also cognizant of risk. They know this is

not a long-term proposition. They've got other pressures on them in terms of what's happening in South Central [Somalia]. They don't want to see their territories descend into that sort of chaos. They're concerned about al-Sha-baab, and they're concerned, I think, about the political risks across the whole of Africa. But whatever we do is going to have to be a combination of incentives and disin-centives. I don't think there's any straight solution which says, "Look, we'll come in and we'll build you a bunch of roads and hospitals and factories, and in return, you stop doing piracy." Provided that the opportunities for piracy continue, then, they'll continue to maximize their income. I think it's pretty logical.

The solution, he believes, lies in coming up with a variety of disin-centives—among them, making the dirty money less attractive.

We're going to say to them, "Listen, we know you guys are involved in it. So we're going to track you down, and we're going to make your ability to spend that money very, very hard. Second thing, we're in a position to improve your political prospects, or damage them, and depending on which way you jump on this, so will we." And at the same time, we're going to say, "Look, we recognize that it's not just you but a whole bunch of people involved in piracy, right down to the soldier level, and can't just give it up. They're going to have to have some alternatives, and that means we're going to have to look at bringing money in from abroad." I don't see this as aid money, but has to be money brought in on commercially attractive terms. There's partially an investment community—and it's probably not American—you know, Dubai, Emirates or whatever. I mean, those guys are up to their necks in this business as well. Somalians are deeply involved in that community, and they have looked to Dubai for twenty, thirty years. That's the place where they go and do deals. There's a very large Somali diaspora there. They've got a lot of money, and if the projects emerge in Somalia, they might very well be interested in investing in them.

As with Jatin Dua and Peter Pham, I talked with Martin Murphy about where the ransom money goes and why it has, thus far, never been tracked by the U.S. Treasury Department. Murphy said he has discussed the situation with an insider at Treasury and was told that they just don't have the resources to do the job, which is something I've heard from others in Washington as I was researching the subject. The problem is that Treasury is a relatively small government department, and, as Murphy puts it, "the money hunters are an even smaller bunch." His source told him that "we just do not have sophisticated knowledge of a network. We don't know who's involved. We don't know how the money moves about. What we do know, we have got one huge advantage: We know where the money comes from. We know how it starts. We know it's put in a package together, we know at least who the initial recipients are. But after that, it just disappears."

Martin said one of his sources observed that "piracy is the only business in the world where the money literally drops from the sky." His description of the movement of money echoes those of Dua and Pham.

> At the moment, we can't follow the money because we don't know the nature of the network. Everything is paid, as you know, in hundred dollar bills. And then it is distributed like a flash. It's gone like a flash. Everyone is paid very, very quickly. Now, what happens to that money? I mean there are an awful lot of those hundred dollar bills in circulation in East Africa. Where they go from there, no one knows. Presumably, these guys are smart enough to be able to detect whether they've been colored or marked in some way. They actually take [counting] machines on board to make sure they're being paid correctly. So they're not stupid. I'm sure we could do a helluva lot more. I'm just saying that it isn't happening at the moment. I don't think I've been sold a line; I'm sure that this is just not happening.

Murphy agrees with my contention that if the State Department put pressure on Treasury and it was given the resources, Treasury could go out there and track the money and put a lid on piracy. "Absolutely. I've spoken to other people who have got clues. Most of the piracy [experts], they know who the leaders are. They know who the top guys are who are getting the money. And the organizers. But somehow they're not able to draw the dots between them."

He acknowledged that following the money could likely lead to businessmen and others with a political following or a clan following, but said deciding whether they're good people or bad people shouldn't be the point. "We should be simply looking at them as 'are they useful to us in terms of stopping piracy?'"

> And, you know, we can turn nasty sometime down the road when they're no longer useful, and we'll find something we can get them on—tax evasion, fraud, whatever it is. We can get them later if we want to. But at the moment, we're just interested in how useful they are. And if they haven't got connections, they're useful in terms of being made examples of. You know, "Here's this major leader who hasn't got connections; look what we did to him. We screwed him royally. And we didn't just stop his money. We knew he was operating an airline"—because one of them is supposedly operating an airline—"We knew he had property in Dubai and Nairobi and the Seychelles and London, and we got all that."

That, however, is more fantasy than reality because, from the multiple contacts I've made within the government, including at both the State Department and the Department of Defense, there appears to be no appetite for aggregating the human resources and the cash to go after the Somali pirates. And part of the reason continues to be the myopia of the American public and media: "if it bleeds, it leads" may be the mantra of the twenty-four-hour cable news networks—but unless the blood is American, no one seems to care. Until we put the resources of the entire U.S. government on the problem and generate the will to track down the leaders, piracy in the Horn of Africa will continue to be a national security issue.

CHAPTER 4

Best Management Practices

U.S. FORCES TAKE SHIP FROM SOMALI PIRATES

NAIROBI, Kenya—In a predawn raid with helicopters hovering nearby, 24 American Marines scaled aboard a hijacked ship in the Gulf of Aden on Thursday, arrested the nine pirates on board and freed the ship—all without firing a shot, the American military said.

According to American officials, around 5 a.m. on Thursday, two teams of 12 Marines each motored up in inflatable boats to the hijacked ship, a 436-foot-long German-owned cargo vessel called the Magellan Star. A band of pirates had seized the ship and its crew of 11 in the Gulf of Aden, between Yemen and Somalia, on Wednesday morning.

—Jeffrey Gettleman and Eric Schmitt, New York Times, 9 August 2010

---

et's not take anything away from the U.S. Navy and Marine Corps teams that risked their lives to rescue the crew and capture the pirates on board the *Magellan Star*, but there's no doubt that what was absolutely responsible for the fact that those eleven crew members and their ship didn't end up in a pirate anchorage close by the Somali coast until their rescue by these brave sailors and Marines was a little blue book. What's in that book has definitely prevented multiple felonies, averted tens of millions of dollars in losses, kept hundreds of mariners from becoming hostages, and in the process probably saved a number of lives as well.

I'll come back to the *Magellan Star* rescue operation and why there is concern with the added requirements in the decision process for the commanders at the scene even though everything eventually worked out for the best. But first—the book.

The title is *BMP4*. The subtitle explains it: *Best Management Practices for Protection against Somali Based Piracy*. Version 4 was released in August 2011, and a newer one is forthcoming. The book is a pocket-sized, attractively formatted 90-page manual designed to assist ships in avoiding, deterring, or delaying piracy attacks in the high-risk area. It was developed after years of coalition operations—navies, merchant fleets, maritime security organizations, and the International Maritime Organization—working together to fight one common foe: pirates.

While the authoring agency, the U.K. Maritime Trade Operations (UKMTO), and the multiple commercial and governmental signatories to it are careful to make no guarantees, it's clear from the latest piracy statistics that vessels implementing the broadest array of best practices have regularly sailed the high-risk area—the southern end of the Red Sea, the Gulf of Aden, Somali coastal waters, and Indian Ocean waters that have seen an increase in Somali-based piracy—without being boarded or hijacked.

The best management practices fall into three major categories, all of which are essential to maximize the defense against pirates. First, implement physical ship protection measures; second, register the vessel and report its progress through the high-risk area; and third, take very specific actions when a ship comes under pirate attack.

Before going into detail on defensive measures, a few definitions are in order. *BMP4* states, "A pirate attack as opposed to an approach is where a vessel has been subjected to an aggressive approach by a pirate craft AND weapons have been discharged." An "illegal boarding is where pirates have boarded a vessel but HAVE NOT taken control. Command remains with the Master. The most obvious example of this is the citadel scenario." Finally, "a hijack is where pirates have boarded and taken control of a vessel against the crew's will."

The thinking behind the best management practices (BMP) design is quite simple: if pirates are unable to board a ship, they will not be able to hijack the vessel. Pirates typically board targeted ships from motorized skiffs while the vessel is under way. This may sound odd, but the first active defensive measure and probably the most important against a pirate attack is to have a well-trained lookout posted. On many occasions—recall the takeover of *Danica White*—the pirates were on a ship before the crew even knew what happened. The second active defensive measure is to keep the skiff from approaching the ship. Third is to send

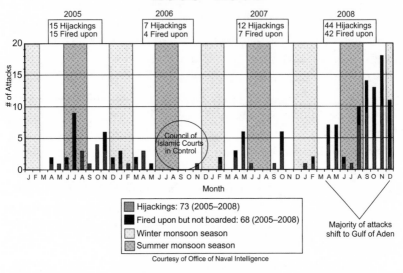

Somali Pirate Activity
2005–2008

2005	2006	2007	2008
15 Hijackings 15 Fired upon	7 Hijackings 4 Fired upon	12 Hijackings 7 Fired upon	44 Hijackings 42 Fired upon

Council of Islamic Courts in Control

Month

Hijackings: 73 (2005–2008)
Fired upon but not boarded: 68 (2005–2008)
Winter monsoon season
Summer monsoon season

Majority of attacks shift to Gulf of Aden

Courtesy of Office of Naval Intelligence

out the SOS notifying UKMTO and coalition naval forces of the attack. Fourth is to keep pirates from climbing aboard. Fifth is to make certain that if pirates do get on board, their access to the bridge is as difficult as possible. Sixth, if they do get to the bridge, they should find that no one is there, that the entire crew is safely locked into what's come to be called a citadel. Locked inside this safe haven, the crew members can control the ship's engine, steering, and electrical functions, and they have the means to communicate with the outside world. Ideally, they should have a supply of food and water to sustain them for up to three days until naval forces can arrive and confront the pirates.

For each of those steps to work, owners or operators of the vessel are presumed to be willing to invest in the physical upgrades and crew training required. However, while mid-size to high-end operators will comply, thousands of ships plying our oceans have owners who won't make the investment and crews who don't have the wherewithal to demand the basic safety measures needed to prevent the vessel from being hijacked. Those cargo ships—think tramp steamers if you're old school—and thousands of smaller dhows or fishing vessels will likely become the low-hanging fruit—easy pickings for the pirates, albeit with

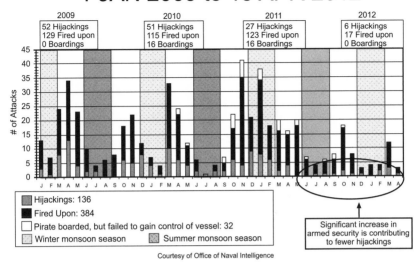

Somali Pirate Activity
1 JAN 2009 to 15 APR 2012

2009	2010	2011	2012
52 Hijackings 129 Fired upon 0 Boardings	51 Hijackings 115 Fired upon 16 Boardings	27 Hijackings 123 Fired upon 16 Boardings	6 Hijackings 17 Fired upon 0 Boardings

Hijackings: 136
Fired Upon: 384
Pirate boarded, but failed to gain control of vessel: 32
Winter monsoon season   Summer monsoon season

Significant increase in armed security is contributing to fewer hijackings

Courtesy of Office of Naval Intelligence

the potential for a much smaller ransom payoff, if indeed any ransom would be paid at all.

With BMP, the first line of defense is awareness. It may seem like a simple thing, but consider that some of the largest cargo ships and tankers on the oceans may have only two dozen crew members—and many of those are belowdecks, in the engine control room. When going through dangerous waters, a 360-degree watch has to be maintained 24/7. The BMP recommendation is that watchstanders should be visible; pirates are less inclined to attack a ship that has obviously prepared for the eventuality. Some vessels have successfully deployed full-size mannequins dressed like ship's crew along the rails just to make their defenses look more formidable.

Recently, when my co-author, Michael Hirsh, was on board Oceania Cruise Line's *Nautica* traveling from Aqaba, Jordan, to Dubai and transiting the heavily pirated southern end of the Red Sea and the Gulf of Aden, the ship's crew was augmented with an unarmed security team whose primary mission was to provide 360-degree observational security day and night. Just keeping a trained eye out for trouble was deemed important enough to bring specialists on board. Even though a cruise ship's primary defense against pirates is its speed, Oceania invested in the additional security team. The ship also held a mandatory pirate-attack drill for passengers, the object of which was to get all off the open decks and balconies and out of their cabins. Passengers were asked to sit on the floor in corridors or the central part of the ship to minimize their exposure to gunfire or RPG attack. *Nautica* was also equipped with long-range acoustical devices (LRAD) on the bridge wings, and while traveling in the high-risk area, remote-controlled fire hoses were clamped to an open deck railing on both sides of the vessel, ready to spray high-pressure water at attacking skiffs.

In the briefing that Hirsh received from the officer in charge of UKMTO in Dubai, Royal Navy lieutenant commander Simon Goodes, several photos were shown of pirate skiffs beginning to close in on their target, and it was often difficult just to see the skiff among the whitecaps until it was very close. Yet it's extremely important to know that an attack is imminent because it gives the master time to call UKMTO and provide the ship's location and other pertinent information.

Goodes said that they want merchant ships to call them if they see something suspicious. "Let us know. We don't mind. We'd rather have calls. Being out here for a few months, you get to know what's what. And there are certain times where we know it's fishermen as opposed to potential pirates." The Gulf of Aden is one of the most fertile fishing grounds in the world; in many cases ships will report they are under attack when in fact it is just fishing skiffs taking in nets or trying to keep larger vessels away from deployed fishing gear.

What they'll tell a nervous captain is, "If it gets within three miles, call us again." But UKMTO doesn't get its hackles up until the suspect boat comes within a mile. "It's difficult to see much detail beyond a mile in a skiff—as to how many people." But that's when they would advise the ship to go to a maximum state of maneuver. "One of our [suggestions], which is in the *BMP4*, is, as a skiff gets close—because they're primarily attacking from the stern or would come in from the stern and run up alongside and start shooting at the bridge to the master—is that the vessel make small alterations in course to create a wake effect, to push the skiffs off. However, we really stress that they must be small alterations, because if you make a larger alteration, of course, it slows the ship down. If you slow it down, they can get on board."

Goodes recalled a successful hijacking that took place when the ship slowed from fourteen knots to six as a result of maneuvering. He pointed out that the small alteration in course need only be between five and ten degrees. "It's not the actual course that does it; it's the actual angle of the rudder, which, depending on the performance of the ship, can slow it down a lot or a little bit. Some ships, you can put a lot of rudder on and it doesn't affect the speed; others, you put a tiny bit of rudder on, and it slows it down." He emphasized that crews have to be trained to respond properly. It's too late to practice the maneuver when they can see the pirates coming.

BMP recommends that ships' masters and crewmen on the bridge should be trained to bring their vessel to maximum speed when they believe an attack is possible. As of this writing, no ship moving faster than eighteen knots has been successfully boarded. Pirates will fire their weapons in the direction of the ship in an attempt to intimidate the master into slowing down. Goodes said, "Some captains will say, 'Well, I'll slow down.' You get a ten-month holiday [in captivity] if you do that. You need to keep the speed up and ignore the intimidation."

When the UKMTO command center receives a call from a ship's master saying he's being attacked, one person stays on the phone with the master, writing notes. Another is looking over his shoulder and then keying the information into an online site known as Mercury. Goodes said, "The previous Merchant Navy officer [running UKMTO] who was quite a character referred to Mercury as Facebook of the military. And it works. Virtually all ships and their commands, and various other places such as the Maritime Rescue Coordination Centers, have access to the Mercury websites on a commercial-in-confidence basis. It's not classified; it's totally unclassified."

When the attack information is keyed into Mercury, everyone monitoring the site knows what's happening. "When we have an attack, the whole section is highlighted; the background color is red. It really stands out." And it serves as an almost instant warning to other merchant ships in the area of the attack. Experience has shown that if pirates mount an unsuccessful attempt to hijack a ship, they will try again in the same general area within forty-eight hours.

Some ships are equipped with LRAD, the long-range acoustical device that can be used to warn the skiffs away. If that proves ineffective, the device can transmit a super-loud, powerful tone that, in theory, causes such severe pain that the pirates would leave. One shipping official I interviewed commented that while LRAD works on fishermen, it doesn't deter pirates.

If the pirates do manage to bring their skiff alongside the target, they'll either use a lightweight ladder with hooks at the top to grab the rail or gunwale, or they'll throw a grappling hook to the ship's rail and clamber up a knotted climbing rope. The most easily boarded vessels are those with low freeboard—a minimal distance between the deck and the water level. Fully loaded tankers—like the hijacked *Sirius Star*—often fall into this category.

BMP identifies a number of schemes to make it more difficult for pirates to board a vessel once they've climbed up the ladder. The most basic is stringing barbed wire along the deck rail, the more the better. Coils of razor wire do an even better job of stopping pirates. Some shipping lines are having electrified fencing installed all the way around their vessel. Masters on some Chinese merchant ships have prepared barrels of Molotov cocktails, ready to light and throw at pirates, although one ship's master reported that the pirates weren't afraid of the fire but of the broken glass bottles because they weren't wearing combat boots—they were all barefoot.

One ship that came under attack while I was patrolling the Gulf of Aden had skipped the Molotov cocktail defense and just smashed bottles and spread the broken glass over the deck. When the barefoot pirates clambered aboard, they had a painful surprise waiting for them. Other ships have carpeted companionways with smashed glass in an effort to keep pirates who have boarded the vessel from getting to the bridge.

Lieutenant Commander Goodes said that the representative of a security company that had come into UKMTO for a briefing told him that a security team boarding a ship in a former Eastern Bloc country persuaded the company security officer to invest in the beer bottle defense. "So they bought three big crates of beer bottles, full, and they drank it on the way down, and then smashed it. Which I would describe as a win-win situation."

One of the more popular and very inexpensive defensive measures is the use of high-pressure water hoses along the more vulnerable areas on deck. It's difficult enough to climb a ladder from a skiff to a moving ship; it can be almost impossible to do it with water pouring down on your head. Commercial vendors of protective equipment have come up with rotary nozzles that cover a large area alongside a ship with heavy spray. Some systems are able to add skin irritants and dyes to the water; others can heat the water to make it even more difficult for a pirate climbing a ladder. The important thing is that these devices are fixed in place and can be operated remotely—no one wants a crew member exposed to hostile fire because he's standing by the railing with a fire hose in his hands.

Should pirates succeed in boarding a ship, the best defense for the crew members is to lock themselves inside a citadel. Crew members secreted inside one need to know that before a naval or military force will attempt to retake a ship from pirate control, 100 percent of the crew must be secured in the citadel; the ship's crew must have self-contained, independent, reliable two-way external communications (VHF is not sufficient); and the pirates must be denied access to ship propulsion.

BMP4 clearly states that "the use of a Citadel, even where the above criteria are applied, cannot guarantee a Naval/Military response." The good news, of course, is that experience has shown that if the crew is locked inside a citadel and the military shows up, pirates most often quickly surrender. It doesn't take them long to realize that the military's rules of engagement are that anyone moving on the ship is a fair target.

One recent example of the success of the citadel defense can be seen in the October 2011 attack on the Italian ship *Montecristo* about 620 miles off the Somali coast and some 200 miles southeast of Oman. The vessel, with twenty-three crew members aboard, was carrying scrap iron from Liverpool to Vietnam. The ship was less than a year old and had been constructed with a citadel. Pirates struck shortly after the Japanese naval vessel that had protected it during transit through the IRTC (Internationally Recommended Transit Corridor) departed.

After transmitting the SOS, the entire crew locked itself in the citadel and, according to one report, took control of the steering and had the ship going in circles. For some reason the crew members did not have radio communication with rescue forces, but they apparently tossed a bottle containing a flashing strobe light along with a message saying that all crew members were in the citadel. The bottle was picked up by rescuers from Royal Fleet Auxiliary ship *Fort Victoria*, which was one of two NATO Operation Ocean Shield ships responding to the SOS. The other was the U.S. Navy frigate USS *DeWert*.

A statement from Italian defense minister Ignazio La Russa said, "Rubber boats circled the *Montecristo*, while a helicopter hovered above. The pirates surrendered right away, some throwing their weapons in the sea, and were arrested." Royal Marines boarded the ship and captured eleven pirates.

Now, let's return to the saga of the container ship *Magellan Star*, which was attacked by nine Somali pirates in a single skiff on 8 September 2010 about eighty miles south of Yemen. You've probably already figured out what saved the crew members from certain captivity. It was their citadel, built to the specifications described in *BMP4*. In this particular case, it almost worked a little too well—even the Marines had a hard time coaxing the eleven crew members from France, Russia, Poland, Bulgaria, and Ukraine out of their impregnable refuge.

It all began shortly after dawn when the CTF 151 flagship, the Turkish frigate TCG *Gökçeada*, responded to the SOS from *Magellan Star* and was joined quickly by the Aegis cruiser USS *Princeton*, which had been only fifteen miles away. Arriving on the scene, they discovered an abandoned skiff with two outboard motors floating nearby. Throughout the next twenty-four hours, the rescuers were in radio or phone contact with the crew. It's worth noting that *Magellan Star* and another cargo vessel were attacked almost simultaneously in the same waters—they were both observed on radar "steering erratically"—but MV *Olib G*, a Greek-owned chemical tanker, was quickly hijacked by the pirates and forced into Somali territorial waters before CTF 151 ships could intervene. The decision was quickly made to concentrate forces on *Magellan Star*.

The details of the rescue were reported by U.S. Marine captain Alexander Martin, commander of 2nd Platoon, Force Reconnaissance Company. He also held the title of 15th MEU Maritime Raid Force commander. Martin wrote about the mission in a Naval Institute blog and discussed it on the blog radio show "Midrats." His outfit was aboard USS *Dubuque*, which made what he describes as "an impressive twenty knots—not bad for the third-oldest ship in the Navy"—to get to the captive ship. Even at her age, *Dubuque* was an impressive platform for this type of mission. An amphibious transport dock, the 570-foot vessel carried elements of Marine Medium Helicopter Squadron 165 out of MCAS Miramar, California, that included two medium-lift helicopters plus four gunships to provide both aerial surveillance and support. In addition, a battalion landing team from 1st Battalion 4th Marines out of Camp Pendleton provided snipers in an overwatch position as the boarding teams conducted their assault.

By the time *Dubuque* reached the scene, *Magellan Star* was dead in the water with her crew locked inside the engine room citadel. All three naval vessels reported good communication with the captive crew.

So the good news was that the owners of *Magellan Star* had spent the money to build and equip a citadel that met all the requirements of *BMP4*, and apparently the crew members had rehearsed what they needed to do in the event of an attack that they couldn't thwart. The bad news was something the Marines quickly discovered: the ship had absolutely no other defenses against the pirates. It was operating at slow speed with a low freeboard. It had no razor wire strung around the deck, no fire hoses at the ready. It was a prime target for the pirates. Apparently, the crew members' game plan was that if they couldn't outrun pirates, they would hole up in the citadel and wait for the cavalry to arrive.

Perhaps that's not a terrible plan if your vessel is going to remain in the IRTC, where naval vessels and their helicopters are reasonably close, but in my view it's irresponsible for shipowners to send their vessels and crews into dangerous waters without offering them even the most basic of the antipiracy devices (other than speed). It's a good bet that if Jürgen Salamon, the managing director of the Dr. Peters Group, which owned the ship, had been part of the onboard crew rather than sitting in his office in Dortmund, Germany, the ship would have been better prepared. Being attacked by pirates and then locked inside a tiny room hoping that rescue comes before you run out of food and water doesn't do anything positive for one's psyche.

According to Captain Martin, by 1200 or 1300 his team members were ready to launch the assault to retake *Magellan Star*. They had adequate time to adjust their basic plans to deal with that type of vessel. They had practiced opposed or hostile boarding twenty or thirty times off Los Angeles, Long Beach, San Diego, and out in the South China Sea. The only thing they'd never done was assault a ship that was dead in the water. While it may sound as though that should be easier, they discovered that when the Navy coxswain driving the RHIB is holding it against the side of a ship that's tossing, the freeboard rapidly changes from six to fifteen feet, and that offered a challenge that had to be overcome with tactical decisions that got them a foothold on the ship.

So if they were ready to go at 1300—literally, dressed with weapons checked—why did they wait until dawn the following morning to launch the assault? Here's my take on a real problem in our modern military.

They didn't go ahead because the Turkish commander of CTF 151 didn't have authority to issue the order; the skipper of *Dubuque* couldn't issue the order; and the honchos at NAVCENT in Bahrain who should have issued the order couldn't or wouldn't issue it. CENTCOM and the Joint Staff? Ditto. SecDef at the Pentagon? Same. No, nothing would happen until someone at 1600 Pennsylvania Avenue said it could happen.

Aboard *Dubuque* the waiting was nerve-wracking. Captain Martin described it this way:

> A brief anecdote from those hours we spent at alert-30 in the small confines of that side port that would be our final position before we launched the assault: "Hey sir," yelled SSgt Homestead who was talking to Captain Doug Berblaauw, the ANGLICO Det OIC managing air up on the bridge wing, "the execute order's now at the three-star level." Everyone looked at each other half suspiciously.
>
> Then reports came to us about the pirates on board. They were armed. They were aggressive. They were pointing their weapons at the warships. They were making demands. They were non-compliant. They refused repeated attempts by the *Princeton* to surrender. They said they would stay on and fight.
>
> "They'll say go now," someone said, "won't they?" We waited and waited. "Hey," Homestead yelled, "listen up, the decision is now at CENTCOM." Pause. "General Mattis!" someone said, and the entire platoon ignited in a spontaneous cheer. A second pause. A sergeant remarks, "Man, now it's gonna take even longer," he said, jokingly. "Whatcha talking about man, it's General Mattis! We're golden." [James H. Mattis is a four-star Marine in command of U.S. Central Command. At various times in his career he's been called Mad Dog Mattis and Warrior Monk.] "No brother, now we'll have to wait for him to get aboard . . . you know the General will wanna be with us on this hit." Everyone laughed and felt relieved . . . this was going to happen after all.
>
> An hour later, still waiting, we asked each other, "I wonder what the hold up is?" Darkness was less than an hour away, time was running out. Homestead again: "Hey

guys, the execute order . . ." we all pulled our headsets off one of our ears to best hear him, "it's at the President." From the platoon: silence.

I think it was Staff Sergeant "Big Daddy" Holm who, from right behind me, captured the mood at that moment when he broke the brief silence with that wonderful and all-encompassing euphemism: "Holy shit."

When the order finally came, the operation actually went better than expected: not a shot was fired; no one was hurt. Nevertheless, it wasn't a cakewalk; all the bad guys didn't see the Marines coming, throw down their weapons, and put their hands on top of their heads. Martin said when his men rushed the port-side bridge wing, the first three pirates did surrender. But the other six didn't give up, leading the two dozen Marines in and out of corridors, cabins, and other spaces in the ship's multistory superstructure. Eventually, they had to use sledgehammers to break into a makeshift pirate citadel, and then used flashbang grenades to disorient the pirates, who still had their weapons.

Martin is justifiably proud of his men. "My Marines acted with extreme restraint. They had to clear six or seven decks. They never pulled the trigger—but they could have."

The conclusion of the assault on *Magellan Star* came next. But the Navy and Marine Corps teams from USS *Dubuque* had never rehearsed this type of assault. The Marines and their Navy reinforcements on the ship—perhaps as many as seventy-five different people—and the three warships floating nearby couldn't convince the crew members to come out of their citadel. They were afraid it was a pirate trick, and they weren't giving up their safe haven. It took a three-and-a-half-hour breaching effort with saws, torches, and other tools to cut through various doors and obstructions the crew had built.

Captain Martin writes:

> they finally cut one last hole and called in with a loud-speaker that it was safe, the marines had control of their ship, and to please come out. The ship's captain peered hesitatingly from behind a steel bulkhead, still unwilling to come forward. Sergeant Chesmore ripped an American flag patch from his shooter's kit and held it into the room as a final identification. The captain broke into a huge

smile and immediately called his crew from their hiding places. They ran forward, unlocked the final barricaded door in their 'citadel' and were escorted topside. Excited. Exhausted. And happy to have their ship back.

As I walked the captain up to his bridge, he examined all the cut doors, and burnt hallways and remarked, "Bastard pirates, they really did a number to my ship." Walking behind him I replied, ironically: "Yeah. They sure did."

In the Midrats blog-radio interview, Captain Martin volunteered his perspective on the long delay before they got permission to begin the assault. He said, "There's a belief out there that the decision-making process slows our actions. It actually really didn't; kind of helped us looking back, because had we gone on that ship that afternoon, the pirates were at their maximum level of awareness. And as an offensive measure, to be able to have the night to use some noise and light deception, be able to affect them [was useful]. Basically, to have the initiative at dawn, I think helped us in our assault. They had come down off their khat."

That sounds like something a good Marine junior officer might say, but from where I sit—from where I once sat—it doesn't wash. Who knew whether the crew's safe haven would really keep the pirates at bay for the additional eighteen hours it took to get the go decision? What wisdom could higher authority have brought to this mission that would have changed the plan?

In the early stages of World War II, Adm. Ernest J. King, the commander in chief of the U.S. Atlantic Fleet, issued two "Serials" to his commanders that stressed the important elements of command and control. I strongly recommend that every naval officer striving for command add these documents to his or her "must read" list to understand King's concerns for his commanders as our nation faced the challenges of war. In Serial 053 he stated, "I have been concerned for many years over the increasing tendency—now grown almost to 'standard practice'—of flag officers and other group commanders to issue orders and instructions in which their subordinates are told 'how' as well as 'what' to do to such an extent and in such detail that the 'Custom of the service' has virtually become the antithesis of that essential element of command—'initiative of the subordinate.'"

Each year the Navy and Marine Corps spend millions of dollars training their leaders how to respond in the face of conflict. In the case of

Magellan Star, there was a Marine Force Recon team that had practiced VBSS skills against hostile opposition. The team had all the equipment it could possibly need; there were no additional units that could or would be called in to back it up. I'm not a military psychologist, but I have to think about what it does to have men all kitted up to go, locked and loaded, and then told multiple times, "it's on, it's off, it's on, it's off." What does that do to their efficiency? Maybe you'll say that it had no effect—the results prove it. Okay. Each and every day you have commanding officers of Coast Guard cutters going after some hard-core drug smugglers in the Caribbean. Would they need permission from the national command authority to board a vessel if the master requested help because his ship had been taken over by drug runners? Of course the answer is no. Why should the rules change for a well-trained Marine Force Recon team going after a bunch of teenage pirates? As a retired flag officer who commanded CTF 151, I feel the decision should be made at the lowest level, and then the troops should be allowed to execute under the watchful eye of commanders who fully understand the known knowns as well as the known unknowns, and who can live with the unknown unknowns. What Admiral King stated years ago still holds true:

▶ Train them—by guidance and supervision—to exercise foresight, to think, to judge, to decide, and act for themselves;

▶ stop "nursing" them; and

▶ train ourselves to be satisfied with "acceptable solutions" even though they are not the "staff solutions" [or, in today's Navy, "Power Point solutions"] or other particular solutions that we prefer.

Remember the *Olib G*, the ship that was hijacked by one group of pirates at the same time that another group was attacking the *Magellan Star*? Apparently, the crew of eighteen on board the *Olib G* didn't have a citadel to hide in or the ability to make their ship go dead in the water until help arrived. As a result, they were forced to take her to a pirate anchorage off the Somali coast, and there they sat for sixteen months while a ransom was negotiated. The original asking price was $9 million; the pirates settled for $3 million and released the ship and crew on 8 January 2012. It's a good bet that it would have been a lot less expensive for the owners, not to mention the negative impact on the crew after more than a year in captivity, if they had followed BMP.

Let's get back to Best Management Practices for a wrap-up. Here's a summary of six "Do Nots" from *BMP4* for ships transiting the high-risk zone for Somali piracy.

▶ Do not be ALONE: Report to UKMTO and MSCHOA; use the IRTC; keeping AIS turned on is the preference of coalition naval forces.

▶ Do not be DETECTED: Keep track of NAVWARNS; use navigation lights only.

▶ Do not be SURPRISED: Increase vigilance—lookouts, CCTV, and radar.

▶ Do not be VULNERABLE: Use visible and physical ship protection measures.

▶ Do not be BOARDED: Increase to maximum speed; maneuver vessel.

▶ Do not be CONTROLLED: follow well-practiced procedures; use citadels; deny use of ship's tools, equipment, access routes to bridge.

BMP4 is available as a free e-book download from www.witherby-ebooks.com. Hard copies of the booklet can be obtained from UKMTO and other supporting organizations. *BMP5*—and possibly 6, 7, and 8—will be forthcoming, because one thing we've learned about Somali pirates: they adapt.

Here's one final note on BMP from Captain David Bancroft (RN, ret.), who, while stationed at UKMTO from 2007 to mid-2009, had much to do with the development of the BMP. Bancroft told me,

> It took the merchant community some time to come to grips with the fact that the navy had no magic answers, and that they too needed to take action—even today, some still do not do so. The basic fact is that proper implementation of BMP is a proven factor in vessels not being taken. BMP is not a menu to choose from, but rather is something that should be implemented to its fullest extent, up to and, wherever a proper risk assessment shows a need, including the use of armed teams on board.

CHAPTER 5

Should Merchant Ships Be Armed?

In my experience, getting an unequivocal answer from the U.S. State Department to just about any question you might ask is nearly impossible. That's why I was startled when, in the fall of 2011, I asked Donna Hopkins, State's coordinator for counterpiracy and maritime security, about armed security forces on cargo ships and she responded, "Completely in favor of that."

We need to view that in the context of history: Except for brief periods, as in World War II when the U.S. Navy put Naval Armed Guard crews aboard merchant ships, the notion of arming privately owned cargo vessels was anathema. We didn't want foreign vessels with guns on board coming into our ports, and vice versa.

Then Hopkins elaborated. "Through an interagency process, we came just a few weeks ago to a White House–level agreement that the United States would advocate for privately contracted armed security on board all commercial vessels. Parts of the industry weren't happy about that, Coast Guard was ambivalent, but we all agreed that would be the policy."

Clearly, the tide has turned with respect to putting armed security guards aboard civilian ships. A few years back, the stated policy of the UN International Maritime Organization (IMO) Maritime Safety Committee (MSC) was that armed guards were not a recommended way to deal with the threat of piracy. But in May 2011 the MSC approved interim recommendations for flag states regarding the use of privately contracted armed security personnel (PCASP) on board ships in the high-risk area of the Red Sea, Gulf of Aden, and Indian Ocean. To be clear, the MSC's recommendation did not include arming the crew members of these ships, which no one—from shipowners to seafarer's union—wanted. Its recommendation spoke to the notion that specially selected and trained guards hired from private security firms could do the job.

There appears to be no question that armed guards used in conjunction with best management practices have had a significant impact on Somali piracy. The International Maritime Bureau (IMB), which has been monitoring piracy worldwide since 1991, issued a report in January 2012 stating that the number of Somali incidents increased to 237 in 2011, up from 219 the year before. But the number of successful hijackings dropped from 49 in 2010 to just 28 in 2011. The director of the IMB, Pottengal Mukundan, said that "pre-emptive naval strikes, the hardening of vessels in line with the best management practices and the deterrent effect of privately contracted armed security personnel have all contributed to this decrease."

The statistic that stands out is this: no civilian ship with an armed security team on board has been successfully pirated. Based on that fact, it would seem that—at least until the Somali piracy problem can be dealt with at its source, on land—placing armed guards on ships is the answer. But it's not that simple; tough problems such as this one never have simple answers.

Stephen L. Caldwell is director of maritime security and Coast Guard issues for the U.S. Government Accountability Office. He's the captain of the ship in the U.S. government tasked with providing briefings, reports, and testimony on the subject of maritime security to congressional committees as well as to individual members of the House and Senate. He agreed with the pirate's point of view as expressed to me by my former boss at NAVCENT, Vice Adm. Bill Gortney, the view that says, "They will not shoot at me. I will get their money. And no one will arrest me. It's a good job."

"It's the easiest model," said Caldwell. "Very attractive. Low risk."

So are armed security teams the way to go? Do we want to say, "Navies of the world, back out. The private security teams can do it"?

"If you look at the resource equation," Caldwell said,

> you've got a billion-dollar warship—whether it's U.S. or Dutch or German or Chinese or Indian—you've got this billion-dollar flyswatter to swat a fly, and that's what the funny part is. The approach works in terms of the convoy or defining the clearly defined security area—when you're

in the Gulf of Aden and you have the Internationally Recognized Transit Corridor. But once you spread out to the whole Indian Ocean, there aren't enough ships in the navies of the world to cover it. And so, in that way, it's kind of more efficient [to have armed security teams on merchant ships]. From the U.S. perspective, these aren't U.S. ships, they're not U.S.-registered or crewed or flagged, and so, to some extent, why does our navy have to protect all that?

If you let the people going there decide what their protection needs are and deal with them—that's kind of what's happening. Because the flags of convenience, the Marshall Islands, Liberias, Panamas, they don't have any navies or they don't have navies that go hang out in the Gulf of Aden to protect ships. Is that where we want to go? It's almost, in some ways, a Band-Aid until something happens on land.

But then there are the pesky details. Such as, when is it okay to lock and load, and who gives the command? As a U.S. Navy admiral, the commander of a joint international task force, I could authorize a helicopter crew to fire warning shots in front of a pirate skiff in an effort to stop it from leaving the area. But even I didn't have the authority to authorize a shooter on board that helicopter or a ship to put a round through the outboard engine, much less fire with intent to hit one of the pirates. Additionally, there were different rules of engagement for each foreign navy ship participating in the coalition under my command. To try to put rounds through engines or bad guys, I had to seek permission from higher headquarters. It was frustrating, annoying, and unnecessary, not that I feel strongly about it. We're either out there to stop the felonies of armed robbery, piracy, and attempted murder on the high seas or we're not. Operating in this middle ground made us ineffectual at best. If these same restrictions had been in place for the naval commanders in the Pacific during the famous maritime engagements during the Guadalcanal campaign, the numbers of U.S. Navy ships in "Iron Bottom Sound" would surely have doubled.

Caldwell and I discussed the possibilities of for-profit companies getting into the business of putting armed guards on board ships at sea. He said,

You don't want anybody on there that's trigger happy. If you get the high-end security teams, these are either ex-SAS [Special Air Service] people out of the U.K., or they're [former] U.S. Special Ops people. And those people are very professional. They want to just do their job and get out of there. They're not going to be shooting people—they're going to be using economy of force and other kinds of principles to make sure things happen as smoothly as possible in avoiding incidents. Their goal is incident avoidance. There is, maybe, a concern if this becomes so widespread and cost becomes enough of a factor that people start going to the lower-cost denominator—the cheapest guys in town—they'll be getting people that aren't so professional or experienced.

To that point, at my last count there were 196 companies advertising their services providing armed guards for ships passing through the high-risk area, and the number seems to be rising monthly. Stephen Carmel, the senior vice president of Maersk Line, Ltd., the American division of the world's largest shipping company with more than 1,300 vessels, made a point of telling us that the security companies with whom Maersk has contracted will hire only former U.S. Navy SEALs for the job. It doesn't get any better than that in terms of quality of training. But Maersk is the Tiffany of shipping companies. It can handle a security fee of $50,000 per transit of the danger area without serious concern. (Truth is, Maersk is considerably less concerned about the economic impact of piracy than it is about any of a dozen regulations imposed on its operations by various international and U.S. government agencies, including Congress.) But there are thousands of shipowners that are more, shall we say, at the Wal-Mart end of the business, and while they don't want to send their vessels and crews out there unprotected, they're not buying top-shelf security.

While a proposal such as "put armed guards on the ships" seems to be such a simple way to deal with a difficult problem, it's a good bet that the devil is in the details. The laundry list of issues that the IMO said needed to be dealt with before PCASP will board a ship is lengthy.

The Intersessional Maritime Security and Piracy Working Group of the Maritime Safety Committee met in London in September 2011. It approved four MSC circulars on the following topics.

▶ Interim recommendations for port and coastal states regarding the use of privately contracted armed security personnel on board ships in the High Risk Area

▶ Revised interim recommendations for flag states

▶ Revised interim guidance to shipowners, ship operators, and shipmasters

▶ A questionnaire on information on port and coastal state requirements related to privately contracted armed security personnel on board ships.

Even as it acknowledged that it was providing guidance "as to under which conditions PCASP can be contracted to prevent ships falling in the hands of pirates," the IMO chose to print the following sentence immediately following the links to each of the circulars: "IMO does not endorse carriage of firearms by seafarers, or the use of privately contracted armed security personnel on board ships." On its web page titled "Piracy and Armed Robbery against Ships," the IMO chose to highlight several items of revised guidance. Under "Carriage of firearms on board merchant ships," the organization states that

> Masters, shipowners and companies should be aware that ships entering the territorial sea and/or ports of a State are subject to that State's legislation. It should be borne in mind that importation of firearms is subject to port and coastal State regulations. It should also be borne in mind that carrying firearms may pose an even greater danger if the ship is carrying flammable cargo or similar types of dangerous goods.
> Non-arming of seafarers:
> ▶ The carrying and use of firearms by seafarers for personal protection or for the protection of a ship is strongly discouraged;
> ▶ Carriage of arms on board ship may encourage attackers to carry firearms or even more dangerous weapons, thereby escalating an already dangerous situation. Any firearm on board may itself become an attractive target for an attacker;

▶ It should also be borne in mind that shooting at suspected pirates may impose a legal risk for the master, shipowner or company, such as collateral damages. In some jurisdictions, killing a national may have unforeseen consequences even for a person who believes he or she has acted in self defence. Also the differing customs or security requirements for the carriage and importation of firearms should be considered, as taking a small handgun into the territory of some countries may be considered an offence.

With respect to the "use of unarmed security personnel" the IMO highlighted the following:

▶ The use of unarmed security personnel is a matter for individual shipowners, companies, and ship operators to decide.

▶ The use of unarmed security personnel to provide security advice and an enhanced lookout capability could be considered.

As to the use of privately contracted armed security personnel, this is the revised IMO guidance:

▶ The use of privately contracted armed security personnel (PCASP) on board merchant ships and fishing vessels is a matter for a flag State to determine in consultation with shipowners, operators and companies. Masters, shipowners, operators and companies should contact the flag State and seek clarity of the national policy with respect to the carriage of armed security personnel.

▶ All legal requirements of flag, port and coastal States should be met.

▶ If armed security personnel are allowed on board, the master, shipowner, operator and company should take into account the possible escalation of violence and other risks.

In case it hadn't yet been made clear, the IMO added this:

▶ New interim recommendations and guidance (MSC.1/Circs. 1405 and 1406) do not change IMO's position on the use of armed personnel—seafarers should not be armed and the carriage of PCASP remains a matter of decision for the shipowner, after a thorough risk assessment, to request and the Flag State to decide. Flag States should have a policy in place on whether or not the use of PCASP will be authorized and, if so, under what conditions.

▶ While providing guidance as to under which conditions PCASP can be contracted to prevent ships falling in the hands of pirates, IMO has clarified that it neither endorses nor institutionalizes the practice or the carriage of firearms on board merchant ships.

The issue wouldn't be nearly as complicated if the ships only sailed from Tampa to Texas. But as soon as international borders are crossed and foreign waters traversed, the complications multiply exponentially. Let's try to translate the IMO guidelines for an American-owned container ship of Liberian registry, sailing with a Filipino crew under a Croatian captain, carrying cargo owned by a German company from Japan to Italy with a stop in Salalah, Oman. The PCASP only needs to be on board the ship while it transits the high-risk area. Where do the armed guards board the vessel? How do they get there? Do they bring weapons and ammunition with them? How many countries have to approve their passage through their airports and seaports? What happens to their weapons when they enter the port in Salalah? What happens when they enter the Red Sea, which, technically speaking, has no international waters but belongs to a handful of countries on either side? How do they deal with the Egyptian-owned Suez Canal? At this writing, Egyptian authorities require a letter of certification on the number of weapons and the employer of the armed guards on board. Where do the guards disembark? What happens to their weapons and ammo? Could the guards pick up another ship going in the other direction, back through the pirate-infested area? What if they need new or different weapons and ammunition?

And what happens if the ship comes under attack and the armed guards shoot someone? Or get shot? Who provides medical care? Who investigates the incident? Keep in mind that I'm not a lawyer, just a retired admiral. If I can come up with a list of questions that can fill half a page, imagine what a tag team of military and civilian lawyers from international agencies, governments, and corporations can dream up.

Stephen Carmel of Maersk is remarkably candid about the situation. He describes the debate over arming merchant ships as a pain in my butt right now. You know, the official position of the U.S. government—and you get the people giving speeches about this all the time, Deputy Undersecretary of State for Terrorism and all that kind of stuff—that the solution to piracy is arming ships, right? And we actually have armed—all our ships that trade in that area now carry armed security. But the interesting thing is the Suez Canal. The Egyptian authorities—they're a little alarmed, because of course, if you trade in that area, you're going through the canal. They said, "If you want to continue trading through the canal and you have armed security teams on board, we want some sort of certification from your flag state that you're doing this in according with flag state law." We have that certification from the Marshall Islands and a couple of others. The U.S. government has refused to provide it. The State Department punted it over to the Maritime Administration, one of the most inept government organizations in existence, and they just don't do it. They won't do it.

And that, he said, will cause real problems for his American-flagged ships passing through "the Ditch."

Once the Egyptians start enforcing that, what we're going to have to do is put our weapons ashore at the south end of the canal or pick them up at the south end of the canal, which, by the way, puts us in violation of our arms exports license. The other thing that's interesting is, there's no rule on anybody's books globally on how to deal with armed merchant ships. [And that's the case because] the world, a hundred years ago, made a concerted effort to get rid of arms on merchant ships.

Nobody has any rules on this. In the United States, anyway, they've chosen to deal with it through standard arms trafficking regulations, which is mindboggling to me, because that's not the business we're in. So we actually have an arms export license, and by the way, the only country we've ever had our arms seized in is the United States. Part of that license says that we're not allowed to take weapons off the ship, but if we can't get through the canal with them on the ship, we're going to have to. So, catch-22: we either stop trading or deliberately violate our arms export license. This is a major mess.

Carmel told me that Maersk has been using small craft at the south end of the Suez to take the guards off the ships, but the weapons stay on board. "Once we're armed, we are armed everywhere we go. There's no international protocol for entering clearance for armed ships; there's no protocol for training internationally; there's no protocol for what appropriate weapons are; there's no protocol for potential liability. So we're fine with arming the ships. But we would like somebody to give us the cover we need to do it legally. That's a major open issue."

I posed a scenario: pirates are attacking. Who has the authority to fire at the pirates? Is the master the ultimate authority? Carmel said, "That's one of the reasons why, at least me personally, I am very opposed to putting active duty [military] security teams on board. Because if they're active duty, it's not the master. Terry, when you were out there, it would've been you who has the authority. And I bear the liability for what they do. So, we have very specific violence escalation protocols, and the captain's the one that says, 'Okay, shoot.'"

Proposals to put armed military teams on board high-value target merchant ships crop up occasionally at websites that cover maritime security. One proposal had teams embarking from a military mother ship at one end of the high-risk area and picked up by another mother ship at the other end. The theory is that this would limit the need for warships to cover the entire ocean. While U.S.-flagged ships carrying sensitive military cargo are already assigned armed guards, this is not a plan that has found any favor in either military or commercial shipping circles. Recently the U.S. Navy retrofitted the amphibious transport docking ship USS *Ponce* as an "afloat forward staging base" to be used primarily by Navy SEAL teams in the Persian Gulf. The unofficial description of *Ponce* was a mother ship. Pentagon spokespeople indicated that the vessel would be available for secret commando missions offshore. Fighting piracy was not specifically mentioned but could quite possibly be one of the required missions.

While Steve Carmel wouldn't provide a written copy of Maersk's protocols for armed guards on board their ships, he did offer a taste. "LRAD first," said Carmel.

The manufacturer of LRAD, the long-range acoustic device, said one model "provides a directional audio broadcast that can safely communicate with high intelligibility far beyond standoff distances. LRAD 2000X operators have the ability to issue clear, authoritative verbal commands, followed with powerful deterrent tones to enhance response capabilities." They claim voice commands can be clearly understood over a distance of eight thousand meters. An LRAD can project warning tones of 153dB effective at a range of more than three thousand meters. The human threshold for sound-induced pain starts at around 130dB. A jet engine at one hundred feet measures 140db. "We know LRADs don't work on pirates, but they work on fishermen. So it's an intent discriminator."

Then he jumped from the equipment to the operators. "We worry a lot about liability. I want to make sure that the guys out there will keep their heads, and they don't shoot at people that shouldn't be shot at, but [if they shoot] at the people that should be shot at, they hit 'em. So every single one of them is a former SEAL. Very professional, and they do a lot besides just ride around and wait for pirates. They help in training the crew. They do security assessments for us."

After both on- and off-the-record conversations with Carmel, I learned that the logistics side of the armed-guards question is easier to deal with than the head game—creating workable ROEs and then making sure they're honored. It's why Maersk hires former SEALs.

In a military environment, the ROEs are super specific—not just when an action may take place, but who has the authority to authorize it. Who can be armed? Under what circumstances are weapons displayed? When can weapons be loaded and rounds chambered? When can warning shots be fired? When can disabling shots (at a boat's outboard engine, for example) be fired? And when can shots be fired at human targets?

To be clear, there is no distinction, as some seem to think, between shooting to wound or shooting to kill. If I authorize my crew to eliminate a threat, the protocol is to aim for body mass. And that's a kill shot.

For Lt. Cdr. Simon Goodes, who was the Royal Navy officer in charge of UKMTO, the British Maritime Trade Operations in Dubai, the rules of engagement are very important. UKMTO serves as the primary point of contact for merchant vessels transiting the high-risk area and is the liaison with military forces in the region. Recall that when

Maersk Alabama came under attack, the first call Captain Phillips made was to UKMTO.

In his office just off the small but very busy command center that UKMTO staffs 24/7 on the grounds of the British Embassy, Lieutenant Commander Goodes felt it important to define an attack before getting into the subject of use of lethal force.

> We only define it as an attack if the merchant vessel is fired upon from the skiff or mother ship, or there is a physical attempt to board, which is actually trying to put the ladders or ropes on board. If it's a situation where a skiff is coming close and the armed security team is firing multiple weapons at the skiff but they don't fire back, that's not an attack.
>
> The attack is only if the skiff is firing at the merchant vessel because, especially around here, bear in mind that all the skiffs carry AK-47s to protect their catch. And the armed security team may be firing on innocent fishermen. That's not an attack; that's a lack of knowledge of the area. There have been multiple reports of swarm attacks by skiffs. To the best of my knowledge, we are not aware of any.

UKMTO gets reports via telephone and e-mail, and the vast majority of attack reports come from fishing boats. He said it's possible that there may be one or two pirate skiffs hiding within the fishing fleets that come out and attack cargo vessels, but he also said, "It may have been that there's an armed team on board the vessel that thinks, 'Oh, they're pirates! Bang-bang-bang-bang-bang, that's an attack. Must've been somebody; there were shots fired.'"

Goodes is sure that innocent people have already died at the hands of supposedly trained armed guards aboard merchant ships. "I think there have been tragic incidents already. But it has not got to the ambulance chasers yet. I believe there have been innocent people, innocent fishermen killed already."

He draws that conclusion based on a close reading of after-action reports. "When an after-action report says, 'They approached and we fired flares. They came closer, so we fired warning shots, and we clearly saw all six shots hit the water,' that's not the sort of thing you write in an after-action report. When a warship finds a body in a skiff an hour later, that would indicate to me [that the circumstances need to be questioned]."

Lieutenant Commander Goodes said that there were authorized armed guards aboard merchant ships from the beginning of his tour at UKMTO in July 2011. "Some flag nations were approving armed guards, others were turning a blind eye, and other vessels were doing it, risking the wrath of their flag nation."

I asked him a very direct question about the death of innocents at the hands of armed guards. Would he go so far as to suggest that in some corporate suite somewhere people are basically saying, "So, we kill a few fishermen out in the middle of the Indian Ocean. They're never going to sue us. Who's going to know?"

His response was cautious. "'I don't know' is my best answer to that. But human nature or analysis of human nature would indicate there must be a proportion of humans that would take that view. Is that vague enough?" Then he laughed. But he continued in all seriousness, leading to a discussion of how the military from different nations each has its own unique way of dealing with pirates, and how the pirates have become cognizant of those differences. "I mean, different nations have different robustness in their approach. And on a national, governmental scale, as well as individually, it's interesting to see different reactions from the pirates against nationals of particular countries."

He wouldn't go on the record, but it's fairly well known that the Indian navy takes an especially aggressive approach in dealing with pirates. He said that Oman, which has a huge investment in the Sultan Qaboos container port in Salalah, is also known to be aggressive. And of course those of us who've been on patrol out there have heard the stories about the Russians, whose naval vessels might catch pirates one afternoon, but by the following morning the pirates have disappeared. "It's very dark out here, and it's a big ocean," is what they'll say if asked. Sort of a fill-in-the-blanks-yourself answer.

The belief that innocents have died at the hands of some of the privately contracted armed guards was echoed by Jatin Dua, the Duke University PhD candidate who lived among the Somali pirates for nearly half a year, and who provided us insight into the pirates' operations. Speaking of people who were actually fishermen—not pirates posing as fishermen—he said, "I can verify fishermen have been lost at sea or other things have happened because of some of these security contractors. You know, most of [the fishermen] are armed when they go; Yemeni fishermen, especially, will be armed. And there have been confrontations at sea, and then these stories sort of circulate. [Fishing] is more dangerous now because they'll be shot by the pirates or you can be shot by the ships themselves because they mistake you for pirates. And, unlike the navies, they shoot first and then ask questions later."

So now that there's a body of experience with putting privately contracted armed security personnel on merchant ships, what's the conclusion? Unfortunately, there's no simple answer to the question. In a perfect world, I'd prefer that merchant ships were unarmed. But with hundreds of seafarers held hostage for ransom over ever-lengthening periods of time, it's difficult to argue against it. However, no matter how effective the security teams have become, they are no replacement for the capabilities that naval warships can bring to the fight. This is not the time for the victory parade on piracy.

And speaking of seafarers held hostage, there's yet another twist to the question of liability related to armed guards aboard cargo ships: what's the liability of a shipowner who knows his vessel is plying pirated waters but doesn't embark armed guards to protect the crew? Eight crew members who were aboard *Maersk Alabama* when Captain Phillips was kidnapped have sued Maersk for damages. They claim the company violated the Jones Act in that it was negligent in not providing armed guards in known dangerous waters; they have also sued for breach of the warranty of seaworthiness, which requires shipowners to furnish a fit vessel.

Attorneys Darren Friedman and Lauren Smith with the civil litigation firm Foreman Friedman, PA in Miami and Chicago said, "It is foreseeable that a court could find a vessel traveling the east coast of Africa to be unseaworthy because of the absence of appropriate security measures, including armed guards." They said that there is an emerging consensus that "from a liability standpoint, this may mean that in order to satisfy their duty to crewmembers to provide a fit vessel and a safe place to work, shipowners need to begin hiring armed guards to protect crewmembers while their vessels are travelling in high-risk waters." They add, "It is important to note that, while the use of armed guards may be beneficial evidence in a lawsuit brought by victims of a pirate attack, it will not prevent a lawsuit from being filed."

There appears to be one unintended consequence of armed ships successfully warding off pirates. In late 2011 the U.K.-headquartered risk mitigation firm AKE Group released an analysis that said, "This combination of lower success rates and increased use of armed guards will cause an escalation of violence, and will lead pirates to focus their activities in areas further south." The company predicted that the high-risk area will continue to increase, with more attacks expected to take place off the Tanzanian and Kenyan coasts as well as toward the Indian coastline.

Having been out there chasing pirates, I continue to be annoyed by a confusing U.S. government policy that opts for merchant ships defending themselves with lethal force against pirate attacks but that still requires our military to engage in what I guess is best called thwart-catch-and-release.

Maybe the powers that be in Washington are hoping that the pirate leaders will figure out that attacking an American-flagged ship can be a terminal error, so they'll look elsewhere for easy pickings. And frankly, given the proclivities of the American public and the media in this country, unless it's an American ship under attack, or an American citizen kidnapped, it's not really big news. So the policy, while annoying and not effective in the long run, works.

There's one final element to this question of lethal force that needs to be addressed: what happens when the armed guards on a cargo ship blow a skiff out from under the pirates, leaving half a dozen or more of them clinging to wreckage somewhere out in the Indian Ocean. Article 98 of the United Nations Convention on the Law of the Sea (UNCLOS) Treaty clearly states that a ship's master is required "in so far as he can do so without serious dangers to the ship, the crew or the passengers: to render assistance to any person found at sea in danger of being lost." Now what?

CHAPTER 6

Crime without Punishment

Okay, I'll be the first to say it. We need a prison ship. Actually, the combined navies fighting piracy in the Gulf of Aden, the Red Sea, the Arabian Sea, and the Indian Ocean need a prison ship. Call it an oceangoing Gitmo. Or don't. But until someone comes up with something that gets us out of the catch-and-release game we've been playing with these pirates, that's what we need.

Why? Because we're getting pretty good at catching Somali pirates—and both the attacks attempted and successful attack numbers have dropped now that a coalition of navies that at one time or another has included the naval firepower from the United States, Australia, Canada, China, Denmark, France, Germany, Greece, India, Italy, Japan, Korea, Portugal, Pakistan, Malaysia, Seychelles, New Zealand, Saudi Arabia, Russia, Singapore, Spain, Sweden, Turkey, South Africa, and the United Kingdom has figured out how to catch them in the act, and even before the act. The problem is that once we catch them, there are limited options in place to charge them, try them, convict them, and imprison them.

In late January 2012 Fifth Fleet commander Vice Adm. Mark I. Fox said that countries with navies collaborating on the piracy mission were holding seventy-one captured pirates. Fox told the *New York Times*, "There is not a repeatable international process to bring them to justice. We lack a practical and reliable legal finish."

While the State Department continues to insist that it is committed to bringing pirates to justice and that Secretary of State Hillary Clinton is not happy with the practice of catch and release, no viable solution to the problem has emerged. Hence the need for a prison ship. Permit me to explain with a vivid example.

In January 2012 six Somali pirates attacked the bulk cargo ship MV *Sunshine* about one hundred miles off Oman. It was a by-the-book approach: brandishing AK-47 assault rifles and a rocket-propelled grenade launcher, they came alongside their target, threw a grappling hook, and then tried to affix a ladder to the vessel. While the captain on the bridge radioed for help, crew members trained fire hoses on the pirates. Then the ladder broke. That was bad enough, but things were about to get worse because the pirates had opted to attack a ship that was just a few miles away from the aircraft carrier USS *John C. Stennis* and its accompanying task force, including the guided-missile cruiser USS *Mobile Bay*.

The commander of the *Stennis* strike group checked the radar images, saw that they were just a few miles from the scene of the crime, and said, "These might be the dumbest pirates ever." Within minutes, one helicopter was hovering over the six pirates in their skiff. Hoping to find the mother ship for those pirates, Rear Adm. Craig Faller ordered additional helicopters to check out other vessels in the area.

While a boarding party captured the half dozen pirates near *Sunshine*, two Navy helicopters discovered the fishing boat *Al Mulahi* roughly 175 miles southeast of Muscat, Oman. It caught their interest because it was carrying a skiff identical to the one that had just been captured. There was a problem, however. The dhow was flying an Iranian flag, and there were no Somalis visible on deck. Given U.S. relations with Iran, sending a boarding team at this stage was out of the question.

But someone came up with a brilliant plan. The pirates attacking *Sunshine* had thrown their weapons overboard, so the boarding team acknowledged that they couldn't be arrested. They gave the pirates food and water and turned them loose. What the Somalis didn't know was that a helicopter from *Mobile Bay* was tracking them—and they headed right back to the Iranian dhow.

Meantime, the guided-missile destroyer USS *Kidd*, which was serving as flagship for CTF 151, steamed at full speed toward *Al Mulahi*. It took several hours to cover the 120-mile distance, and when it got close, it contacted the dhow on bridge-to-bridge radio and asked if there were any foreigners aboard. The answer was no. However, aerial surveillance had revealed that there were Middle Easterners aboard as well as Somalis. *Kidd*'s crew also could see that some of the clothing hanging to dry was Somali. According to reports from a *New York Times* reporter who was aboard *Kidd*, there was a brief standoff during which the Somalis remained hidden and forced the Iranian captain to speak with the Americans.

Among *Kidd*'s crew were sailors able to speak many languages; one of them, CPO Jagdeep Sidhu, spoke English, Punjabi, Urdu, and Hindi. Listening to the radio conversation, he heard the Iranian captain use an Urdu phrase. Sidhu responded, and the captain eventually said in Urdu, which the Somalis didn't understand, "We need help. Please help."

That request was good enough for the commander of CTF 151, Pakistani rear admiral Keleem Shaukat, to authorize a boarding. Two RHIBs carried the VBSS team members to the boat, and once they boarded the vessel, they discovered six Somalis hiding near the bow and nine more in a cargo hold. They offered no resistance. A search turned up four assault rifles and ammunition. The captain of the dhow, Mahmed Younes, said he and his crew had been held hostage by the fifteen pirates for more than two months—and it was the second time in recent years that he'd been taken captive by Somali pirates.

All fifteen pirates were taken aboard *Kidd* and then flown to *Stennis*, where they were locked in the brig. The crew of the fishing boat was given food and fuel, and it sailed back to Iran.

And therein lies the problem. Fifteen Somali pirates were in American custody, first on *Stennis* and eventually handed off to the newly arrived aircraft carrier on station, USS *Carl Vinson*. The cargo ship they had attacked was Greek-owned but sailing under a Bahamian flag. The attack took place in international waters but within the exclusive economic zone of Oman. And they had hijacked an Iranian vessel and kidnapped its crew. Those were the crimes. But what were the real options for punishment? As it turns out, despite the possibility that any one of several countries could claim jurisdiction and prosecute, there weren't many.

Even Captain Younes was cynical about the situation, telling the *Times*, "The punishment should be for the crime. They should be taken to court and tried. At any cost they should not be let go, because if you let them go they will come back stronger and harass more people. Every time these navies' countries let them go, the pirates just laugh at that."

After considerable negotiating and hand-wringing, and after an attempt to have several different countries each take a few of the pirates for trial didn't work, the Republic of Seychelles ultimately agreed to accept the lot of them. While the diplomats were figuring things out, the pirates got a tour of the best the U.S. Navy has to offer. They went from the *Stennis* brig to the *Vinson* brig. Next stop was the destroyer USS *Momsen*, which was heading to the Gulf of Aden and which was where the pirates needed to be situated for their final move. *Momsen* didn't have the space to accommodate them, so they were moved to the amphibious transport dock USS *New Orleans*, which offered sumptuous accommodations on the American plan. Once the deal was done, they were flown by helicopter to the U.S. base in Djibouti and placed aboard a C-130 for the flight to the Seychelles.

State Department spokesperson Victoria Nuland issued a statement that said, "We appreciate the Seychelles' regional leadership on counter-piracy, as seen in their willingness to prosecute and incarcerate Somali pirates, as well as their plans to host a regional intelligence coordination center to support future piracy prosecutions." Given that the Seychelles are on record that their pirate-holding facilities are overburdened, I'm going to take a guess and say that the United States offered a financial inducement to sweeten the deal.

At this writing, I'm told that there's a lot of wheeling and dealing going on to find countries—plural—willing to try those fifteen pirates. Kenya may take two; the Seychelles another two. The rest? Who knows? I'm half-wondering if the pirates are going to be offered a choice of where they'd like to be tried.

Any notion of an efficient legal process in this matter and others like it is a pipe dream. Who's going to pay for witnesses to attend multiple trials in locations on two continents—or way out in the middle of the Indian Ocean? Who's going to gather the evidence and prepare cases that can be successfully prosecuted in the judicial systems of a variety of countries?

My former staff judge advocate at CTF 151, Cdr. Pete Koebler, one of the most seasoned maritime lawyers I've ever known and my right-hand man, provided a memo that offered greater detail on the difficulties of prosecuting pirates. First problem: "It is not enough to say that international law allows for universal jurisdiction over piracy. In order to legally prosecute suspected pirates under a nation's own domestic laws, the nation concerned must normally also have adopted some sort of domestic criminal law concerning the topic of piracy."

He said that, ideally, the law would mirror the broad definition of piracy found in international law, but that nations that have not historically been directly affected by piracy might not have laws that apply to the current circumstances. Then he offers this concern:

> Even assuming a particular nation does have a domestic law on point, such a nation may well be concerned about the precedent it will set whenever it elects to prosecute a particular set of suspected pirates. Having done so in an individual case, will they now be honor bound by the court of popular opinion to prosecute all similarly situated suspected pirates in the future? Even if it will not break the national treasury to prosecute a particular set of suspected pirates, can the nation afford to prosecute the numerous other similar groups of suspected pirates who may well be captured later that very same year?

For the United States, piracy is one of the offenses against which Congress is delegated power to enact penal legislation by the Constitution. The document addresses piracy in Article 1, Section 8. It gives Congress "the Power . . . To define and punish Piracies and Felonies committed on the high seas, and Offenses against the Law of Nations."

Since 2009, the United States government has taken quite a few pirates to trial.

▸ 2009—MV *Maersk Alabama*, 1 prosecuted (3 killed)

▸ 2010—USS *Nicholas* attacked, 5 suspected pirates captured; USS *Ashland* (LSD 48) attacked, 6 suspected pirates captured

▸ 2011—SV *Quest* attacked, 2 pirates killed, 13 pirates captured (4 hostages killed)

▸ 2012—Saeed Abdi Fooley pleaded guilty to piracy of Jean and Scott Adams' yacht *Quest*

What these cases have in common is that the victims or intended victims were American citizens or American ships. Our government was willing to commit the resources to collect the evidence and bring witnesses to the trials. But not every country has that ability. Back to Pete Koebler's brief:

The stronger the evidence is against the suspected pirates, the more likely it is that a nation will be willing to prosecute them. An ideal case would be one involving the capture of some suspects shortly after they have actually attempted to pirate another vessel and in which there were multiple witnesses who are willing to identify their attackers in court, as well as, perhaps, even photos or videos they took of the piracy attempt. Also, not unlike drug runners who are prepared to throw their contraband overboard before capture, there are certainly pirates who are well prepared to dispose of any incriminating evidence which might be used to help prove their true intent in the event it appears they might be captured while traveling about the Gulf of Aden.

Think back to the pirates who attacked the *Sunshine* and hijacked an Iranian fishing boat to use as a mother ship. Certainly, the American sailors involved in their capture would be able to testify, but what about the merchant seamen aboard *Sunshine* who fought off the pirates? What about Captain Younes? If Iran isn't going to try those pirates— and that's a good bet—are the mullahs going to send Captain Younes and his crew abroad to testify at a piracy trial? The pirates were caught red-handed just like so many others we caught when I was out there. But I wouldn't bet on their trial, much less on conviction.

While we were at sea, Pete Koebler shared my frustration at our inability to prevent pirate attacks by capturing Somalis who, in our view, were clearly bent on mischief. He wrote,

> There were also several occasions when we rescued some Somalis at sea and it seemed that regardless of what their true intent may have been when they set out to sea, no nation would likely be willing to prosecute them for anything. On the one hand, if a large number of young men from Somalia are floating about in a skiff in the vicinity of the International Recommended Transit Corridor through the Gulf of Aden, then it is difficult to imagine a particularly good reason for them being there absent an intent to commit piracy. On the other hand, if there are no grappling

hooks, no ladders, no masks, and no weapons aboard the skiff when it is boarded, then it is equally difficult to imagine a successful piracy prosecution of such individuals. A defense attorney would likely be able to argue successfully that there is simply insufficient evidence to prove they are pirates. In fact, even if some weapons are found aboard the skiff, the outcome of a trial for piracy is still somewhat unpredictable if the individuals have not yet made their intent absolutely clear by attempting to pirate a vessel. After all, pirates aren't the only ones with weapons in the Gulf of Aden. Some legitimate fishermen reportedly carry firearms in the Gulf of Aden in order to defend themselves from pirates and as a means to warn other vessels not to run over their nets accidentally.

Even when we've been able to get a country to accept captured suspected pirates for prosecution, there have been no guarantees that crimes will be punished. The country of first resort to try pirates has been Kenya, which signed a memorandum of understanding with the United States in January 2009, with the United Kingdom in December 2008, with the European Union in March 2009, and with Denmark in August 2009. But as more pirates have been captured on the high seas, the Kenyan justice system has found itself overwhelmed, and the welcome mat has been wearing thin.

This book would not be complete without including my favorite episode of the problems that navies face in getting pirates to the right country for prosecution. In January 2009 the *Absalon* captured five pirates who were attempting to hijack a Netherlands Antilles–registered freighter. After extensive negotiations between the two countries, the Dutch government agreed to try the suspected pirates. You would think that would be the hard part. Not so fast. The first major issue: how do you get the suspected pirates to the Netherlands? Fortunately, the *Absalon* was returning to Bahrain for a port visit. The Bahraini government reluctantly approved the transfer from the *Absalon* to a KLM flight heading to Amsterdam. Story over, right? Not so fast. *Absalon* had to remain at anchorage until the night of the transfer of the pirates to the airport. Once arrangements were confirmed, *Absalon* headed to her berth at Mina Salman. What could happen next?

Once the suspected pirates boarded the KLM flight to Amsterdam, the pilot asked who these young chaps were. Pirates, he was told. Not on my plane, he said. The pirates' cover broken, everyone headed back to *Absalon*. The pirates finally made their trip to the Netherlands on a Dutch military aircraft.

An unclassified diplomatic cable dated 16 July 2009 originating from the U.S. Embassy in Nairobi and released by WikiLeaks summarized the situation at the time, when one hundred Somali piracy suspects were being held in Kenya.

> The manner of delivery and quality of evidence, as much as the number of transfers, has dampened Kenya's enthusiasm for piracy cases. A few cases were delivered by EU countries (including Italy and France) with little prior consultation with Kenya and/or with weak evidence. The large number of deliveries in quick succession (more than 70 suspects within three months) resulted in these newer cases receiving less attention from police, prosecutors, and courts than earlier cases. Consequently, the informalities and weaknesses of the Kenyan Judicial system became more pronounced. For example, some defendants made initial court appearances without defense counsel, assigned prosecutors, or translators. In one recent case, defense lawyers successfully stalled proceedings when the magistrate suspended witness testimony (including that of civilian witnesses flown in from Manila) in order to consider the defense motion challenging the court's jurisdiction. While the motion is not expected to succeed, delays of this kind may make it extremely difficult to ensure the timely appearance of both civilian and military witnesses in the future. Care must also be taken to ensure that defendants' human rights are respected in practice.

The cable continued, noting that the Kenyan parliament had passed the Merchant Shipping Act and had rewritten penal code provisions dealing with piracy, and that most of the language repeats provisions of UNCLOS. However, it goes on to state: "The international community's assistance, fact-finding missions, invitations to conferences, advice, expectations, and scrutiny threaten to overwhelm this small and antiquated criminal justice system's ability to absorb it all, particularly at a time when the government of Kenya is focused on its larger political crises and pressing need for progress on the reform agenda."

The cable then summarized a case in which I had a personal interest, the attempted hijacking of MV *Polaris*, which is discussed elsewhere in this book:

> On June 30, 11 U.S. Navy and Coast Guard personnel (accompanied by Navy and Coast Guard JAG officers) and two Filipino seamen were assembled in Mombasa to testify in the trial of seven Somalis accused of piracy. The suspects were captured by the USS Vella Gulf on February 11, 2009, after they attempted to seize the MV Polaris, a Marshall Islands–flagged vessel. They were turned over to the Kenyan authorities on March 8. Trial was scheduled for July 1–2 and July 7. However, only one U.S. witness testified before the magistrate suspended proceedings to consider a defense motion challenging Kenya's jurisdiction. The magistrate is expected to deny the motion when he rules on July 16. (Note: The High Court of Kenya has rejected the same jurisdictional challenge made earlier on appeal by defendants captured by the U.S. Navy and convicted in 2006. This ruling is generally viewed as binding on this issue.) However, the case is likely to be continued until September due to lack of courtroom availability, so the witnesses were sent home with the hope that they may be able to return when trial resumes. Logistics and expenses for the Filipino crew members' participation in the trial were arranged by the Marshall Islands maritime organization and the private shipping company that employed them. (Note: A similar motion challenging jurisdiction was also made during the week of June 29 during the piracy trial of nine Somalis caught by the German Navy and handed over to Kenya on March 11, and it also resulted in a delay of that trial.) Post's Department of Justice Resident Legal Advisor and Bernadette Mendoza, the Deputy Chief of Mission from the Embassy of the Philippines in Nairobi, traveled to Mombasa to meet and

assist the witnesses and participated in pretrial conferences with prosecutors. Ms. Mendoza indicated that her government remains very concerned about the impact of piracy on its seafarers, and noted that there are currently 46 Filipino seamen being held hostage for ransom in Somalia, the largest number from a single country.

The cable went on to list a variety of impediments to the smooth processing of piracy suspects through the Kenyan judicial system while recognizing that "the international community must be as vigilant as possible in ensuring that the fundamental rights of piracy suspects turned over to Kenya are protected." Frankly, the cable doesn't give me much hope that, given that Kenya has been the best place to try piracy cases in that part of the world, the justice system is going to play a major role in impacting piracy. And the final comment in the cable from the American Embassy to the State Department confirms my thinking:

The capture and prosecution of Somali pirates can play only a tiny role in the overall solution to the piracy problem in the region. Interdictions and prosecutions should continue, as should efforts to improve the prosecutorial capacity of regional states. However, even increased and problem-free prosecutions are likely to do little to deter pirate activity given the economic and political situation in Somalia, plentiful and vulnerable merchant shipping, and the willingness of shipowners and/or their insurers to pay large ransoms. Further, Kenya's justice system (and those of its neighbors) can only accommodate a limited number of cases, and can only absorb and benefit from moderate and sustained international assistance. In light of these facts, we should continue to discourage excessive focus on and uncoordinated efforts at rapidly building prosecutorial capacity in the region.

In 2010 Kenya took the action that an inferential reading of that State Department cable could have predicted: it announced that it would no longer accept suspected pirates for trial. Since then there have been some exceptions, but for the most part Kenya is no longer the go-to country when one has pirates in the brig.

The State Department, which is on the receiving end of cables like that, continues to say that Somali piracy is an issue to be dealt with, that working alongside other nations to defeat it is important, and that piracy should be prosecuted. But it hasn't devised a solution to the problem I was faced with on the water—what can we do with pirates that we catch?

Donna Hopkins is a former classmate of mine at the Surface Warfare Officer Department Head School. She's a team leader working for State's Bureau of Political-Military Affairs. She said the pirates' seizure of the *Faina* carrying Russian tanks and munitions to Kenya "perked up everybody's attention" and made them recognize that piracy "was more than just a transient, low-key threat."

In September 2008, shortly before the UN Security Council was drafting Resolution 1851 calling for an international body to coordinate counterpiracy naval operations, the Bush administration's National Security Council issued its own counterpiracy policy. Hopkins said, "Starting from the top, it called for naval operations working on delivering judicial consequences to piracy to help the prosecution problem, working with industry to make sure they were doing more to protect themselves, and then working on the public diplomacy, strategic communications." Early in 2009 a group was added "to concentrate on the pirate enterprise at shore, going after the leaders and the financial flows. And that's really about intelligence, law enforcement, and financial intelligence fusion aimed at picking up a half-dozen or so, two dozen or so, pirate leaders ashore."

Frankly, Donna told me about so many contact groups, resolutions, dual-track approaches, and working groups about national-level discourse, intergovernmental discourse, and strategies that are multipronged interagency, multilateral, and multisectoral that I came away from the conversation understanding why military people and diplomats have a difficult time collaborating to solve a problem. Just like every warship working the Gulf of Aden needs interpreters who speak Somali and other local languages, we also need people who can interpret between our own two career fields.

When all was said and done, she said, "You won't find this in the execute orders, but I think there's an unwritten rule to do catch and release. Because there's too much opportunity costs associated with having these guys on your ship for sixty days. And while I understand that from a tactical point of view, from a strategic point of view, it's a really bad, bad thing to do." Speaking candidly, she said the catch-and-release policy is "stupid," observing that it has had a real effect on the pirates—in a way that is bad for the good guys. "The pirates that we've subsequently picked up are almost always repeat offenders and have now gotten smart enough from having been apprehended multiple times. One guy said he'd been picked up five times and subsequently released by different ships. Very savvy. They want to get rid of the evidence and say nothing. There's no way to prosecute them."

Cdr. James Kraska is an expert on the subject, both from a policy standpoint and from the point of view of an attorney, a seasoned Navy judge advocate. He's written extensively about piracy and in 2011 published a book on the legal aspects of dealing with the problem titled *Contemporary Maritime Piracy: International Law, Strategy, and Diplomacy at Sea.* Commander Kraska, a professor at the U.S. Naval War College, has served as oceans policy advisor for the director of strategic plans and policy, Joint Chiefs of Staff, where he developed global counterpiracy policy for the U.S. armed forces and represented the Pentagon in counterpiracy policy at the National Security Council and the International Maritime Organization.

Our conversation began with his explanation of why Somalia has an inexhaustible supply of young men willing to become pirates.

> With 75 to 80 percent unemployment—if you have a job, you might make $100 a month. As a militia member, you might make $80 or $100 a month, and it's fierce fighting. I mean, it's not for sissies. Whereas piracy is relatively safe, and if you get caught, you'll probably get released. So what's not to like about that? You've got a pretty decent shot at earning a huge amount of money. Back then [in 2008], it was maybe $15,000 for a low-level pirate; now, it can be $150,000, and that's for a low level, just a regular gun carrier, just a hired muscle off the street. And that's a huge amount of money. It can take care of their family and their parents, he can retire in Kenya, buy a house and live on easy street. It's an enormous attraction to be a pirate. I mean, there's no deterrence if you're putting them back on the beach.

But on the other hand, practically, what else are you going to do? There's just not a lot of good options. It has become less and less acceptable to just put pirates on the beach. I want to say estimates are as high as 90 percent or more [that] we've caught and released. And so there are a lot of criminal cases going on all over the world. But, to what end?

Kraska then provided insight into the nature of prosecutors.

The big fear in the United States [is] that the Department of Justice doesn't want to do—and this is normal of any prosecutor, even a military prosecutor—they don't want to prosecute anything unless they're going to win. Prosecutors don't bring cases that they might lose. And so they don't want to bring a case in which it's going to be difficult and it's going to be expensive. The defense is going to do things like call you, the admirals, as a witness. And who else? They'll call people in the Pentagon, I mean, the defense counsel is going to sort of make as much of it as they possibly can. And the defense is going to throw up all sorts of claims. I mean, you've heard them all, "This is a poor fisherman. He got caught up. He's a victim, too. He was kidnapped. Everybody's got an AK-47, and they all have to have one to defend themselves." And so, you face the real possibility of an acquittal, and then what do you do? You've got a Somali in the United States, and you kick him out the door with a green card, basically, because you're not going be able to send him back because then the NGOs and the refugee sort of apparatus kicks into gear. And then you own him, and that's always the fear. And then if you're successful, the very best you're going to get is, you know, you give them three hots and a cot for the rest of their life or they're going to drive a taxi or sell falafel on the streets of Chicago or whatever it happens to be.

Kraska said that "in the metaphysical sense, the solution is not going to be discovered out on the ocean." He believes the United States should support AMISOM—the African Union Mission in Somalia—which was begun in early 2007 by the Peace and Security Council of the African Union and was supported by a succession of United Nations Security Council resolutions.

On 21 June 2011, the Security Council met to discuss a UN study about the cost of establishing piracy courts both in Somalia and outside the country. Estimates were that a three-year period would cost more than $24 million, much of which would be consumed by building or rebuilding physical infrastructure to hold the suspected pirates under humane conditions, and to try them in an appropriate environment. The study focused on courts in the semi-independent regions of Puntland and Somaliland. Funding for the courts would be borne by the UN Development Program and the UN Office on Drugs and Crime.

The notion to establish what is described as an extraterritorial Somali antipiracy court in another country would require the cooperation of the Transitional Federal Government (TFG) in Somalia, which the experts we've spoken with believe has a very tenuous hold on the country. The UN's undersecretary-general for legal affairs, Patricia O'Brien, said in her presentation to the Security Council that in order for this plan to proceed, an agreement would have to be negotiated between the TFG and the country willing to host the court to "regulate their respective rights and obligations." The precedent for such an arrangement is the trial of the Lockerbie Pan Am Flight 103 bombers, in which the United Kingdom and the Netherlands agreed in 1998 that a Scottish court could conduct a trial in the Netherlands. The difficulties in establishing such an arrangement with other African nations are significant, considering that at the time the Security Council heard the proposal, 1,011 suspected pirates were being held by twenty countries, and many of them had already been convicted by courts in those countries. One suggestion to make the extraterritorial court function is to recruit international law experts to participate in the legal process.

Jack Lang, the former president of the foreign affairs committee of the French National Assembly, prepared the UN report. His charge from Secretary-General Ban Ki-moon was to identify steps that can be taken to assist countries in the region, as well as other countries, "to prosecute and imprison persons who engage in piracy; and explore the willingness of States in the region to serve as potential host for any of the options for potential new judicial mechanisms."

The delegate from India said, "Piracy is not only a threat to the freedom of maritime navigation; it has destabilizing effects on global and regional trade and on security and is jeopardizing the lives of seafarers, who are the lifeblood of the international economy. . . . We support the establishment of any extraterritorial court outside Somalia in which Somalis have an ownership, the courts that are manned by Somali judges and prosecutors in accordance with Somali law."

The delegate from the United Kingdom expressed greater concern over prison capacity in Somalia than for court capacity in countries that have been willing to try accused pirates. He said,

> It is of note that there is a greater willingness among regional partners to prosecute suspected pirates than there is to hold those convicted, and that the Somali administrations are willing to accept post-trial transfers from courts in the Seychelles, and in principle from others, too, once similar agreements are reached. The United Kingdom welcomes the stated intention of the authorities in Somalia to work with the United Nations on specialized anti-piracy courts within Somalia and on prisons within Somalia to provide more capacity in both areas as soon as possible.

It was suggested by the Portuguese delegate during the Security Council debate that the perfect location for an extraterritorial court would be Arusha, Tanzania, which is about 240 miles west of Mombasa, Kenya, because there were courtroom space and ancillary facilities being vacated by the International Criminal Tribunal for Rwanda, which was downsizing.

Meantime, the Russians argued for a functioning court both in Somaliland and in Puntland, with an additional extraterritorial court with international participation. The Russian delegate made a point of saying that just going after the pirates perpetrating the attacks would be unacceptable. "To fight the scourge of piracy, we should concentrate our efforts on targeting those suspected of financing and planning acts of piracy. They are the most responsible for and the real masterminds of the majority of piracy incidents off the coast of Somalia and should therefore be the principal aim of our action."

The Portuguese delegate agreed, adding,

As the report underlines, consultations with a number of Member States, INTERPOL, the United Nations Office on Drugs and Crime, the Department of Political Affairs and the Monitoring Group of the Security Council Committee established pursuant to resolution 751 (1992) suggest that the identities of key leaders of pirate networks and their location and political connections are widely known. Many of them are reportedly within Somalia. Therefore, any solution that is aimed at prosecuting such persons cannot be detached from the legal environment of where they actually live. That is why a solution must be based on Somali law, even if initially through an extraterritorial court justified by the current security situation in Somalia and the need to ensure safe and swift investigation and prosecution.

The delegate from the United States, Ambassador David B. Dunn, leaned away from internationalized courts and toward establishing an effective court system in Puntland and Somaliland, hoping that, with UN assistance, those courts could achieve international standards, which would then permit the transfer of suspected pirates to Somalia for prosecution within three years. He said, "We believe that building on the ongoing efforts in Somalia along those lines may be the most effective and efficient way to help meet the goal of the Lang report for the Somaliazation of the anti-piracy effort."

He then tossed water on the notion of an extraterritorial piracy court, saying, "Based on the report's findings, it is clear to us that an extraterritorial Somali piracy court is not a viable option due to opposition to the idea from Somalia itself and the host of constitutional, procedural, security, financial and logistical issues identified in the report. The Somali authorities have been clear that they do not support that idea."

As I've researched the subject, I asked time and time again whether it was reasonable to expect that Somali officials who I had been told were getting their cut of the multi-million-dollar ransoms that had been paid could be expected to participate boldly in an effort to step up prosecutions, not just of the actual pirates, but of the top dogs. So I think it's tragic that the United States seems compelled to take a position against real trials outside the territory of Somalia.

One issue that needs to be addressed in the fight against piracy is the failure of the U.S. Senate to ratify the 1982 UNCLOS, which has been ratified by 161 countries. After making numerous changes to satisfy our lawmakers, there has been very little movement in the Senate to bring the convention to the floor for a vote. The convention gives the military the tools to fight piracy on the high seas. Over the past two decades every chief of naval operations has testified that for the U.S. Navy to join with our coalition partners and show the leadership to maintain security and allow the free flow of commerce, it is a must for the treaty to be ratified. As Adm. Vern Clark testified before the Senate Foreign Relations Committee in October 2007, "We cannot remain outside the Convention and convince other nations that we truly believe in the importance of the rule of law when we are not party to the Convention which provides legal certainty throughout the world's oceans." The treaty does not limit the power of our maritime forces in any way, shape, or form and must be ratified.

One of the experts with whom I've discussed this situation is Georgetown University law professor Mark V. Vlasic, a former White House Fellow and special assistant to Secretary of Defense Robert Gates. Vlasic previously served as a prosecutor at the UN war crimes tribunal in The Hague. He draws a straight line between our ability to fight piracy in the Gulf of Aden and the ratification of the convention, saying,

> Sadly, no matter how skilled our navies are in the Gulf of Aden, they are still effectively searching for the veritable needle in a haystack, as they patrol a vast region with a relative handful of ships. We cannot fight piracy with our fleet alone, and fortunately, we have another weapon available to our efforts. That weapon is the Law of the Sea Convention, which makes piracy a universal crime, and subjects pirates to arrest and prosecution by any nation.

> The Convention specifically spells out criminal laws and jurisdiction throughout world's oceans. It locks-in freedom of navigation, asserting that no state may subject any part of the high seas to its sovereignty. It gives every state the right to sail ships flying its flag on the high seas, conduct military exercises, fight illicit drug trafficking, and gather intelligence—all essential to our national

defense. For these reasons, our military commanders have long advocated for its ratification.

As for dealing with captured pirates, I wish I had reason for optimism. The fact is, after all the United Nations meetings, and international conferences from Dubai to London, there appear to be no efforts directed at taking down the pirate bosses and financiers. Similar to the war on drugs in America, where our jails are filled with lots of small dealers, getting the kingpins is a stated goal but often proves elusive. Even America's approach to dealing with the skinny young guys in the skiffs out at sea has diminished since the time I was out there commanding CTF 151. Now it seems the coalition only goes after suspected pirates after they've attacked a ship, which I consider a highly passive approach to the problem. The active approach—going after mother ships or land-based operations—is virtually nonexistent. And although I hate to say it, even the U.S. Navy has backed down on the mission. We haven't had a U.S. flag officer in command of CTF 151 since January 2010.

The only place where there appears to be an appetite to capture, try, and incarcerate pirates is in the Seychelles. After the island nation agreed to a role as a de facto regional center for holding and trying suspected pirates, there was enough international financial support to allow for the construction of a new prison that could hold sixty inmates. Because the Seychelles, a former British colony, has a common law–based legal system similar to those in other former colonies and the United States, it was able to use jurists from other Commonwealth nations to conduct trials. By the end of 2011, the new prison was already more than two-thirds full.

I feel compelled to end this chapter where I began: with a rant about the idiotic policy of catch and release. This is the hardest part of the antipiracy mission for me and countless others to understand. The United Nations has given us the power to go after the pirates with numerous Security Council resolutions, and with UNCLOS we have the legal authority to prosecute these buccaneers. It was like the movie *A Bridge Too Far.* You expend all the effort and manpower to capture the suspected pirates (heaven forbid I forget myself and actually call them pirates). They have all the materiel needed to commit the crime, and in some cases they do commit a crime, but due to pressure from various governments, including our own, we release them. In most cases, if they haven't done it already, we take their weapons and pirate gear and throw it into the sea for King Neptune to use. In so many cases, my JAG, the Coast Guard LEDETs, and the NCIS agents actually said we had solid evidence to send the suspected pirates to trial, but the shore lawyers said, "No!"

The odd part about the whole strategy was that we were ordered to give them a warning just before we let them go. "Look guys, we know you've been bad, but don't do this again." Sure, we may have collected biometric evidence so that if—when—they were picked up again, we'd know they were repeat offenders. But that didn't matter. My guess is that most of them stayed pirates. We hadn't given them a good enough reason to find another occupation. I can't help repeating what my former boss in NAVCENT, Vice Adm. Bill Gortney, stated so eloquently about being a pirate, "There is no reason not to be a pirate. . . . The vessel I'm trying to pirate, . . . they won't shoot at me. . . . I'm going to get my money. . . . They won't arrest me because there's no place to try me." What a business model. And as for my suggestion at the beginning of this chapter that what we really need is a prison ship? Well, I suppose I was just kidding. Wasn't I?

CHAPTER 7

To Pay or Not to Pay

In 75 BC, according to Plutarch's *The Life of Julius Caesar*, pirates in the Mediterranean captured Caesar and demanded a ransom of twenty talents, a measure of silver worth about a quarter-million dollars today. Caesar laughed, told them he was worth fifty, and sent his followers to raise the money. When the ransom was paid and the great emperor was released, Caesar immediately set sail from the harbor of Miletus, returned to the island where he'd been held prisoner, and captured most of the pirates. He took them to Pergamon, an ancient Greek city, and, after holding them for a short while in prison, crucified the lot of them, as he had told them he would do while they were holding him for ransom.

Pirates are no longer a problem in the Mediterranean, but the Gulf of Aden and 2.6 million square miles of the Indian Ocean are now their hunting grounds. Today, a quarter of a million dollars wouldn't ransom a tramp steamer from warlords who have gotten a taste of real money. And thus far the likelihood of a pirate receiving a death sentence is not very high, the nighttime practices of certain of our allies guarding Pirate Alley notwithstanding. Thus, the tale of Caesar might appear to be more picturesque than important, but I'd suggest the Somalis would do well to read Plutarch.

At the start, let me put my biases on the table. I was personally touched and affected by hearing Capt. Mark Genung describe standing by the hijacked MV *Faina* for more than a hundred days aboard USS *Vella Gulf*. Twice, and sometimes three times, daily he spoke by radio to the first mate, who had taken over as captain when the master died shortly after the hijacking. The pirates who took *Faina* ultimately received a ransom of $3.2 million to free the ship, its cargo of Russian tanks and munitions, and the twenty surviving crewmen.

Mark saw firsthand the consequences of being held hostage, the terror of never knowing if the pirates—given to making occasional threats apparently just for the fun of it—were going to torture or kill the hostages because negotiations were going badly. Mark and his crew relayed messages from families back in the Ukraine, Russia, and Latvia to the captives. He was in a position to demand proof-of-life appearances on deck by the hostages, and aside from what he was being told over bridge-to-bridge radio, he could see for himself their physical deterioration. So when I hear officials of the U.S. Department of State say, publicly and privately, that there are no circumstances under which ransoms should be paid, I tend to think, "Easy for you to say."

In early March 2012, I participated in a panel sponsored by the U.S. Chamber of Commerce, which began with an address by Assistant Secretary of State for Political-Military Affairs Andrew Shapiro. His comments on payment of ransom were precise:

> When a vessel is successfully hijacked, our foremost concern is always the safety of the crew, regardless of nationality. The U.S. government is acutely aware of the dilemma that shipowners face when ships and sailors are taken hostage. While the safety of the crew is critical, industry must face the fact that submitting to pirate ransom demands only ensures that future crews will be taken hostage. A vicious cycle has formed where ever-rising ransom payments have not just spurred additional pirate activity, but have also enabled pirates to increase their operational capabilities and sophistication. The average ransom is now at $4 million per incident and has reached as much as $12 million. Ransoms paid in 2011 totaled $135 million. Piracy, as a result, has gone from a fairly ad hoc, disorganized criminal endeavor to a highly developed transnational criminal enterprise. In short, they have developed a successful business model that is hard to break.
>
> The United States has a long tradition of opposing the payment of ransom, and we have worked diligently to discourage or minimize ransoms. But many governments

and private entities are paying, often too quickly, serving to reinforce this cycle and incentivizing future hostage-taking. While some may consider this the cost of doing business, every ransom paid further institutionalizes the practice of hostage-taking for profit and promotes its expansion as a criminal enterprise both at sea and on land.

The issue of ransoms is no doubt an emotional one for all involved—especially the families and friends of those who are hijacked. And we recognize the unease within industry that believes government involvement will only prolong the hostage situation and increase the cost of the hijacking. Nevertheless, we strongly encourage flag states, shipowners and private parties involved in hostage crises to seek assistance from appropriate U.S. government sources in their crisis management procedures. Continued cooperation between industry and government and, most importantly, the mutual exchange of information is critical.

The American maritime industry should also know that this Administration will do everything it can to ensure the safety and security of American citizens threatened by pirates. This Administration has taken bold aggressive action when necessary, such as the rescue of the captain of the *Maersk Alabama* in 2009 and the rescue of an American hostage and a Danish hostage in January of this year. The United States has also actively prosecuted pirates involved in attacks on U.S. vessels. To date, that totals 28 persons involved in several attacks.

Before making his case for refusal to pay ransom, Assistant Secretary Shapiro had provided some comparative numbers on piracy. In January 2011, he said, pirates held thirty-one ships and 710 hostages. In early March 2012 they held eight ships and 213 hostages. What he didn't say was that the length of time hostages are being held has risen as pirate organizations have realized that the costs of holding hostages longer are more than repaid by the increase in ransom payments they receive. And the number of hostage deaths has also risen.

To the pirates it's just business, but to the shipowners it's more than that. While I'm not going to go all gooey and say that the tough-as-nails

▲ The Danish flexible support ship HDMS *Absalon* (*right*), the guided-missile cruiser USS *Vella Gulf*, and the guided-missile destroyer USS *Mahan* transit the Gulf of Aden as part of Combined Task Force 151. —*U.S. Navy photo by MC2 Jason R. Zalasky*

◄ The amphibious transport dock ship USS *San Antonio*, January 2009, served as my first flagship when I was commander of CTF 151. —*U.S. Navy photo by MC3 John K. Hamilton*

◄ The amphibious assault ship USS *Boxer* was my fourth flagship during my command of CTF 151 in early 2009. —*U.S. Navy photo by MC2 Oscar Espinoza*

◀ The guided-missile cruiser USS *Monterey* was the third of my four flagships while I was commanding CTF 151. —*U.S. Navy photo by MC2 Michael D. Cole*

▶ An SA-330J Puma helicopter approaches the Military Sealift Command dry cargo and ammunition ship USNS *Lewis and Clark*. I was told not to call it a "prison ship" even though special accommodations had been built to hold captured Somali piracy suspects until they could be released or sent somewhere for trial. —*U.S. Navy photo by MC3 Scott Pittman*

▶ The guided-missile cruiser USS *Vella Gulf*, shown here conducting a high-speed turn during a torpedo evasion exercise, was the second of four flagships and the most successful at catching pirate suspects during my tour as commander of CTF 151. —*U.S. Navy photo*

◀ A McKnight family reunion in Jacksonville, Florida, with my sons, T and Tyler, and my wife, Lisa. Tyler is a Navy helicopter pilot. —*McKnight family photo*

▼ In October 2008 Lisa and I were there the night Arnold Palmer received the Lone Sailor Award from the Navy Memorial. Golf is a passion of mine, so this was a huge thrill. —*Photo courtesy of Dr. Howdy Giles*

▲ On one of our many visits to the Danish navy's *Absalon*, we were given a demonstration of its joystick-controlled weapons systems. Standing, left to right: Capt. Mark Cedrun of USS *Boxer*, Capt. Dan Termansen of *Absalon*, and me. —*U.S. Navy photo*

▲ One of the highlights of my time as commander of CTF 151 was visiting the PLAN flagship *Wuhan* while under way in the Gulf of Aden. We saw very few crew members during our tour of the immaculate but somewhat outdated vessel. I was never quite sure what the Chinese Special Forces members guarding me with fixed bayonets were worried about. —*U.S. Navy photo*

▲ NBC News chief Pentagon correspondent Jim Miklaszewski and I enjoy a laugh during his visit to *Vella Gulf*. I had to tell Mik that since a Russian admiral was coming to visit, the powers that be had ordered him and his crew to leave. He told me he'd been thrown out of worse bars. —*U.S. Navy photo*

▲ The commanding officer of the Chinese flagship *Wuhan* explains his combat systems capabilities to me and my team during our visit to his ship in the Gulf of Aden. This was a rare opportunity for U.S. Navy personnel to visit a Chinese warship under way. —*U.S. Navy photo*

◄ Jatin Dua, a Duke University PhD candidate in the Department of Cultural Anthropology, spent several months observing and interviewing Somalis involved with piracy. Here he's in a vehicle leaving Bosaso Prison, where he interviewed a pirate leader who continues to operate and give instructions via cell phones. —*Photo courtesy of Jatin Dua*

▲ Dr. J. Peter Pham is director of the Michael S. Ansari Africa Center at the Atlantic Council in Washington. He's shown here doing "field work" in Mogadishu, one of the places in Africa he regularly visits. —*Photo courtesy of Peter Pham*

◀ Prior to my departure as commander of CTF 151, I visited the Turkish warship TCG *Giresun* and presented an American flag to Captain Cenk Dalkanat for his outstanding support to the coalition. —*U.S. Navy photo*

▲ On 25 September 2008 the MV *Faina*, a RO/RO carrier with a cargo that included thirty-three Soviet T-72 tanks, other weapons, and ammunition, was hijacked by Somali pirates. The ship had been bound for Mombasa, Kenya. Concerned that the cargo not fall into the hands of al-Shabaab terrorists, the U.S. Navy destroyer USS *Howard* pursued the hijacked vessel until it anchored about eight miles off one of the Somali pirate camps. *Howard* was relieved by USS *Bainbridge*, which remained nearby for more than one hundred days. The Americans negotiated an agreement with the pirates, permitting them to resupply in exchange for regular radio or phone contact and regular opportunities for the crew of twenty-one to appear on deck for "proof of life." Note the armed pirates in the lifeboat beneath the hostages and on the deck above them. —*U.S. Navy photo*

▲ The *Faina* cargo hold carried these 1970s-era Soviet-built T-72 tanks, which the pirates apparently did not know were on board the vessel before it was hijacked. —*U.S. Navy photo*

▲ Capt. Mark Genung, commanding officer of USS *Vella Gulf*, watches as one of his ship's helicopters makes a pass over the anchored MV *Faina*. The acting captain of the hijacked vessel credited the presence of the American sailors with giving them hope and keeping them alive during their more than four months of captivity. —*U.S. Navy photo*

▲ In November 2011 Royal Navy lieutenant commander Simon Goodes was the OIC at the UKMTO facility. —*Photo by Michael Hirsh*

▲ Vice Adm. Bill Gortney, commander of the U.S. Fifth Fleet based in Bahrain, speaks with Capt. Mark D. Genung on the weather deck of USS *Vella Gulf*. —*U.S. Navy photo by MC2 Jason R. Zalasky*

▲ This is the operations center of UKMTO on the grounds of the British Embassy in Dubai. Ships entering the high-risk area are advised under best management practices to register with this office and to make contact in the event of suspected pirate attack. The video screens display the Mercury home page, which has been described as "Facebook for mariners." In the event of suspected pirate activity, Royal Navy personnel at UKMTO post the location, which then pops up in red on screens on board ships monitoring the Web site. —*Photo by Michael Hirsh*

▲ This boat photographed by Jatin Dua is likely the Puntland Coast Guard vessel that came out to meet us when Combined Task Force 151 was compelled by higher authority to release a batch of suspected pirates that we'd caught. My JAG officer and the Coast Guard law enforcement detachment on board felt there was enough evidence to bring them to trial. —*Photo courtesy of Jatin Dua*

◄ These are the only two functioning boats belonging to the Somaliland Coast Guard based at Berbera. They're used for harbor patrol and for picking up suspected pirates who are released by coalition naval ships. —*Photo courtesy of Jatin Dua*

▲ The 1,090-foot-long very large crude carrier MV *Sirius Star*, with its cargo of 2.2 million barrels of Saudi oil bound for the United States and its crew of twenty-five, was hijacked on 15 November 2008, 450 miles southeast of the Kenyan coast. Until then, Somali pirates had never ventured that far out to sea. The ship was the largest ever taken by pirates. It was released from a pirate anchorage near Harardhere, Somalia, on 9 January 2009 after payment of a $3 million ransom. —*U.S. Navy photo by AW2 William S. Stevens*

◄ On 12 December 2007 pirates released the MV *Golden Nori*, a Japanese chemical tanker whose hijacking on 28 October set off fears that terrorists would use its Israeli-bound cargo of highly flammable benzene as a floating bomb to block a narrow strait or even the Suez Canal. A day later, the ship was refueled by the dock landing ship USS *Whidbey Island*. The release of *Golden Nori* marked the first time in more than a year that no ships were held by Somali pirates. —*U.S. Navy photo by SN David Brown*

▲ Admiral Metin Atac, the Turkish chief of navy, and I discuss counterpiracy operations during his visit to the Gulf of Aden with Captain Cenk Dalkanat, the commanding officer of the Turkish frigate TCG *Giresun.* —*Photo by Lt. John Fage, USN*

◀ A Russian Helix KA-27 helicopter assigned to the Russian destroyer *Admiral Vinogradov* investigates a fishing trawler in the heavily pirated Gulf of Aden. While not part of CTF 151, the Russian naval forces worked closely with us and on at least one occasion sent their helo to support our ships actively in pursuit of pirates.

—*U.S. Navy photo by MC2 Jason R. Zalasky*

▲ On 12 February 2009 pirates attempted to hijack the Indian-flagged merchant ship MV *Prem Divya*. A helicopter from *Vella Gulf* fired two warning shots, and VBSS team members took nine suspected pirates into custody. —*U.S. Navy photo*

▲ VBSS team members in rigid-hulled inflatable boats from *Vella Gulf* apprehend suspected Somali pirates. This group of nine was the second group of pirates apprehended in a twenty-four-hour period by *Vella Gulf*. This capture put us over our allotted quota of pirates to be captured and led to my firsthand experience with the concept of catch and release. —*U.S. Navy photo by MC2 Jason R. Zalasky*

ScanEagle is a small, long-endurance UAV carried by several of the U.S. Navy vessels participating in CTF 151. The UAV has a ten-foot wingspread and an average cruising speed of about 70 mph. It carries high-resolution cameras and can function in daylight or at night. The UAV is launched from a pneumatically powered mobile ramp (above left) and is recaptured (above right) using what's called a Skyhook retrieval system. During the *Maersk Alabama* saga, ScanEagle provided nighttime images (below) of the lifeboat in which Capt. Richard Phillips was held hostage. ScanEagles were first deployed by the Navy in 2005. —*U.S. Navy photos*

▲ Sailors on the *Vella Gulf* bridge wing are on alert while the ship's VBSS teams are deployed in boats to intercept suspected Somali pirates. The device at left is an LRAD, which can be used as both a loud and long-range acoustic device. In this case it is used to direct the suspects to keep their hands in the air and in other cases as a transmitter of audio tones so long they can drive off attacking pirates —*U.S. Navy photo by MC2 Jason R. Zalasky*

◀ Skiffs being towed by a suspected pirate mother ship are destroyed by weapons fire from the guided-missile destroyer USS *Momsen* (DDG 92) after the ship disrupted an attack on a commercial oil tanker transiting the Arabian Sea. —*U.S. Navy photo by HTC John Parkin*

The attack on the MV *Maersk Alabama* drew worldwide attention when four Somali pirates kidnapped Capt. Richard Phillips and attempted to get him to Somali beaches on board a lifeboat taken from the ship. The *Arleigh Burke*–class guided-missile destroyer USS *Bainbridge* (DDG 96) was first on the scene and was joined by the *Oliver Hazard Perry*–class frigate USS *Halyburton* (FFG 40) (upper left). Their mission was to keep Phillips alive and keep him from being taken to Somalia. The two ships played "good cop/bad cop" with the pirates. A helicopter from *Halyburton* (upper right) deliberately harassed the pirates to raise their anxiety level. Ultimately, *Bainbridge* took the lifeboat under tow. One pirate came on board for medical treatment, and SEAL Team Six snipers killed the other three. The lifeboat with the bodies was towed to *Boxer*, which can be seen in the distance (center). Captain Phillips was brought on board *Bainbridge,* where he was given a brief medical exam and greeted by Capt. Frank Castellano (lower right) before being transferred to *Boxer* for more extensive medical treatment. —*U.S. Navy photos*

corporate types who run the world's shipping companies will say that their seagoing crews are just like family, those who make their living from the sea do have a bond to each other. At that U.S. Chamber of Commerce program that dealt specifically with the question of paying ransom, I was very impressed with the remarks of Svein Ringbakken, the managing director of DNK, a Norwegian association that provides insurance for vessels against war risk. Previously he had been the general counsel of INTERTANKO. He is a lawyer who understands the psychology of his industry and the people in it.

Ringbakken had listened to Secretary Shapiro's pitch against the payment of ransom to free ships and crews and then was asked for his thoughts. He said,

> When it comes to the actual payment of ransoms from industry, if the U.S. has U.S.-flagged ship taken, I think you have a pretty decent expectation that you might get help from somewhere. If you have a ship taken, they want to have her and the crew released.
>
> If you are, however, in a number of other ship registration countries, [that may not happen]. It is not necessarily because they may care less about their ships, [but] because they may not have the means to go in and do what the U.S. and France have done on a number of occasions.

Then he drove the point home. "The shipowner has a duty of care; he really needs to do whatever he can to take care of these people. And at the end of the day—it's not desirable—but in these scenarios in Somalia, that involves a ransom payment. Unfortunately."

I believe it is of no consequence that mariners may earn a bonus for signing on to a ship going through the high-risk area; acceptance of that minimal payment is not a waiver of expectation that your employer will do whatever is possible to see that you come home to your family. Just as shipowners are expected to provide a safe working environment for their crews (and companies have been successfully sued by crew members whose ships were not prepared to defend against pirates), there is an unwritten agreement that most owners acknowledge—that they have an obligation to redeem their employees from the hell of hostagedom.

The European Union Naval Force (EU NAVFOR) released records at the end of 2011 showing that more than 2,300 crew members had been taken hostage in the preceding three years, and that ransom payments in 2011 were at least $135 million compared to around $80 million in 2010. The British government's position on ransom payment mirrors that of our own. The Foreign Office released a statement at the beginning of 2012 saying it has a "clear and long-standing policy of not making or facilitating substantive concessions to hostage-takers, including the payment of ransoms." Under pressure from the maritime industry, including insurers, the Brits have stopped short of making ransom payments illegal, but they urge private firms not to pay "because we believe that making concessions only encourages future kidnaps."

Lt. Cdr. Claude Berube, who teaches courses on maritime security challenges and naval history in the political science department at the U.S. Naval Academy, has studied Somali piracy and the payment of ransoms. He observes that the payments have increased substantially since the first large ship, *Feisty Gas*, was taken near Somalia. "In 2005 they were ransomed off for about $315,000. Now the ransom is, on average, about $4 to $5 million." He said that back then neither the ransoms nor the insurance rates for ships passing through the high-risk area were high enough to get companies concerned. Now, the tipping point has been reached, and companies are willing to spend money to protect their ships from pirates.

But ships are still being taken, and government proclamations aside, Lieutenant Commander Berube doesn't see an end to ransom payments.

> We continue to pay these ransoms, but the thing is, how can you stop paying ransoms? At any one point in time, you're going to have at least three hundred mariners from around the world who are in Somalia. You stop paying those ransoms, what happens to those individuals? And that's why, quite frankly, the Indian mariners, some were threatening to go on strike, they're having a much greater problem now trying to man some of these ships that are going through the Indian Ocean because the mariners see that they run the risk of being out for—it used to be thirty to ninety days. Now, it's up to a year or more.

Donna Hopkins lives and breathes Somali piracy on a daily basis as the plans and policy team leader in the State Department's Bureau of Political and Military Affairs. This is where the diplomatic element of the American counterpiracy policy is orchestrated. She said it was the hijacking of *Faina* in late 2008 with its military cargo that got Washington to focus on piracy. "That perked up everybody's attention, and shortly after that, the *Sirius Star* was ransomed for millions of dollars. That was the first multi-million-dollar ransom and its major cargo [$100 million dollars worth of Saudi oil headed for the United States]. That's the first time the U.S. government really perked up. The Navy had been out there floating around; intervened and intercepted a couple things, but then it became clear that this was more than just a transient, low-key threat."

Hopkins was able to provide some insight into the thinking that's going on in the State Department with respect to ransom payment.

> I think one thing that we're seeing now is that the pirates have [come] to overstep themselves in a few ways. They've gotten very greedy with the ransoms. If they'd kept the ransoms reasonable, they probably would be a whole lot better off financially than they are now. It's my theory that there's a new generation in town. It's no longer the mom-and-pop, gentleman's agreement—I'll take your ship, be nice to your guys; you give me a little bit of money. It's a whole new generation of criminals here. They want maximum return on minimum investment and they're not above killing and torturing people.

That is precisely why the blue-chip shipping companies are willing to pay to get their crews out of captivity. Hopkins said that the initial killings by pirates of the four mariners aboard the sailboat *Quest* might have been the result of one or two pirates getting stressed out and deciding that the way to end the situation was to kill the hostages. "It didn't do any good for their business model," she said. "Apparently, lots of pirates are really, really pissed off about that. Messes up the business."

That led me to relate a true story to Donna—whom I've known for more than twenty years. I told her that I'd spoken with Capt. Gordan Van Hook, USN (Ret.), now senior director for innovation and concept development at Maersk Line, Ltd., about the kidnapping of Captain Richard Phillips from *Maersk Alabama*. He said that Fifth Fleet headquarters (HQ) had made it clear to his company that the lifeboat carrying Phillips and four Somali pirates would not get to Somali shores. "We made it clear to them," Van Hook said, "that we were worried about Phillips and that we didn't want anything to happen to him, and that if it came right down to it, we'd rather pay the ransom and get him free, and have him aboard *Bainbridge*."

The response from Fifth Fleet in Bahrain? "It was, 'That's how you feel?' And we said, 'Yeah,' and they said, 'Okay, understand.' And by that point we knew that we no longer had any say in what was going to happen."

Then I asked Van Hook a hypothetical question. What if the lifeboat had gotten to Somalia and it came to paying the ransom or not? You've got the State Department and, I believe, the Defense Department saying, "Our policy is, we don't pay ransom. We don't want anybody paying ransom." As a private company, it's your guy out there. How do you advise Maersk when your own government is saying "don't do it"?

Captain Van Hook thought for a moment and then said, "If it's a terrorism-type thing, we wouldn't be allowed to. But if it's just a strict criminal kidnapping, there's not a law that says we can't pay ransom. So we would be able to pay a ransom in that case. Our feeling was at that time—and this was the established business model out there—pay the ransom, get the guy back, end of story. Our number one concern is the safety of our people. Nobody likes to pay ransom; nobody wants to pay ransom; but given no other choice, we pay the ransom."

And if the government comes back and says that by doing so, you're just encouraging the pirates? "Okay, that's fine. But you're going to sacrifice our people to make a point? I understand—we all understand—that we may not have a say in it. But given a say in it, we're going to do whatever it takes to [rescue our people]—otherwise, people won't sail with us. Nobody's going to sail with us if the deal is, we're not going to pay the amount. And you have to remember, back at that time [of the *Alabama* incident], nobody had been killed."

Then he reminded me of something that is often forgotten.

> I used to make this point until I got told to shut up. More people had been killed, at this point, by naval forces than had been killed by pirates out there, because the INS *Tabor*, an Indian frigate, had shot up a Thai fishing boat

that was a mother ship. It had pirates on board, but they ended up killing eight or nine Thai fishermen in the process. So the established business model was, you pay these guys off, and the ransoms weren't even that much. And when you're talking about a trillion dollars worth of trade that goes through there annually, this is not even floor sweepings we're talking about.

Martin Murphy, who has arguably spent more time just thinking about Somali piracy than anyone I'm aware of, doesn't buy into the notion that the Somali pirates have gotten greedy and inflated their ransom demands.

I think that implies that there's some sort of central authority figure that is able to get greedy. I think what you're seeing is more and more actors coming into the situation and wanting a slice of the pie. But they've also had effective negotiators. They've increased from what was the original ransom for the *Feisty Gas* back in 2005, about $300,000, and then it jumped and went over a million. They've gradually wound it up to the $4 to $5 million range, and they're making a very good living. Getting greedy? I just see it as, you know, the good negotiator.

Peter Pham, a colleague of Murphy's at the Atlantic Council, also doesn't buy into the assessment that the pirates overstepped their bounds with greedy ransom demands. "They realized that there was a low tolerance for people being held captive, and that they could use the people to leverage higher payments. They sort of figured out, 'We're only getting a million dollars, and the boat's worth twelve, the cargo's worth another ten, and the grief at the foreign ministry—we could at least get two out of this.' And two became three, and three became four."

In my conversation with Stephen Carmel, the senior VP of Maersk Line, Ltd., who was their man in charge when the *Maersk Alabama* was taken and pirates were holding AK-47s to Captain Phillips' head, he made the point that the pirates, rather than getting greedy, are taking advantage of their position.

Like any good businessman, they're going to press their price points to see where they can go. But also, you've got to remember, the success rate is down to about 12 percent or so—somewhere in there. Their costs are going up exponentially; it's a lot more expensive [to successfully hijack a ship now]. It takes more of them, it takes them longer. Basic economics says they've got to charge more to get the same level of return. In the old days, back in the *Danica White* days, again—Terry, you well know—when the Ukrainian ship [*Faina*] got hijacked, the side port door was open and the ladder was down. A kindergarten class could've hijacked that ship; it wasn't that tough. Now it's hard work for them.

Having been in the hot seat, Carmel is in an excellent position to comment on the notion that the payment of ransoms could be made illegal.

There is an Executive Order out there that spun a lot of people up, but it did not outlaw paying ransoms. I think you would have difficulty saying that merely because someone kidnapped somebody and is asking for a ransom, that makes them a terrorist. That's a pretty big stretch because they're clearly not. We certainly would not want to see the dots connected between piracy and terrorism; no one, at this point, has demonstrated that dot connection. And I can tell you, in my mind, there are some parts of the government that would love to see that connection made, simply to use terrorism financing laws to stop the payment of ransom. That said—and this is me, personally—is it wouldn't have stopped the payment of ransom. It's relatively easy to arrange for payment in a lot of places. England, by the way, has a law on the books now that specifically exempts ransom payments from any terrorism financing laws, even if the connection's made. So, in England, it's legal to pay ransoms, even if the connection between pirates and terrorists is made.

Summing up, Steve Carmel not only thinks it's a bad idea, but it couldn't be enforced. "My view is, all that does is criminalize the victim, and it's going to divert resources of the government into attempting to prosecute the victim where those resources really should be dedicated to breaking down the financial networks of the pirates themselves."

And that's something I was told by everyone I asked, that it isn't happening because the Treasury Department doesn't have the staff, the budget, the mandate, and the wherewithal to follow the money. At the London conference on Somali piracy held in February 2012, the United Kingdom announced the creation of an international task force on pirate ransoms, saying, "It would bring together experts from across the world to better understand the ransom business cycle and how to break it." Call me a cynic, but rather than another international group, I'd rather have one very direct order—and the budget to go with it—from the Oval Office to the Treasury Department to field a task force to follow the money, and then to make it happen.

What is happening now within the administration is just knee-jerk reaction to frustration, to the inability to effectively deal with the problem. Martin Murphy said,

> I think they're seeking a silver bullet to try and solve it, and one that's going around is making, apparently, the payment of ransom illegal. I think that people really haven't thought through the implications of that, and there's one school, which is in the State Department, which says, "Hey, look—come on, we'll make the payment of ransom illegal, and it might take a couple years, but eventually the pirates will stop because they're not making money."
>
> And then you say, "Well, there's going to be people—three, four, five hundred seafarers trapped."
>
> "Well, that's a small price to pay." And I think that's callous, because eventually they'll stop feeding them, they'll sell them to al-Shabaab, they'll sell them to somebody else. Or just let them die.
>
> The second thing is that most of these guys come from third-world countries who are nominally our allies, the Philippines and Indonesia, and I think there will be some political blowback there. I think the most worrying thing that hasn't been talked through is the fact that if the payment of ransom is made illegal, seafarers and crews will very rapidly refuse to cross [that area]. The shipowners

will refuse to go into the area because of liabilities, and
seafarers will refuse to sail if they feel they're at any level
of risk. And you've got a real chance that trade across the
Arabian Sea will dry up, including the oil trade.

Murphy continued, "What worries me is that a number of people
in the U.S. government just don't get that. One or two people, it's been
made very clear to them by the insurance industry and by people who
know that this is the potential end game. And it'll come very quickly
if it happens, and they'll say, 'Oh, okay, I've got it now.' But there are
a number of other people—not so much in government, maybe on the
Hill—who just don't get this."

And I certainly agree with that. We've got people who are serving
in Congress now who don't know who the secretary of the navy is.
Don't know how navies and armies work. They don't understand how
it all comes together, and they just don't care.

Murphy said in England this condition is called sea-blindness.
"People just don't recognize how dependent we are on international
trade. As far as they're concerned, you know, bananas come from Wal-
Mart, they don't come from Guatemala."

And then there's the issue of the thus-far veiled threat that our government could go after Americans who pay ransom to pirates under the
theory that the pirates are terrorists. Pham has closely watched as the U.S.
Treasury Department's Office of Foreign Assets Control invoked sanctions, in Executive Order 13536 dated 10 April 2010, against a few of
the major pirate figures, notably Mohamed Abdi Garaad and Abdullahi
Abshir (aka Boyah). The theory is that they've been designated terrorists, so ransom payments could not be made to them legally. "How the
Department of Justice would prove that your ransom payment went to
Garaad or Boyah, I have no idea," said Peter, "but you can only specu-
late." He said that he's not sure the Department of Justice could meet the
legal burden of proof. "But they certainly can make your life miserable
by insinuating that your ransom payment went to a designated terrorist
and now you're dragged up on terrorism finance charges."

Ultimately, with respect to the payment of ransom by a U.S. shipping company, I suspect that those paying close attention will discover
that there are laws, there are rules, there are suggestions, and then there
is what can only be read between the lines. My conversation with Donna

Hopkins turned back to the question of ransom; I told her that Gordan Van Hook had said that if the pirates had gotten Captain Phillips ashore, Maersk would have paid the ransom. Here's her response:

Hopkins: Oh, he would have, but he would've had a whole bunch of people breathing down his neck, and those pirates would not have gotten away alive. He would not have been allowed to conduct that transaction hands-off.

McKnight: Because he's an American citizen?

Hopkins: Yeah. Can't have that. There is almost no limit to the steps the U.S. government will take to prevent ransoming for American citizens. Effectively. We call it "no concessions." It's not that we won't negotiate, not that ransom can't be paid, but the transaction will not terminate the way the ransom-takers want it. And that's all I'm going to say about it.

My guess is she probably said enough. And my suggestion is that perhaps the Somali pirates would do well to read Plutarch and remember Caesar.

CHAPTER 8

Attack on the Maersk Alabama

Now let us speak in hushed tones, for we will be saluting those whose name cannot be mentioned and whose very existence must not be acknowledged, except with a wink, a knowing nod, and a White House briefer's innocuous mumble about of "an additional set of U.S. forces." Yes, they drop out of the sky like superheroes, do their bit to make the world safer for mere mortals and kidnapped mariners, and then vanish into the night, never to be officially spoken of outside secure rooms in the inner circles of the Pentagon. But, c'mon, people, kids in sixth grade know about them. Hell, they want to grow up to be one of them.

It's pretty hard to keep them a secret when one minute an American sea captain is being held captive in a lifeboat by desperate Somali pirates with the DTs from khat withdrawal, and the next, the captain is safe, one pirate is in custody, and some poor yeoman on a U.S. Navy ship is trying to figure out where and how to file forms in triplicate authorizing the disposition to a foreign government of three non-American bodies, each of whom suffered a single, fatal, presidentially authorized gunshot wound to the head.

There is a logical sequence to telling such a story, and while I agreed that during the conversations, as a condition of obtaining exclusive interviews with senior naval officers who were involved every step of the way, I would not utter the mythic name of certain "nonorganic forces," I made no such pledge for the content of this book. Therefore, despite the official fiction that all they are is dust in the wind, I'm about to tell you the untold story of the rescue of the captain of the hijacked MV *Maersk Alabama* by several hundred U.S. Navy personnel on board two warships in the Somali Basin. (Yes, Capt. Richard Phillips wrote a book about his rescue, but he was in the hijacked lifeboat—he really had no idea what was going on to free him. My point is, most of that story has been untold until now.) The rescue personnel include at least a half dozen members of SEAL Team Six who parachuted into the Indian Ocean with their sniper rifles, did their thing, and then vanished like the Lone Ranger, leaving the world wondering, Who were those masked men?

The groundwork for the positive resolution of the MV *Maersk Alabama* hijacking actually took place a couple of months before the 508-foot container ship with a crew of twenty was taken by pirates on 8 April 2009. That's when Steve Carmel recognized that there had never been any dialogue between commercial shippers and the American government on what would happen if a U.S.-flagged vessel were hijacked. Carmel's division of Maersk operates roughly fifty U.S.- and Marshall Island–flagged vessels, including about twenty-five commercial container ships plus various tankers, roll-on roll-offs (ROROs), multipurpose ships, and so-called gray hull ships operated for the Military Sealift Command (MSC).

Carmel pressed the government to do something, and the initial result was a meeting—he calls it a "tabletop"—at the company's Norfolk headquarters with industry and Coast Guard officials, one O-6 from the Office of the Chief of Naval Operations, and representatives from the MSC and FBI as well as from the Department of Transportation's U.S. Maritime Administration. The result, said Carmel, who is a graduate of the U.S. Merchant Marine Academy and a former master of tankers in worldwide trade, was, "We got everyone's attention that this is a little bit more complicated of an issue than anyone was thinking."

The U.S. Coast Guard took the bull by the horns. Just two weeks before *Alabama* was hijacked, a group convened under the guidance of Coast Guard deputy commandant for operations Vice Adm. Brian M. Salerno and director of prevention policy for marine safety, security, and stewardship Rear Adm. James Watson in the Commandant's Briefing Room at HQ in Washington. The group included U.S. Navy Rear Adm. Brian Losey, who was at the time the National Security Council staff point man for combating terrorism. Losey had a long career with SEAL units, including commanding SEAL Team One and commanding the Naval Special Warfare Development Group (DEVGRU), which would figure prominently in what was to happen shortly off the Somali coast. Also in the room were Robert "Turk" Maggi, the State Department's coordinator for counterpiracy and maritime security, and Brad J. Kieserman, the coordinator of what is colloquially known as MOTR, the Global Maritime Operational Threat Response Coordination Center. Kieserman had been the first chief of the Coast Guard's Operations Law Group, had spent eleven years at sea, including time as commanding officer of a cutter, and had participated in dozens of search-and-rescue operations.

The theme of the session—which sets a new standard for calling something prescient—was what to do if one of Maersk's feeder ships in the Arabian Gulf gets pirated. (A "feeder" in shipping industry parlance is a seagoing vessel with a capacity of between three hundred and one thousand twenty-foot equivalent units [TEU]. Feeders typically collect shipping containers from smaller ports and transport them to central container terminals, where they're loaded onto long-haul ships, some of which can carry almost 15,000 containers.) The participants went into specific detail about what would take place if Somali pirates hijacked an American ship. "When we finished," Carmel said, "we had a list of personal phone numbers, and who talks to whom, and who makes what decisions on each side of the fence, which in a situation like this is 90 percent of responding to it. We understand what each side's equities are."

While it was relatively easy to assign most responsibilities, one major issue remained unresolved: "One of the things we were adamant about," Carmel recalls, "is that in the event of a piracy event, we did not want to see an attempt to retake the ship. Especially if we didn't know where the crew was, or they weren't all secure. We absolutely didn't want to see that happen without intense conversations with us."

While nothing was engraved in stone, Kieserman agreed that, for the time being, that call would be Maersk's, and nothing would take place along those lines without extensive coordination. Within a few days, the shipping company had dispatched Gordan Van Hook to meet with officials at Fifth Fleet HQ in Bahrain and reinforce the notion that there are American-flagged ships plying heavily pirated waters. Van Hook had been hired upon his retirement from the Navy in September 2008, in part because of his ability to interface with the Navy on piracy issues, and he had already worked with the Office of Naval Intelligence and Fifth Fleet on issues related to several near misses with some of Maersk's ships working the East Africa theater from the major container port of Salalah, Oman, to Djibouti in the Horn of Africa. He said one of the company's primary concerns was that "there wasn't great awareness by either the Department of Defense or the Department of State that U.S.-flagged ships were operating out there."

In Bahrain, a meeting scheduled for twenty minutes between Van Hook and Vice Admiral Gortney lasted more than two hours. Van Hook said the Fifth Fleet commander essentially said there was no doubt that if something happened, he would get the mission, but nobody had yet told him to plan for it. As a result of the meeting, Van Hook gave Fifth Fleet access to the company's FleetViewOnline, the system the company uses to track its ships. Van Hook was sobered by his discovery that there was no awareness by the Navy of ships carrying cargo for the State Department or the U.S. Agency for International Development through the high-risk area.

At the conclusion of that visit, Van Hook went to Salalah, where he'd arranged to ride one of the Maersk feeder ships to see firsthand what their antipiracy measures looked like. He had two ships to choose from: *Maersk Georgia* and *Maersk Alabama*. "*Alabama* was going down to Mombasa; it was going to be a much longer transit. I looked at it—it was going to be weeks I was going to be out of pocket. So I decided I'd ride *Maersk Georgia*, which was going from Salalah to Suez through the Gulf of Aden. 'Well, that's a hotter area anyway; I'll see more,' I thought."

Fortunately for him, Gordan's crystal ball was having a bad day. It was while he was aboard *Georgia* that he learned *Alabama* had been captured. If he had chosen *Alabama*, he would have been front-page news, and I don't mean that in a good way. But he wasn't lacking for excitement aboard *Georgia* because, at a safe distance, he witnessed the hijacking of the 32,000-ton, 600-foot MV *Malaspina Castle* and crew of twenty-four. "We heard them on the radio; we could see them on the horizon. It was a bulk freighter. We had an Indian Navy frigate right on our starboard beam, and you could see her trying to fire up another boiler, and all the smoke is going up. This is an Oleander-class Brit frigate, so it's ancient, probably thirty years old. They couldn't get in the game fast enough because when these things happen, it's a fifteen-minute drill. It's all over once pirates are onboard. They've got control."

Telling the story in the grill room at Washington's Army-Navy Club, Van Hook seemed to be reliving the moment, and he was frustrated. "Everybody kept saying, 'why don't we bring back the convoys?' Convoys weren't going to work. No way, because you could be convoying right behind one of these guys, and the pirates speed up, come right up and jump onboard, and that's it. All the old-timers who were saying 'bring back convoys,' they didn't know what they were dealing with. This isn't a U-boat war; this is maritime crime at sea."

And when he got word that *Alabama* had been taken by pirates? "I thought *Alabama* was okay because she could make eighteen knots. So I called Fifth Fleet and they kind of gave me a little bit of shit because it was like, 'Gordan, I thought you told me your ships were fast enough and this wasn't going to happen.' I said, 'Well, looks like the paradigm has changed.'"

He got off *Georgia* at Port Suez, took a flight to Nairobi and then to Mombasa, where he set up headquarters at the Maersk Kenya office and waited for the crisis team from the office in Norfolk to arrive and help him manage the situation, which quickly became a matter of dealing not only with Fifth Fleet but also with a press corps that began swarming all over the city. By this time, Maersk knew that Captain Phillips was off *Alabama* and being held in the ship's lifeboat by four Somali pirates wielding AK-47s, and that USS *Bainbridge* was on the scene. But I'm getting ahead of the story. Let's back up.

~∞~

On 7 April 2009 the U.S. Maritime Administration released an advisory recommending that ships stay at least six hundred nautical miles (almost seven hundred statute miles) off the coast of Somalia due to an increased threat of piracy in the Somali Basin. It's likely that the increase in activity closer to the long Somali coastline was a direct result of the deterrent effect naval forces were having by concentrating in the Gulf of Aden—Pirate Alley.

The officer in charge of UKMTO in Dubai at that time, Royal Navy captain David Bancroft, told me he believed the pirates were using Korean and Taiwanese tuna fishing vessels as mother ships with what he said was "local security" on board.

> I gave the advice to stay 200NM off the coast in April/ May 2007. At the same time, vessels being taken often saw the pirates claim they were 'Somali Coastguard.'

Indeed, some had been trained as such by Hart Security back in 2003, I believe. When they boarded a vessel, they often claimed that they were not hijacking the vessel but were arresting the vessel for some MARPOL (marine pollution) or fishing infringement, and the ransom was not a ransom but was called a fine. By taking people outside of 200NM my intention was to take away any chance of a legal excuse being used to help the pirates. Once outside of 200NM it would be very clearly piracy.

I've said more than once that pirates generally adhere to their version of the Jesse James Rule of Robbery—"We rob banks because that's where the money is." In the case of the Somali pirates, they worked the Gulf of Aden heavily because that's where most ships bound for or exiting the Suez Canal travel. But with warships of CTF 151, Operation Atalanta, the Chinese, and the Russians concentrated there, the pirates weren't averse to looking elsewhere.

On 1 April, *Maersk Alabama* sailed from Port Sultan Qaboos in Salalah, heading down the eastern side of the Arabian peninsula and into the Gulf of Aden, initially bound for Djibouti in the Horn of Africa via the IRTC and then on to Mombasa, Kenya. Captain Richard Phillips was aware of the warnings, but he—like the pirates—knew that the world's merchant fleet delivered cargo where it needed to go, and he hadn't signed on for a leisurely cruise to tropical islands.

In this case, among the ship's cargo scheduled to be offloaded in Mombasa were containers reportedly carrying some four thousand metric tons of corn belonging to the UN's World Food Program destined for Somalia and Uganda. Other containers held one thousand metric tons of vegetable oil being sent to refugees in Kenya.

Alabama arrived in Djibouti on 5 April and began discharging cargo. I didn't know it at the time, but in a bizarre coincidence, I was there at the same time. I had turned over command of CTF 151 that morning, Palm Sunday, to Rear Adm. Michele Howard and was flown by helo from *Boxer* to the huge American base in the Horn of Africa. I caught a flight in the afternoon that took me the 1,100 miles across Yemen and Saudi Arabia back to Bahrain, where I would debrief with Vice Admiral Gortney and the deputy commander of the twenty-four-nation Combined Maritime Forces, Royal Navy commodore Tim Lowe.

The 6 April session lasted an hour, and I left feeling good about the praise that had been heaped on me but unsettled because the issue of what we would do with pirates that we captured wasn't anywhere close to being resolved. I told the commanders the same thing I had told Howard: If we're going to catch pirates, we have to figure out ahead of time what we're going to do with them. We're like the dog catching the car. The legal issues had to be dealt with. The government of Kenya had just told us, "We've got too many, so don't give us any more. We won't accept them." We were bouncing back and forth between being aggressive and nonaggressive in our pursuit of pirates. It bothered me that we were kind of saying, "Okay, let's just be in the defensive mode rather than the offensive mode because we don't want to keep them on ships for a long time while we figure out how to get rid of them." I was still annoyed about the whole midnight express mess, where the Danes could proactively ferry their pirate prisoners ashore from *Absalon* and pass them to local Puntland officials, but my decision-making chain of command—which inevitably seemed to run all the way to the Pentagon and the State Department—freaked out at the thought of engaging in such an innovative, no-red-tape, middle-of-the-night solution.

About the time I was finishing up at Fifth Fleet HQ in Bahrain, *Alabama* departed Djibouti and steamed due northeast, back into the heavily pirated but somewhat protected waters of the Gulf of Aden en route to Mombasa, Kenya. Relatively soon, however, the ship would turn south into the Indian Ocean, mirroring the Somali coastline all the way to Mombasa.

The distances we're dealing with are vast. Here's an easy way for anyone familiar with the map of the United States to think about it: the Somali coastline is roughly equivalent in length to the U.S. East Coast from Maine to Miami. *Alabama* has a top speed of eighteen knots— just under twenty-one miles per hour, which means she can travel no more than five hundred miles in a twenty-four-hour day. So following a course that takes this ship five hundred or more miles farther offshore than it would normally travel, and then back in to its intended port, and doing the same thing on the return trip, could easily add as many as four days to a voyage.

Before Somali piracy had become a problem, the customary route for southbound vessels traveling around the Horn of Africa was within twenty miles of the coast. But in 2005, when piracy became a force to be reckoned with, captains began going up to two hundred miles offshore. It put them beyond the range of pirates who were launching their skiffs from the beach but significantly increased the length of a voyage from Djibouti to Mombasa.

We've already taken note of the fact that although the pirates appear to be uneducated teenagers, they and their superiors have a knack for adapting to changing circumstances. Thus, when merchant ships began sailing a couple of hundred miles off the coast, the pirates started hijacking fishing trawlers and sometimes even larger boats and using them as mother ships. This greatly expanded their range, and it forced shipping companies to consider sending their vessels hundreds of miles offshore to transit from Suez to Mombasa, and on down the east coast of Africa.

The U.S. Department of Transportation's Maritime Liaison Office had issued a precise warning to mariners on 1 April, the day *Alabama* departed Salalah: "Recent activity suggests that pirate activity off the east coast of Somalia has increased. Attacks have occurred more than 400 nautical miles offshore." It went on to suggest that ships traveling along the coast of Somalia and Kenya move to the east side of the Seychelles Islands and Madagascar. Presumably such repositioning would require ships to run a much shorter east–west pirate gauntlet than if they made their entire north–south voyage closer to the coast.

Well aware of the dangers, Captain Phillips opted to roll the dice and struck a course that would keep *Alabama* about three hundred miles off the coast. I suppose one can imagine him having an internal Dirty Harry–type conversation: "Do you feel lucky, captain?" And he did the math. It's a big ocean. According to a U.S. Navy press release, the high-risk area that the pirates were working at that time was roughly four times the size of Texas, or the size of the Mediterranean and Red Seas combined. *Alabama* could just as easily run into a mother ship five hundred or one thousand miles offshore as three hundred. He had a schedule to meet. And he was responsible for operating his ship economically, which is to say, he had to keep an eye on how much fuel he was burning and how long he was taking (although there's never been any indication that his bosses at Maersk pressed any of its skippers to take unnecessary risks in the interest of saving bunker oil).

Just a few hours out of Djibouti, the crew of *Alabama* got a rude reminder of how quickly things can turn ugly. Phillips found his ship being pursued by three pirate skiffs with their mother ship following about eight miles behind. He describes the incident in chilling detail in his book, *A Captain's Duty*. Suffice it to say here that had it not been for heavy seas forcing the pirates to turn away, *Alabama* would have been taken during that attack.

On Tuesday, 7 April, when the U.S. Maritime Administration issued an advisory recommending that mariners stay at least 600 nautical miles—690 statute miles—off the coast of Somalia, *Alabama* was southbound, roughly 300 miles off the Somali coastline. The seas had calmed and would be of no help if she had another encounter with armed pirates in skiffs that could easily overtake the vessel. Before he went to bed that evening, Captain Phillips posted his special captain's night orders: "From here down to Mombasa, potential is high for a piracy incident. Keep a wary eye."

I left Bahrain that afternoon for Dubai. My nonstop United flight to Dulles was cancelled, so I was rebooked on the 8 April Lufthansa red-eye departing Dubai around 1:40 a.m. to Frankfurt, connecting to the 11 a.m. United flight that would get me into Washington around two in the afternoon. When I landed at Dulles, I turned on my Blackberry and found at least a dozen emails. "Go get 'em, Terry." "Knock 'em out." "Proud of you." All that kind of stuff, and I'm thinking, what the heck are they talking about. So I grabbed a copy of that morning's *Washington Post* and there it was. The *Maersk Alabama* had been hijacked by pirates and was being held for ransom. Talk about mixed emotions. I confess to feelings of combat envy coupled with intense pride and confidence in the sailors I'd left behind aboard *Boxer*, *Bainbridge*, and *Halyburton*. This is what we'd trained for. They would handle it while all I'd be able to do was watch CNN and make an occasional phone call to try to learn the real story. Damn!

Two days earlier, Steve Carmel had driven from Maersk's headquarters in Norfolk to participate in a two-day discussion of piracy at the ONI. Just before midnight on the night of 7 April—which is not quite 0800 East Africa Time on 8 April—he got a call from the company's operations office. The Ship Security Alert on board *Alabama* had been activated. He quickly packed and departed Suitland, Maryland. It would be a fast three-hour drive back to Norfolk.

While on the highway, Carmel began working the phone tree that had been established at the MOTR meetings just two weeks earlier. His

principal contacts were Brad Kieserman, Rear Adm. Frank Thorp, who
was the Navy's chief of information (and, now retired, is senior vice
president for communications and marketing at the USO), as well as
the people he'd just been meeting with at ONI. From Carmel's perspective, everything was working seamlessly. In short order, he had sat in on
a couple of the MOTR conference calls; he was confident that he was
being given all the information available.

Just so you understand the geography, MOTR's situation room is
at Coast Guard HQ in Washington. When an incident is being worked
by secure video teleconference, there can be as many as six or seven
faces in split screen on the large monitors in the room. But some MOTR
calls have as few as four and as many as fifty participants. MOTR's job
is to facilitate. As Brian Wilson, MOTR's deputy director, puts it, the
organization's job is to connect senior levels of the U.S. government and
at times connect operational levels. MOTR is not in charge because
there's no command-and-control element. There's no ability to give
orders. It's designed to develop "a unity of effort" and to get the facts
right—even when the facts are constantly changing. The first MOTR
call for the *Alabama* hijacking took place five and a half hours after the
silent alarm was triggered on the bridge of the ship. There have been
times when a MOTR call has occurred more quickly, but Wilson said
experience has taught them that "it's more prudent, sometimes, to wait
until we have good fidelity on the facts." For MOTR to work well, he
said, requires the right level of seniority. "We've had several high-profile
cases with generals, admirals, ambassadors. It's a flexible process. And
then others that are more routine can have a lieutenant."

Maersk's situation room in Norfolk had been built for daily use but
with crisis management in mind. Company staffers drilled and practiced
regularly. The room has banks of computers and three big flat-panel
displays, and, using an adaptation of Inmarsat, they're able to track and
communicate by voice and data with their ships around the world. They
can select any ship on the displays, place it on a map of the region, and
overlay heading, speed, weather, and other data.

I know from personal experience that the pirates are inconsistent
when it comes to cutting off communications from a hijacked vessel.
Sometimes they do; other times they don't. When *Alabama* was hijacked,
the pirates never cut off Inmarsat; as a result, the Maersk situation room
didn't lose track of her. That's the good news. The bad news was that

every newsroom in the world with an enterprising reporter figured out how to use Inmarsat to call the phone on *Alabama*'s bridge. Inmarsat told Maersk that the volume of calls to the ship was so extreme that it actually slowed down communication to the entire Indian Ocean area. Carmel said this quickly became a problem. "This is where the Navy and Admiral Thorp, in particular, were invaluable. Inmarsat worked with us to block a lot of that stuff from coming."

Then there was the flip side of that problem.

> We had the crew, as it's happening, trying to call out to negotiate with the *Today* show and Associated Press and everyone else. They're all snapping pictures of the pirates with their cell phones, so they're all trying to sell pictures and interviews. So, we got control of communications outbound from the ship as well, to cut that off.
>
> One of our displays is CNN—the world gets its news from CNN—so we're going to monitor what's going on. And the number of people getting up and speculating about what was going on and being completely wrong about it was just incredible. At one point we're sitting there, and Larry King says, "We're gonna go to a break, and then when we come back, we have the ship on the line, and we're gonna have an interview with them." I almost fell out of my chair! I mean, I just could not believe what I just heard. We called Admiral Thorp and asked him to get on with CNN and get them to cancel that. And he did it.

From Carmel's perspective, communications between Maersk, the Navy, and the Coast Guard couldn't have been better. Initially, he was on the MOTR conference calls—he still holds a top secret-SCI (sensitive compartmented information) clearance—but at some point other government agencies on the line got uncomfortable with a representative of the shipping company being on MOTR, so he dropped off. Nevertheless, he didn't feel out of the loop because Brad Kieserman would talk with him after every MOTR call and relate everything that had been discussed. "I was not uncomfortable because the communication between Brad and I was intense and thick, and open and honest and objective, so there was never a doubt in my mind that I knew what was happening, and I don't think there was ever a doubt in his mind that our skirt was completely open and they had everything we had."

The same level of trust existed between Maersk and the Navy. "We had virtually an open line between our situation room and the guys out in the Fifth Fleet MOC [Maritime Operations Center, Bahrain]. I'd say I probably talked to Naval Intelligence every half hour, if not more frequently. And the DEVGRU guys were here a lot."

Okay, he said it: DEVGRU. One of those names that dare not cross the lips of mere mortals without blessing from on high, or at least proper clearance. Even though it has a Wikipedia entry that is reasonably accurate, the Pentagon insists it's still in the "if I tell you I'll have to kill you" category. The U.S. Naval Special Warfare Development Group is commonly known as DEVGRU and informally known by what Wikipedia says is "its former name, SEAL Team Six, . . . one of the United States' four secretive counter-terrorism and Special Mission Units." Just assume that everything DEVGRU does is highly classified, which, for the purposes of a retired admiral writing a book, makes talking about what they may or may not have done a bit limiting. But I'll press on.

Steve Carmel told me that "part of our deal in all this was giving the folks that needed it copies of the ship's plans, specifics of construction. Once Phillips ended up in the lifeboat, the DEVGRU guys in particular, we were giving them lifeboat plans, information on materials. Actually we arranged for one of those guys to meet one of the other feeders [MV *Maersk Arkansas*] with an identical setup and lifeboat out in the Middle East so they could survey what exactly they were dealing with."

To answer a question now that will become relevant a bit later in this saga, no, the guy from the organization that does not exist didn't test fire a weapon at the windshield on *Arkansas*' lifeboat. But Carmel said, "We gave them an awful lot of very, very specific information about construction and strengths and that sort of stuff."

What had actually happened on *Alabama* was a classic takedown of an unarmed merchant ship by Somali pirates who had no qualms about opening fire on the ship's bridge. It happened near dawn. One pirate skiff began chasing *Alabama*. Captain Phillips said his ship was making 16.8 knots when the chase began. He sent his chief engineer to the engine room to keep an eye on things and pushed it up to a maximum 18.3 knots. It was immediately clear that there was no way they'd outrun the pirate skiff; it was bounding across the relatively calm water at better than 21 knots. So *Alabama* began racing maneuvers, zigzagging to create a treacherous wake that the books said would make it more difficult for the pirates to come alongside.

UKMTO has made a point of telling mariners that one of their best defenses against attack is speed. In the 2010 edition of its book *Best Management Practices for Protection against Somali Based Piracy* it says, "To date, there have been no reported attacks where pirates have boarded a ship that has been proceeding at over 18 knots." And then it is added, in boldface type, "It is possible however that pirate tactics and techniques may develop to enable them to board faster moving ships."

When it became obvious that *Alabama* wasn't going to outrun the pirates, Phillips hit the ship security alert button, sounding the silent alarm that would alert Maersk headquarters in Norfolk and put a rescue operation in motion. But as I've already mentioned, it's a big ocean, and the military ships involved in antipiracy activities were concentrated hundreds of miles north of *Alabama*, in the much more heavily traveled sea lanes of the Gulf of Aden. While I thought that Fifth Fleet would quickly be able to get a P-3 Orion surveillance aircraft out of Djibouti tasked to find and track the hijacked ship, getting surface vessels to give chase and intervene was going to take time, and time was something Captain Phillips didn't have a lot of.

There have been many stories about how the pirates have been taught or told not to aim at the mariners, just to fire their automatic weapons or RPGs at the ship, close enough to scare the captain into stopping. In the attack on *Alabama*, when the pirates were about a quarter-mile away and closing in, they began shooting at and hitting the superstructure close to the bridge. This group of four pirates apparently had not received the memo about just aiming to scare, not to kill. Rounds from at least one AK-47 were pinging into the metal on the bridge wings behind which crew members were crouched down.

After arming himself and his first mate with emergency signal flares that theoretically could be fired at the pirates, Phillips ordered the mate to call UKMTO and report that they were under attack. If one of the flares hit a pirate, no question it would stop him. If they really got lucky, they might hit a gas can in the boat and blow the thing sky-high. But a flare gun is not a precision target pistol, especially if the shooter is on a moving ship and the target is in a small boat going roughly twenty-five miles an hour. *Alabama* also had several fire hoses blasting down from the deck, but they proved ineffective.

In a relatively short time, the pirates maneuvered alongside and hooked the top of a twenty-foot ladder to the fish plate—the narrow strip of steel plating that projects upward at the edge of the deck. Five seconds later, one pirate was on the deck using a rope to haul up a bucket carrying a loaded AK-47. He wasn't intimidated by the signal flares. By this time, most of *Alabama*'s crew members had been ordered to lock themselves into the engine room or the aft steering compartment, from which the vessel could be operated. The captain and eventually three crew members locked themselves on the bridge.

Soon after, they heard shots fired from the deck level and knew the pirates had shot the locks off the cages that were supposed to prevent access to the superstructure. Just seconds later, the pirate that Captain Phillips would come to call "Leader" was standing near the bridge door with an AK-47 assault rifle, looking at him through the window. "Relax, Captain, relax," Phillips recalls the man saying. "Business, just business. Stop the ship, stop the ship." It had taken the pirates about five minutes to capture the bridge of *Alabama*.

CHAPTER 9

Hostage in the Lifeboat

USS *Bainbridge*, commissioned in November 2005, is one of the U.S. Navy's newer *Arleigh Burke*–class guided-missile destroyers. The 9,200-ton displacement vessel is 509 feet long with a 66-foot beam. Her four General Electric turbines have 100,000 total shaft horsepower and can drive *Bainbridge* at 30 knots—just under 35 mph. The vessel's hull was designed to permit high speed in high sea states. When the ship is coming at you head on, she looks like a very nasty knife slicing through the water. *Bainbridge* was built to carry a pair of SH-60 Seahawk helicopters, but when the *Maersk Alabama* hijacking went down, she was operating without choppers. In their place, she had launch-and-recovery facilities for the Boeing ScanEagle, a UAV with a 10-foot wingspan that can stay airborne for more than twenty hours. It has an operating range of roughly sixty miles from the ship and a maximum speed of 85 mph.

At about 0900 on the morning of 8 April, Cdr. Francis "Frank" Castellano, the skipper of *Bainbridge*, was doing a planned maintenance spot check in one of his radar rooms when the phone rang. "Sir," said his tactical action officer (TAO) in the combat information center (CIC), "you need to come back to combat right now. We just got a call from Fifth Fleet that a U.S. merchant ship has been pirated approximately three hundred miles to east-northeast of *Bainbridge* and we're the closest ship. They need us to get there now."

Bainbridge had come through the Suez Canal in mid-March, had participated in antipiracy patrols in the Red Sea as part of CTF 151 when I was in command, and then continued in what Castellano describes on-the-record as "typical Fifth Fleet maritime security operations, struggle against violent extremism, counterpiracy, etc." When the call came that morning, she was close to the Somali coast, north of Mogadishu, with ScanEagle up doing some surveillance. I'll go out on a limb here and guess that the mission had something to do with supporting U.S. Special Ops forces in Somalia, and perhaps Kenya, who were keeping tabs on terrorists of the Islamist militant offshoot al-Shabaab, often thought to be loosely affiliated with al-Qaeda. That those missions are taking place is well known among the academics and think tank types who pay attention to such things.

It's worth mentioning here that U.S. Navy ships can simultaneously be part of multiple task forces. When I was out there, I was dual-hatted, as they say, as commander of international Combined Task Force 151 and of Task Force 51, which is a U.S.-only operation. My successor, Admiral Howard, was also dual-hatted, as were the captains of *Bainbridge* and *Boxer*. This is important because the rules of engagement are not the same for CTF 151 and TF 51. When *Bainbridge* was tasked to rescue an American ship, crewed by American merchant mariners, she was responding as part of TF 51, deliberately making it a U.S. operation under U.S. commanders, operating under U.S. rules of engagement, and communicating on radio frequencies that were not shared with international partners aboard CTF 151 ships. Those ROEs are designed to make it crystal clear to our ship commanders and their staffs when they can use deadly force. Over the next few days those ROEs were to become very important to Frank Castellano.

There are times in the military where you're tasked to do something that you're not fully prepared to do. And then there are times when the stars align—I'm not talking about flag officers here—and you're blessed with an abundance of resources. Because *Bainbridge* had been doing sneaky-Pete surveillance work, not only was she carrying ScanEagle, she also had what Castellano calls a "robust intel team" that included a lieutenant (junior grade) and two intelligence specialists as well as a senior chief intel specialist, Joel Steinbach, who were all temporarily assigned to the ship. As part of permanent company, Castellano also had a very senior lieutenant commander, John Byron Vernon, and his experienced cryptological team. They were the guys who Castellano immediately assigned to gain situational awareness about what was going on.

By the time the skipper got to the CIC, the ship had already changed course and was heading toward the hijacked *Alabama*. Initially, *Bainbridge* could only make twenty knots because the crew had to recover the airborne ScanEagle, which was out near the end of a very long radio-controlled leash. About an hour later, word came from Fifth Fleet MOC: "Crank it up to 30-plus and do best speed in order to get there."

With his intel team, Castellano began reviewing the standard TTPs—tactics, techniques, and procedures—for a piracy incident. He needed to know what the pirates were doing, how they were behaving. He told me,

> Typically, they have their mother ship along with the attack vessel, which would be a skiff. They'll board, take control of the ship, and then bring in reinforcements. And that was really the concern from higher HQ, why they wanted us to get there fast. I was told to increase speed to max because while there were an unknown number of pirates on board now, they knew reinforcements would be coming, because that's just the way the pirates' TTPs are.
>
> The first initial guidance was to get out there, gain situational awareness, and actually to covertly monitor—see what was going on and prevent further reinforcements of the pirates, but not kind of tip our hand that we were there.

Even at full speed, *Bainbridge* was going to take about ten hours to reach *Alabama*. That gave Castellano the luxury of time to think, time to formulate a plan that was initially just based on the information relayed to UKMTO in Dubai by Captain Phillips. After a bit, *Bainbridge* was able to gain intel from the P-3 out of Djibouti, which provided *Alabama*'s position as well as info on suspected mother ships.

About the same time that *Bainbridge* had been given her new assignment, Fifth Fleet also sent orders to USS *Halyburton*, an *Oliver Hazard Perry*–class frigate, to join the fray. Officially, the ship was given a change of operational command (or was "chopped," as they say) to the all U.S. Navy Task Force 51. *Halyburton* is a bit smaller and older than *Bainbridge* but was carrying two SH-60 Seahawk helicopters. She'd been part of the NATO task force patrolling two segments of the IRTC in the Gulf of Aden. The Portuguese rear admiral in command of the NATO force was decidedly unhappy to lose her—and especially her helos—to the *Alabama* rescue mission. Just the day before, those helicopters had stopped a group of pirates who were setting up for an attack, and had forced the Somalis to toss their weapons into the sea.

The problem for *Halyburton*'s CO, Cdr. Michael Huck, was that she was 722 nautical miles from where his bosses wanted her to be, but he couldn't make top speed heading south to join *Bainbridge* because he had to be conscious of fuel consumption; there are no floating gas stations in the Somali Basin. Making twenty-two knots on one turbine, *Halyburton* would take thirty-two hours to arrive on station. *Bainbridge* would be going it alone for a long time.

Early in the evening of 9 April, as *Bainbridge* was closing in on *Alabama*, Castellano received word that the merchant ship's crew had retaken control of the vessel. Then they learned that the pirates had taken Captain Phillips hostage and had him in a lifeboat. "We didn't initially have an idea of what the lifeboat was. We had assumed it was like a RHIB." Then information began pouring in.

Castellano said,

> I ended up getting a phone call from Maersk's command center, and they actually gave me Richard Phillips' name, they actually gave me the first mate's name. And they also gave me the Inmarsat number for *Alabama*. I ended up talking to the first mate, and he gave me a rundown. He said, "This is what happened." Told me about the four pirates, told me how many AKs and handguns they had on board. I asked him if they had any explosives or RPGs. He gave me a description of the lifeboat. I talked to the chief engineer who had jumped the pirate leader. He told me the story of how he wrestled the pirate leader and what injuries he thought had been sustained by the pirate leader.

Castellano ascertained that there was a standoff going on between the hijacked ship's crew and the pirates. The bad guys had Captain Phillips in the ship's lifeboat, and the crew had the injured pirate in custody.

> [We learned] that the lifeboat was actually a covered lifeboat. They were basically using *Alabama* to block the lifeboat's progress, and then they came to an understanding with the pirates on the lifeboat that they would just

kind of settle down for the night, with the pirates on the
lifeboat just hanging off the quarter waiting for daylight
so they could talk. What I got was that the pirates were
trying to convince the *Alabama* crew to let them back on
board at first light, and then they could go ahead and do
the prisoner exchange.

Castellano, however, didn't believe the pirates' end game was a
prisoner swap. "They did have satellite phones, so in my mind, they
[had called and] were waiting on reinforcements. The P-3 had found
pirate mother ships in the area."

Once everyone up the chain of command learned that the pirates
had taken Phillips hostage, the orders for *Bainbridge* changed. "Now
what we got," said Castellano, "hey, get in there and basically take
control of the situation. I interpreted that as, I'm rolling right up on
them and overwhelming them. What happened was, we had comms
with *Alabama*, both through Inmarsat and also on the radio. I stayed
off bridge-to-bridge [channels], though, because in that area it carries a
long way and I didn't want to tip my hand to anyone listening in."

The news that Phillips had been taken prisoner on the lifeboat
had a huge impact back at Maersk headquarters in Norfolk. Steve
Carmel learned about it in a middle-of-the-night phone call from Brad
Kieserman at MOTR. "The issue that Phillips now is in the lifeboat
changes completely what is happening," recalls the Maersk executive.
"The *Bainbridge* is not there, but as soon as Phillips gets in that lifeboat
and the pirates leave, the hijacking is over. Hijacking's done. This is now
a kidnapping of a single American citizen. Everyone was still involved
that was originally involved, but when you're talking about the kidnapping of a single person, the responsibilities shift. Overseas, when somebody is kidnapped, instantly the FBI is the lead agency. So, as soon as
that happened, the FBI stations two agents in our situation room 24/7."

This was never really made clear when the events were happening,
but sitting at home in the DC suburbs and observing, I could guess that
perceptions about what was taking place and who was in charge were
about to get blurry. If Maersk got its ship back, odds were they were
going to be told they've got less of a stake in the outcome. Going in, it's
common knowledge that the State Department is dead set against any
ransom payments to rescue a crew.

But Carmel had already used the "R" word on MOTR.

> We'd have paid it. I was very clear all the way through
> the process. In fact, on the very first MOTR call I said
> to everyone, "As far as we're concerned, this is gonna
> play out like every other hijacking plays out. I don't want
> any kinetic response from the Navy. If the pirates are in
> control, that ship's gonna go to the coast of Somalia and
> we're gonna pay to get it back." End of story. And that,
> by the way, remains my position, and I really don't care
> what State Department has to say about it. At the end of
> the day, what matters to me is getting the crew back.

As previously made clear in chapter 7, Carmel's colleague at
Maersk, Gordan Van Hook, is just as hard-core on the notion of paying ransom rather than attempting a hot rescue. He had no interest in,
as he put it, sacrificing one of his people so the State Department can
make a point.

Nevertheless, taking Captain Phillips into the lifeboat and freeing
Alabama to sail away with her crew changed the calculus. Maersk's
Carmel described his next encounter with the head of MOTR, Brad
Kieserman.

> So Brad and I have this conversation in the middle of the
> night, and he says, "Listen, different ballgame now." I
> said, "You're right." He said, "We're agreed that I got
> this one now?" And I said, "You got it. I'm in a support
> role now." So the government has got control of this com-
> pletely. And the question, of course, then is why are we
> still involved? It's the kidnapping of a single American
> citizen, why are we involved at all?
>
> And the answer is because everyone understood that
> it was possible that he could end up in Somalia, and we
> knew that if that happened—especially where they were
> probably going to end up going ashore—the chances
> of getting him back were slim. We needed to preserve
> the option of paying a ransom to prevent that, and the
> government couldn't do it. And that's why they kept us
> involved. Because the government, itself, wants to pre-
> serve the option of paying a ransom.

Carmel also shot down one of the stories that began cropping up in the media, that Maersk had been contacted by someone ashore, offering a deal or making demands. But Maersk was prepared for that to happen.

> We actually did have some K&R [kidnap and ransom] specialists over in England who we flew over here to be ready if it got to a negotiation stage, but we were never contacted by anyone for anything.
>
> Now, of course, the *Bainbridge* shows up, the *Alabama* goes to Mombasa, and the lifeboat thing plays out the way it did. We always knew what was going on, or at least as much as they could tell us openly. They're very into specifics about what's in the lifeboat and what they want to know about. It's clear to me what's gonna happen. But they're not gonna tell me specifically.

With Phillips in the lifeboat and *Alabama* back in the crew's hands, *Bainbridge* continued at top speed racing to the scene, and Captain Castellano and his crew planned for their entry into the drama. "We devised a game plan on how we were going to steam in there. We ended up launching ScanEagle—because we have IR [infra-red] capability— at about one hundred miles away." What he wanted was situational awareness now that the P-3 had gone off station.

> So where's *Alabama*? Where's the lifeboat? Were there any pirate vessels in the immediate vicinity? I came in with no lights on, came in at thirty-plus knots. I manned all my gunnery stations. We set up additional lighting, kind of force protection bright lights. Had the "big voice" [loud-speaker system] out there.
>
> Since *Alabama* was close to the lifeboat, I was concerned going in there, whether there was going to be any exchange of gunfire. At about six miles out or so, I basically directed *Alabama* to move away from the lifeboat, about two miles to the east, so that way it gave us a clear shot on—I don't want to say "a clear shot,"—I mean more from a ship-handling perspective, a clear path to the lifeboat. I rolled in there lights off, and got in nice and

close to the lifeboat. It was real dark. I don't think they saw me coming because at about three hundred yards or so, we hit the lifeboat with lights and big voice, with the Somali interpreter talking to them.

It's not routine to have a Somali interpreter on board U.S. Navy ships sent to the Indian Ocean. *Bainbridge* apparently had one to provide assistance to the special ops mission the ship was supporting, and it was a good thing he was there. Just being able to precisely translate between parties when lives are at stake is a major plus. But in this case the interpreter was able to do much more than just facilitate conversations; he was able to provide a cultural perspective on the young Somali men holding Phillips captive, providing details that would prove useful in the hours and days ahead.

Castellano said his interpreter told him that Somalis, even though they're great fishermen and have proven themselves to be effective pirates, are fearful of the combination of night and being on the ocean. Their habit at night is to huddle down in the bottom of their boats. "We would see it later on in the deployment. We'd look at fishing boats through our night vision sights and it would look like they were abandoned, but you'd roll up on them and there were folks lying down in the bottom of the hull of those skiffs because they're kind of trying to hide from the water."

The Somali interpreter also provided a basic lesson in the geopolitics of his country that would prove useful during negotiations with the pirates, whose goal would shift from capturing a ship for ransom to getting back to Somalia with the captain as their hostage. He also told Castellano that the pirates usually chew khat leaves because it has a stimulating effect similar to—but less intense than—cocaine or methamphetamine, and it helps ward off seasickness. It turned out the pirates had run out of khat, and Castellano would turn that to his advantage during negotiations by offering them cigarettes to help take the edge off.

The pirates did not react well when *Bainbridge* lit up the place. In Castellano's words, "They were pissed." The Somalis had told *Alabama*'s first mate, Shane Murphy, that they didn't want the military involved, and they threatened to kill Phillips. "Pretty much as soon as we rolled up there and blasted them with the lights and sirens and big voice, they panicked."

That's when Castellano began his role as negotiator—something the Navy doesn't routinely train its captains to do. He tried to calm the pirates down, to convince them to give up. The pirates were verbally posturing; there was no brandishing of weapons at *Bainbridge*. The upshot was an agreement to take it slowly and talk again after sunrise. *Bainbridge* shut down the noise and lights, maintaining station around the lifeboat throughout the night, circling it like a shark.

Castellano was grateful for the time to analyze the situation. "I'm thinking, how are we gonna get him off? I have a very good VBSS team, they're great. But they're not trained for combat action, to do a hostage [rescue] kind of thing. I don't have sniper rifles on the ship; I've got good old M-4s and M-16s and the 50-cals and everything else, but nothing where I could—I basically had iron sights. So it's not like my gunner's mate is up there for a sniper thing."

Through the entire situation, *Bainbridge*'s skipper was getting emails and chats and intel via all sorts of channels. "It was pretty much constant, and everyone wanted to help. I don't mean that in a negative way, but it was actually fairly overwhelming."

There was no question that Castellano was and would be the on-scene commander throughout the operation. Admiral Howard aboard *Boxer* was in command of TF 51 but was close to Djibouti when it all started and would not arrive in the area until shortly before the final curtain. Fifth Fleet's orders were to secure *Alabama* so that it didn't get pirated again by removing her from the area. There'd been intel from both the P-3 that had flown overhead and from other sources that there were several cargo vessels already being held by pirates that had changed course to converge on *Alabama*, plus one, MV *Stolt Strength*, a chemical tanker carrying phosphoric acid that had been hijacked the previous November with its crew of twenty-one Filipinos, that reportedly got under way from anchorage near one of the pirate ports with the intent of heading out to sea to reinforce the pirates now in the lifeboat.

BAINBRIDGE DECK LOG POSITION 02-47-7N 050 049E
1322 2009 04 09 PAI SPEED 6
18 PERSONNEL EMBARKED M/V ALABAMA SECURITY FORCE

Castellano's response was to put together a group of sailors, a gunner's mate (GMC), and one of his boarding officers, a young lieutenant (junior grade)—he called them the Alabama 18—and put them aboard the recently hijacked ship. "We loaded them up with some M-60s [machine guns], M-4s, shotguns, grenades, everything else. Basically, the mission tasking to the JG was, 'Bring *Alabama* to Mombasa safely. Self defense rules of engagement apply.' He had intel on the situation, and I also gave him one of our satellite PRCs so he had secure comms back to us. He was a Naval Academy guy, and it was basically a 'message to Garcia' [mission]. And then I grabbed the GMC and said, 'Chief, make sure he doesn't fuck things up.'"

While that was happening, another group aboard *Bainbridge* had come up with a way to put batteries for Captain Phillips' radio, medicine, and some water on a wooden pallet and float it to the lifeboat. Early on, the notion of just motoring over in a RHIB didn't play well with the Somalis.

Conversations between the *Bainbridge* skipper and the pirates began again and immediately went downhill. Castellano recognized the scenario was one of an irresistible force meeting an immovable object, "Because they didn't want to give up, and we didn't want to give up. That's when they made a statement that said, 'We're going to Somalia. You can either tow us there or follow us there, but we're going. And we're going to make it to Somalia or we're all going to die out here.' That was the first time the situation turned into a black-and-white situation."

Shortly after 2300, the deck watch on *Bainbridge* heard shots fired aboard the lifeboat. The log entry initially said the shots were fired at Captain Phillips, but that portion of the entry was stricken.

BAINBRIDGE DECK LOG 2009 04 09
2301 ALL AHEAD FULL 16 KNOTS
SHOTS FIRED ~~AT CAPTAIN PHILLIPS~~ BY PIRATES
3 FLARES FIRED BY BAINBRIDGE

In Washington, the president had been receiving regular briefings on the events unfolding off the Somali coast. At 1400 EST on Friday, 10 April, the National Security Council Deputies Committee, which is responsible for day-to-day crisis management of policy issues affecting national security, met in the White House Situation Room "to review issues related to ongoing piracy situation." At 2000 that evening, the White House press office reported that "POTUS [President of the United States] requests readout of Deputies Committee meeting. National Security Council gives POTUS telephone update on current situation and conclusions of Deputies Committee. POTUS gives Department of Defense policy guidance and certain authorities to set of U.S. forces to engage in potential emergency actions."

Aside from the obvious—an American citizen had been kidnapped from an American ship—the White House and Pentagon had another quite significant reason to come down hard and fast on the pirates. *Maersk Alabama* is part of the Maritime Security Program, which means the U.S. government actually subsidizes her operation as part of a fleet of active, commercially viable, militarily useful, privately owned vessels to meet national defense and other security requirements. About sixty U.S.-flagged ships are part of the program. Their owners agree to make their ships and commercial transportation resources available upon request by the secretary of defense during times of war or national emergency. That's the primary reason that, by law, every crew member on *Alabama* must be a U.S. citizen.

Later in the evening of 10 April NBC's chief Pentagon correspondent Jim Miklaszewski reported, "It was determined that the more advanced skill set of SEAL Team Six was needed." On the MSNBC .com website, he writes: "The White House and military also laid out the three primary objectives of the mission: 1) try to negotiate for the peaceful release of hostage Captain Phillips. 2) keep the lifeboat from reaching the Somali shore. 3) use lethal force if the Captain's life is in imminent danger."

Having now been confronted by the give-me-Somalia-or-give-me-death edict from the pirates, Castellano needed help. Through Fifth Fleet, he was put in contact with an FBI hostage negotiator trainer at the FBI Academy at Quantico, Virginia. The agent—Castellano recalls his name as Frank DeLorenzo, but when I asked to interview him for this book, the FBI denied his existence—gave him talking points, guidance, and direction. Castellano remembers him saying, "You shouldn't be the only one negotiating. You need to take a step back." He asked the skipper if there was anyone on his crew who had experience with this sort of thing. Admittedly, it was a long shot. But the question paid off.

"It turns out that my senior chief intel specialist [IS] had had training in the past, just from his intel background, and he became the negotiator." Castellano didn't hesitate to put SC Joel Steinbach (now master chief) on the phone with the FBI agent to get a moment-by-moment tutorial. "The interpreter, my senior chief IS, XO [executive officer], and I were up on the bridge wing, basically doing the negotiations."

In my conversation with Castellano about the negotiations, he paused at this point and reflected on a major lesson he learned from the Somali translator at a critical moment in the negotiations. It had to do with the cultural significance to the pirates of what was transpiring, and with their cultural background. "We didn't have that, so we were approaching things from a Western mindset. And our Somali interpreter was able to kind of temper that. You know, where we love to operate in the gray, there's a lot of realism in Somalia. Harsh conditions and everything else, it's black-and-white. And where our mentality of life being precious—that's not in the forefront of Somalis' minds."

I interrupted. "Did that necessarily mean that when they said, 'we're either going to get this to Somalia or we're going to die out here,' that in their mindset, that wasn't that big a deal?"

"Yeah," responded Commander Castellano, "Yeah, it wasn't a big deal. There's a saying, *inshallah*, God willing." The negotiating team members were already concerned about Captain Phillips' long-term well-being, but this new understanding of the Somali psyche meant they really had to step up their game.

The FBI hostage negotiator had told them that at least once a day, if not twice—in the morning and the evening—they should demand a proof-of-life. Castellano said it meant "talking to Phillips, reassuring him that we were there and that we were going to get him back, and seeing if there was anything he needed."

On the first morning *Bainbridge* was on station, they did a proof-of-life. That evening, they spoke by radio with Captain Phillips again. But in the early morning hours, he tried to escape. As Phillips tells it in his book, the pirate he called Tall Guy was "standing in the open door with the moonlit water behind him. The boat was rocking slightly in the swells. He reached out a hand to get a grip on the door frame. Then both hands were in front of him. It was calm enough that he didn't have to hang on." The pirate was relieving himself when Phillips snuck up behind him and shoved. Tall Guy went into the water, screaming. Phillips debated for a moment whether to grab the pirate's gun from the deck, turn, and fire at the three sleeping pirates, or to try and escape. He dove into the water. Tall Guy's screams instantly awakened the other three pirates, and they began firing their AKs at Phillips, who tried unsuccessfully to swim away from Tall Guy.

Castellano recalls that the pirates wanted his crew to see what they were doing to their hostage as punishment for the escape attempt. "They dragged him back and they bound him. We saw them smacking him. They left the door open so that we could see. They all took a few whacks at him, punching him in the stomach and about the head and shoulders. That was the low point because we felt helpless."

The incident changed things both for Phillips—he was now tied up all day long—and for Captain Castellano. "The next morning, the pirates would not allow us to talk to Phillips. They said he was a bad guy. He didn't listen to them. He tried to escape, and he was their prisoner now."

Castellano was quite certain what authority had devolved to him.

> It was a case of hostile act, hostile intent. And between their actions, both verbally and physically, especially when Phillips jumped overboard and they started shooting in the water at him—if there was any doubt, it was all washed away then. But I saw this strictly from a self-defense perspective throughout pretty much the whole thing. It's the commander's inherent right to take action when you see hostile intent, hostile act. However, in the back of my mind, and also just in conversations with higher [authorities], the life of the hostage was paramount. You know what I mean? It wouldn't help when they shot at him in the water if I turned the 5-inch gun there and blew the lifeboat out of the water. You can make a case that I responded to a hostile act appropriately. However, if I did that, or even if I unloaded with 50-cal, Captain Phillips was on the gun target line, and he would've been collateral [damage], and then the mission would've failed.

I had to wonder if Captain Castellano, the on-scene commander, had the authority to order the pirates blown to kingdom come if he was reasonably sure that Phillips would survive. As someone who has commanded a U.S. Navy ship as large as and even more lethal than any World War II aircraft carrier, the question of who has the authority to order the use of lethal force is of critical importance. I'm convinced from the evasive answer he felt compelled to give during a conference call interview being monitored by public affairs personnel both at Fifth Fleet HQ and in the New York Naval Public Affairs Office that the answer was yes. Sort of. The conversation went this way:

McKnight: In preparing to talk to you, I read several articles online, and they state specifically that President Obama had previously given you standing orders to take action if you determined Phillips' life was in immediate danger. Is that accurate or inaccurate?

Castellano: There was—and this goes into the non-organic forces [the SEALs, who, I've been told by a source, were actually requested by Captain Castellano]—there was guidance and I would say that that was accurate. What was in the paper. There was guidance from national command authority dealing with the non-organic forces and what we could do. That's about all I want to go into it there.

McKnight: You were comfortable with the fact that you had the authority and that you were, in fact, the on-scene commander?

Castellano: Yes, I don't think there was any doubt about that.

McKnight: Does that include being the one to say, "It's okay to shoot"?

Castellano: I'd rather not go into that. There was national command authority guidance, so—I'll leave it at that. . . . I am ultimately responsible for everything that happens on that ship, no matter who, you know—So I'm either the hero or I'm the goat. And I knew that throughout the whole incident.

It was after that exchange that Castellano got quite reflective.

> I can tell you, you know, you are the officer you are based upon your experiences. My first tour [in a] department head job, I was operations officer on *Cole*. I left *Cole* six months before she got hit. Kirk Lippold was my CO for half of my time as OPS. He's a close personal friend of mine, in addition to being my CO back then. And I tell you, when I went down and brushed my teeth, I looked myself in the mirror and I said, "This is my Kirk Lippold moment." It wasn't a problem, you know what I mean? It was kind of surreal. But I knew it was the closest thing that I could see.

More than two years after the event, Castellano still rethinks that night when Phillips jumped overboard. "I felt kind of helpless when that happened and, reflecting, [I wonder could I] have done something else to have ended this situation at that moment in time? Taken better advantage of what happened?"

But there were no advance indications Phillips was going to jump. If there had been, Castellano said,

> If I had had a RHIB boat in the water constantly, in case he'd jump overboard, to rush in. Could I have had additional guys up on deck with M-4s to put down covering fire, so that way, when he jumped overboard, I could keep pirates' heads down. You know, I was close, but could I have been closer where I could've basically threaded the needle of putting the ship in between him and the lifeboat. That's really a hindsight kind of thing.
>
> I talked to the XO and I talked to the TAO. From a morale standpoint, that was kind of our low point. It was at night, it was like 2300, so you can't tell on an IR sight whether that was [Phillips] going overboard, you know what I mean? Because the way it looked, we saw him jump in—we recorded it on our sight—and if you play it back over and over again, you can tell. But in the moment, it looked like, hey, the pirates were going for a swim. Because it was f-ing hot out there. We're talking 100 degrees plus, and that lifeboat must've been miserable. Why would they not try to take a jump in the drink to cool off?

CHAPTER 10

The Rescue of Captain Phillips

ater in the morning of 10 April, *Halyburton* arrived. Initially, she took up a position just over the horizon from *Bainbridge* and the lifeboat but sent one of her helicopters aloft to begin building a maritime picture. At 1930 Captain Huck got a call from Castellano asking him to get his VBSS team and boat crew in the water and his helo up to stop the lifeboat from making a run for the Somali coast, which was about twenty nautical miles away. At that point, *Halyburton* closed from 10 nm to just 1 nm astern of *Bainbridge*—the traditional "lifeguard duty" position—where crew members observed the 506-foot ship playing an all-night-long, start-and-stop blocking game with the 28-foot lifeboat.

Although *Halyburton* was away from the action, her helo was absolutely in it. Huck was heading from the bridge wing to the bridge when he heard screaming. It was the cameraman on the helo, and he was shouting, "Shots fired! Shots fired!" Reviewing the video, he could see one of the pirates poke his head and an AK-47 out of the lifeboat and begin firing indiscriminately. Then he went back into the lifeboat.

According to Captain Huck, there was a fleeting thought of returning fire, "But it wouldn't have been a win. It would've been a complicated shot. *Bainbridge* is there, you've got RHIBs between us and the guys, any way you look at it [it was too risky]."

In Mombasa that same night, at two in the morning, things were going a bit nuts for Maersk's Gordan Van Hook. *Alabama*'s acting captain, Shane Murphy, had docked the ship with an audience of world media. This was as close as television networks could get to cover the story, and they were all over it much to the chagrin of the Kenyans, who were bent out of shape because this merchant ship was carrying eighteen U.S. sailors armed to the teeth.

Van Hook arranged to get the Navy men quickly bused out of the port area, but they had to leave their weapons behind. The Maersk executive, now clearly in the role of fixer, managed to get all the arms—rifles, machineguns, shotguns, grenades, and ammunition—boxed up and shipped to the U.S. Embassy in Nairobi. Then he had to deal with Kenyan Port Authority officials who felt it was their responsibility to investigate the entire incident. "They wanted to search the ship and make sure there weren't any more pirates on board and that there weren't any weapons on board. The way these things work—they wanted to be paid off in some way. Or they want some cigarettes or some coffee. So you gotta kind of deal with that."

He also had to deal with the twenty-three civilian crew members he had first met in the mess on board the ship. A former ship captain, he said,

> I've talked to a hundred crews. I know how to talk to a crew. I get in there, and I'm the company guy, so they wanted to take my head off. "Why did I put them in this position? We need armed security." That sort of thing. I was trying to explain how we do the whole process of risk assessment, and how we're going to relook at it. They don't wanna hear it. Some of them were more stressed out than others. Phillips was not universally loved by the crew. He was a hard ass, and he had a [defensive] plan where they had sort of a citadel, and they practiced it. And the crew doesn't like to do things like that. So I noted that part of the crew was very supportive of the captain, and then others were kind of silent on it. It was mainly divided between the deck and engineers—the deck people were more supportive.

Maersk put the crew members up in a fancy hotel for a couple of days, threw them a barbeque on the pier, and paid them a bonus plus overtime. Then he told them that the company had chartered a jet to fly them home. Surprisingly, that wasn't good news. "A bunch of them wanted to go back to sea, just keep working. Some of them had only been on the ship for a few weeks, so they were counting on being there for three months, so I got, 'You're sending me home? I don't want to go back to the old lady.' Others were happy. It was a mix. People were under a lot of stress; it was kind of a relief to get them on the plane and on the way back."

Three hundred or so miles away, at about 0815 on the morning of Saturday, 11 April, the lifeboat with the four Somali pirates and Captain Phillips on board got under way and tried to make a run for the coast. Since Captain Castellano had been up all night maneuvering *Bainbridge*, he asked Captain Huck to bring *Halyburton* onto the playing field. The two skippers had devised a new plan: good cop, bad cop. *Bainbridge* would be the ship that offered aid and comfort—food, water, and, eventually, medical care—to the pirates. *Halyburton* would make their lives miserable.

Huck kept a personal journal of the *Alabama* action. For the morning of 11 April, he wrote:

> Did some pretty aggressive maneuvering. Got the LB [lifeboat] on the bow and used fire hoses to harass the pirates. Got that set up and as LB made run we brought them alongside and hit driver in the back bubble (several window panes were busted) with fire hose. They didn't like that either. Also used helo as my free safety to impede progress of LB. The pirates really didn't like the helo. After about 45 min of some very aggressive maneuvering, LB went DIW [dead in water]. Event closed out with BAI [*Bainbridge*] lowering their two RHIBs and surrounding LB with HAL [*Halyburton*], BAI, 2xRHIBs and helo.
>
> Pirates did bring out AK-47 and fired a few shots. Was cognizant of the threat when LB was alongside HAL earlier and stepped away from some open firing lines. Was looking into the bridge so did not see shots but heard them and noticed the excitement level of the bridge wing increase.
>
> There were several times during the maneuvering that we could have taken out driver and other pirate since we were less than 50 ft away but overriding concern was safety of Richard Phillips. The only way we come out winning on this is if Richard Phillips is alive. Demonstrated restraint even though we had the clear shot several times and had been fired on from pirates.

At 1000 on Saturday morning, word reportedly came from Somalia by radio that people identified as "tribal elders" were calling for the pirates to surrender. Huck notes that the pirates didn't get the message until 1530 in the afternoon. There was no immediate response.

Meantime, at 0900 Washington, D.C., time at the White House—1600 on board *Bainbridge*—President Obama received a briefing paper update from the Situation Room. The White House press office eventually released a log that shows this notation twenty minutes later:

> 11 April 2009 0920
> National Security Council gives POTUS telephone update on current situation. POTUS gives Department of Defense policy guidance and certain authorities to additional set of U.S. forces to engage in potential emergency actions.

Once again, we must speak about those who must not be spoken about. The U.S. Naval Special Warfare Development Group—DEVGRU, aka SEAL Team Six—is headquartered at Little Neck, Virginia, close by Naval Air Station Oceana. The White House had previously given the order for the SEALs to head toward the scene of the *Alabama* hijacking. I suspect that the order issued on the morning of 11 April made it clear that lethal force could be used if necessary to rescue Captain Phillips from the pirates. Speculation in the press said the operation had been designated counterterrorism, which allowed the White House and the Pentagon to cut through the red tape that exists when military and law enforcement operations are combined.

Once it was determined that Captain Phillips was, in fact, in the lifeboat and that the pirates were headed toward the Somali coast, there was very little time to delay. SEAL Team Six needed to move fast. There were numerous options, including a battalion of highly qualified Marines in the area aboard *Boxer*, but when it comes to a hostage rescue at sea, there really is only one option: Navy SEALs. (Why would you send in the second team and be questioned later if something bad happened? You need to send the best.) This tier-one force can move fast, and that is just what it did.

Here are the logistics that I've gleaned from a variety of sources. The SEALs flew on an Air Force C-17 Globemaster from NAS Oceana.

The distance to the lifeboat was roughly 8,000 miles. The cruising speed of the C-17 is 450 knots, about 520 mph. The aircraft has a range of 2,800 miles, which means that Air Force tankers had to refuel it at least three times during the minimum sixteen-hour flight. SEALs are understandably concerned about stealth. That tells me that the operation was planned so that they would parachute into the ocean under cover of darkness, probably a high altitude–low opening jump so that the pirates weren't alerted to the passage of the huge aircraft. When the SEALs come, they bring the equipment they'll need to complete the mission, including weapons and boats. We know that there were no sniper rifles on board *Bainbridge*, and while SEALs are trained to use weapons they might encounter anywhere in the world, they prefer their own. There is no mention of SEALs in the *Bainbridge* deck log, no indication when they boarded the vessel, or how many of them arrived. *Halyburton*'s deck log was more specific.

HALYBURTON DECK LOG
0222   2009 04 11   1ST RHIB IS ALONGSIDE
0226   1ST RHIB IS CAST OFF
0227   2ND RHIB ALONGSIDE
0230   2ND RHIB AWAY
0231   3RD RHIB ALONGSIDE
0233   3RD RHIB AWAY
6 SEAL TEAM MEMBERS ON BOARD HALYBURTON
0308   RHIB ALONG STBD SIDE
0314   RHIBS AWAY TO BAINBRIDGE WITH PAX
ON BOARD

Several sources that I interviewed mentioned that in order to get the right forces to the scene as soon as possible, a squad of SEALs working in the Horn of Africa was dispatched to the ships. This group would keep the situation at bay until the Team Six operators dispatched from the United States came in. After this first group arrived on station with all the required equipment to prevent the pirates from getting the lifeboat to the pirate camps on the Somali coast, they were sent to *Bainbridge*.

The details are sketchy on where and when the transfer took place; however, there's mention in Captain Huck's journal of RHIBs going to pick up "village elders," and then those village elders are never mentioned again. Anywhere. What we do know from the logs is that a squad of SEALs ended up on *Bainbridge* with sniper rifles and with authorization from the National Command Authority to use lethal force to rescue Captain Phillips and prevent the pirates from getting him ashore in Somalia.

HALYBURTON DECK LOG
0337 2009 04 11 NAVIGATOR RECOMMENDS HALYBURTON
SHOULD NOT APPROACH SOMALIA
COASTLINE BY MORE THAN 8NM.
BASED ON NAUTICAL CHARTS ON BOARD.

HALYBURTON DECK LOG
0900 2009 04 11 SHOTS FIRED UPON USS HALYBURTON BY
PIRATES WHO HIJACKED M/V MAERSK ALABAMA
0908 LOSS OF HEAT SIGNATURE ON LIFE RAFT
LIFE BOAT IS DIW [DEAD IN WATER]
L BOAT HATCH IS OPEN. PIRATES CAME
UP NO WEAPONS
0914 PIRATES GONE BACK INTO L BOAT
0915 HAVE HEAT SIGNATURE ON L BOAT
0917 GM —— HAS THE M16. ——
ARE MANNED ON THE MOUNT 62 240
0918 CLEAR LINE OF FIRE
0919 PIRATE OUT OF THE HATCH
PIRATE BACK DOWN IN THE HATCH
0920 50 CAL IS NOT TO FIRE
0928 PIRATE LOOKING OUT AFT GLASS AT THE
RHIB AND HALYBURTON TO CHECK OUR
POSITIONS
0946 ANOTHER PIRATE COMES OUT TO
RELIEVE HIMSELF
1000 QM REPORTS 16 NM FROM LAND

HALYBURTON DECK LOG
1047 2009 04 11 XO HAS VISUAL STATED "HE IS ALIVE.
SITTING PORT SIDE. WAS BENT DOWN.
LOOKS UP AND SEES THE SHIP AND SITS
UP STRAIGHT" CAPTAIN PHILLIPS. ONE
PIRATE IS BELIEVED TO HAVE A INJURED
RIGHT THIGH

Now we return to the world of, in the words of former defense secretary Donald Rumsfeld, the known knowns.

At about 1645 on 11 April, just minutes after the president had issued his order, the pirates spoke with the translator and said they were going to start the engine and "make it to shore, no matter what." In so many words, they said they were willing to die.

Captain Huck wrote: "Called in helo and applied some loving care. I also came in real close to impede the progress of LB. Guess pirates were not as keen to get to shore because they stopped after 5 minutes. They started their engines up about 30 minutes later, but once I closed them, they stopped."

HALYBURTON DECK LOG
1736 2009 04 11 IN TERRITORIAL WATERS [less than twelve miles from coastline]

The problem for the skippers of the American destroyers was that they were no longer in a position to just sit there and wait it out. There was a strong northern current that varied from two to five knots, and it was moving the lifeboat ever closer to shore, and although they never got close enough so that anyone standing on the beach could see them— that's about six miles—they did come within twelve and a half statute miles of the Somali coastline, and that was much too close for comfort. Both captains were keenly aware that there were two elements, either of which would constitute mission failure: Phillips ends up on the beach or is killed in the effort to prevent it. It was time for some out-of-the-box thinking.

Huck wrote that as nightfall set in, he was "looking forward to a night of shenanigans."

BAI has suggested that the LB be towed out to sea with grappling hooks since we were at 11 nm from shore and drifting closer to shore at about 2 kts. I expressed my reservations on the towing with grappling hooks option. Concern is how to get close enough to reach LB with grappling hooks without escalating situation and endangering Richard Phillips. My XO suggested that since BAI was closer that they put a swimmer into the water and attach a grappling hook to the prop shroud. Once secured LB could slowly be pulled out to sea. Got a wait one while BAI mulled it over.

Aboard *Bainbridge*, the Somali translator had given the negotiating team on the bridge a useful piece of information. He had learned from conversing with the pirates that their plan was to get a mile or two off the beach and then drive up and down the Somali coast until they figured out where they were. The pirates had a magnetic compass on the lifeboat, but when they struck out for shore, they weren't compensating for set and drift—the speed and direction of the current. Castellano said, "The point that they thought they were going to was about a good eighty miles north of where they wanted to head."

This engagement in psychological operations was also the result of the translator being able to educate the Americans about certain political and cultural circumstances that could come into play. "As we got closer," Castellano recalls, "we started telling them that they were heading to the wrong place. If they get ashore, they're going to end up in a rival clan's area. They're going to kill them, and they're going to take their hostage and bring shame upon them and their families."

The psychological tactic may have played a role in the pirates agreeing to meet with tribal elders at sea to resolve the standoff. Huck wrote, "The point of concession was for LB to proceed east back to sea."

The pirates continued east until *Bainbridge* departed the area. At that point, the lifeboat informed the Americans that they had run out of fuel.

BAINBRIDGE DECK LOG 2009 04 11
2046 ALL STOP LIFEBOAT WENT DEAD IN WATER

Huck ordered his RHIB crew to prepare to bring fuel over to the lifeboat, but *Bainbridge* returned and Huck wrote, "LB was miraculously able to get back underway." That was about 2300. The lifeboat continued moving slowly to the east for about five hours, when the pirates once again claimed to be out of fuel. Huck notes, "Got LB out to 21 nm from shore so possibility of mission success looking better." Knowing that those whose name must not be spoken were en route puts his comment in a different context.

12 April 2009. Easter Sunday. But there would be no time to observe the holiday aboard *Bainbridge* and *Halyburton*. Both ships had their RHIBs in the water during the night. During the same time, the Somali that Phillips identified as "Leader" asked to use the phone on *Bainbridge*.

BAINBRIDGE DECK LOG 2009 04 12
0732 2009 04 12 ALL STOP
0740 ONE PIRATE IS IN RHIB
0744 ONE PIRATE IS ONBOARD 16 YRS. OLD

He was picked up in a RHIB and brought to the ship, where he was given medical treatment for injuries suffered during a struggle with *Alabama*'s chief engineer during the hijacking. Captain Huck wrote in his journal that the "young pirate attempted to work out deal with other pirates to let Richard Phillips go while they made it successfully ashore."

BAINBRIDGE DECK LOG 2009 04 12
1330 LAUNCHED WILLIAM + SUSAN [code names for RHIBs]
1345 ASTOP
1400 WILLIAM WENT ALONGSIDE LIFEBOAT TO TALK WITH CAPTIVE M/V CAPTAIN
1410 WILLIAM LEFT LIFEBOAT WHEN PIRATE

CLOSED DOOR TO LIFEBOAT
1448 RECOVERED WILLIAM + SUSAN

Later in the day the RHIB returned to the lifeboat. The pirates had radioed that Phillips needed a doctor. The corpsman wasn't allowed physical contact with the hostage, but he was able to converse with Phillips, who told him that he thought he'd experienced a touch of heatstroke. The boat dropped off food and some clean clothes—blue pants and a bright yellow shirt. Captain Phillips didn't figure it out right then, but there were people aboard *Bainbridge* who wanted to make sure that he more or less glowed in the dark.

At some point in the afternoon, *Halyburton* got a call from *Bainbridge* directing it to clear away from the lifeboat. Instructions were issued to the officers of the deck to keep the ship at least 3 nm away and for their helicopter to come no closer than 10 nm.

Until that morning, the seas in the area had been like glass. But there'd been a shift in the weather pattern, and things were getting progressively bumpier. A half hour before sunset, with the pirate leader still aboard *Bainbridge*, an agreement was reached to take the lifeboat under tow. Recall that the pirates had earlier claimed they were out of gas, but since they'd also used that as a ploy, no one aboard the ships knew if it was the case or not. There are stories that the pirates were told that their ride would smooth out with *Bainbridge* towing them, and since conditions in the lifeboat were three notches beyond intolerable to begin with, anything that would improve things sounded like a good idea.

BAINBRIDGE DECK LOG 2009 04 12
1723 RAMID [rudder amidships] 5 KNOTS
CONNECTED LIFERAFT FOR TOW
1724 LIFERAFT UNDER TOW OF BAINBRIDGE

A RHIB brought over a towing cable, and in short order the lifeboat was riding smoothly in the protected water behind the slowly moving ship. In his book, Phillips writes that after they were hooked to the ship, he loosened the ropes that had been holding him. The pirate he called "Young Guy" came down the aisle with a flashlight to check on him. Phillips said that he kicked the ropes off his feet and stood up. "The pirates' heads popped up from fore and aft. I walked forward." The pirate called Musso jumped up, saying that Phillips had to sit down, that he couldn't leave.

"So shoot me," Phillips recalled. "I've had enough. I'm out of here."

The captain said that Musso dropped his gun and grabbed him around the waist. Tall Guy came up behind him and grabbed hold of his leg. He took two steps toward the forward end of the boat and then heard a *BOOM!* and saw a muzzle flash from the front.

BAINBRIDGE DECK LOG 2009 04 12
1829 2 KNOTS ONE SHOT FIRED AT RHIB

Phillips writes, "I reeled back, and sat, landing on the third seat. 'What are you guys doing?' I shouted. Young Guy had shot off a round from the front end of the boat." Then, the captain wrote, they heard a female voice from outside asking, "What's going on in there?" The pirates responded, "No shoot! No problem! Mistake!" "It's okay. No problem now! All good."

Phillips described watching Musso and Tall Guy walk up toward the forward hatch. "They were raising themselves up as I slid down to the floor. I was exhausted. I just wanted to rest." And that's when three SEAL snipers in the prone position on the fantail of *Bainbridge*, which had winched the lifeboat to within twenty-five meters, each fired a single shot. Each of the three pirates was struck in the head, a deliberate shot that is used to kill a target while making sure that he doesn't have an involuntary muscle response and pull the trigger on the automatic weapon in his hand.

BAINBRIDGE DECK LOG 2009 04 12
1910 SHOTS FIRED FROM SMALL BOAT AT FLIGHT DECK.
RICHARDS [sic] INSTRUCTED TO EVACUATE.
BAINBRIDGE RETURNED FIRE.
1914 MAN THE BOAT DECK
1918 NO INJURIES REPORTED.

RICHARDS [sic] ESCAPED FROM PIRATES IN RHIB
BOAT
1948 NAV LIGHTS ENERGIZED

HALYBURTON DECK LOG
1919 2009 04 12 AMERICAN HOSTAGE ON
BAINBRIDGE RHIB
1934 BAINBRIDGE RECOVERED RHIB WITH
CAPTAIN RICHARD PHILLIPS ON BOARD
1937 THREATS ARE NEUTRALIZED

When Phillips responded to a voice calling to him from a RHIB and said that he was okay, Castellano said that from the bridge he could hear the cheer that went up from the crew. Captain Huck's final entry for Easter Sunday reads like this:

At about 1930 got called to the Bridge because Richard Phillips was overboard. Manned full SCAT and Boat Deck. Fifteen minutes later received word that pirates were dead and in the LB. Quit lifeguard duties and stayed out of the way—3nm off BAI quarter. Richard Phillips to Boxer at 2015.

The reference to Phillips going overboard was a misinterpretation of something that had come over comms after the shots were fired.

Fifth Fleet HQ in Bahrain released an official account of what had happened. It was reported in the news media this way: "Commander Castellano stated that as the winds picked up, tensions rose among the pirates and 'we calmed them' and persuaded the pirates to be towed by the *Bainbridge*. Vice Adm. William E. Gortney reported the rescue began when Commander Frank Castellano determined that Phillips' life was in imminent danger and ordered the action."

Vice Admiral Gortney, according to press reports, said that just before the shooting, one pirate was behind Captain Phillips pointing an AK-47 rifle at him. The head and shoulders of each of the other two pirates were also visible above the deck of the enclosed lifeboat. Determining that Phillips might be shot at any moment, the commander ordered the action.

Castellano was quoted as stating, "[We] ultimately believed the pirates were about to kill the captain. That's what was the decision point."

There was considerable debate afterward within the military community as to who actually had the authority to order the SEALs to shoot. From where I sit, I believe it's the captain of the ship who has the ultimate authority to say the words, "weapons released." Frank Castellano refuses to be specific about it, but is clear that he knew that the powers that be in Washington had authorized the use of lethal force if needed to save Captain Phillips' life. Other conversations I've had with naval officers lead me to believe that the ground rules change when those whose name must not be mentioned enter the picture. "Special ops guys don't need a surface warfare officer telling them how to do their job," is how one put it. I have to agree.

Captain Phillips was brought aboard *Bainbridge*, was given a quick medical check by a corpsman, and had a very brief conversation with Captain Castellano. Then he was picked up by a helicopter that took him to the recently arrived USS *Boxer*, an amphibious assault ship that has high-tech medical facilities on board. After being examined by a Navy doctor and pronounced in good physical health—he was clearly suffering from psychological stress—he took a phone call from President Obama, who also called Commander Castellano and Vice Adm. William McRaven, commander of Joint Special Operations Command, to express appreciation for the work the military had done in securing Captain Phillips' release.

The conversation with the president was a high point in Castellano's life. For me, it's just cool to hear about it, and it makes me awfully proud. Castellano said:

> It was pretty awesome. Got word to go ahead and call the president through the National Military Command Center. They patched me over to the White House switchboard. Talked to a staffer there who said, "Stand by for President Barack Obama." He wanted to express his congratulations and thanks to the officers and crew of the *Bainbridge* and everybody involved in the operation. You know, we all did a great job. He said that he'd just gotten off the phone with Mrs. Phillips, and she was very grateful and thankful for what we did in saving her husband.

He made mention of the fact that any crewmember who wanted a free meal in Vermont had a place to go—Mrs. Phillips had extended that.

I talked to him, telling him how it was a total team effort, it wasn't just us on *Bainbridge* but everyone involved, *Halyburton*, *Boxer*, the inorganic forces, Fifth Fleet, FBI, the intelligence community. There were a lot of folks involved in this, and it wasn't just us. And then we wished each other a happy Easter. It lasted a few minutes.

After he got off the phone, Castellano got on the 1-MC—the ship's internal loudspeaker system—and told the crew he'd just spoken with the president. "They thought that was the greatest thing. Their morale was so high after the incident. It was a once-in-a-lifetime event. I mean, a once in a two-hundred-year event." The reference is to the last hijacking of an American-flagged ship, when the Barbary pirates were raising hell and Thomas Jefferson was president.

BAINBRIDGE DECK LOG 2009 04 13
0906 LIFEBOAT UNDER TOW OF USS BOXER RHIB
3 PIRATE REMAINS ARE ONBOARD USS BAINBRIDGE

The remains of those three pirates were eventually returned to Somalia in an operation just like the midnight express we did when I was out there to return a batch of pirates to their homeland. The handoff was made in Somali waters to their coast guard.

After all the excitement had died down, Captain Phillips was brought back to *Bainbridge*, which set off to deliver him to Mombasa. The trip took a day longer than expected because the ship was diverted to answer a distress call from another American-flagged cargo ship, MV *Liberty Sun*, which was under attack.

BAINBRIDGE DECK LOG 2009 04 14
2125 IN PURSUIT OF M/V LIBERTY SUN
BEING ATTACKED BY PIRATES

Later a French frigate captured eleven of the pirates who had gone after *Liberty Sun*. One of the pirates told the French news agency that "the aim of this attack was totally different [from the attack on *Alabama*]. We were not after a ransom. We also assigned a team with special equipment to chase and destroy any ship flying the American flag in retaliation for the brutal killing of our friends." It was a claim that was certainly braggadocio; the likelihood that it was factual was minimal. There's never been any evidence that pirates have targeted, or even have the capability to target, ships of specific nations. Their tactics were always to go after ships that had been fortuitously encountered.

When *Bainbridge* docked in Mombasa harbor on 16 April, the crew had the Lynyrd Skynyrd hit "Sweet Home Alabama" blaring from the deck speakers. Unfortunately, because of the delay, *Alabama*'s crew had already been flown back to the United States. Waiting for Captain Phillips on the dock with his backpack, clothes, and—most important—reading glasses was Maersk's representative, Gordan Van Hook. The two men spoke at length in a stateroom on the ship, and there was no question in Van Hook's mind that Phillips was dealing with a lot of posttraumatic stress. He had been alerted to that ahead of time by Captain Castellano, and Maersk had flown two specialists in from Kuwait to help him deal with it. At first, Phillips was resistant, but after a bit of arm-twisting, he agreed to meet with the doctors. The session lasted two-and-a-half hours; afterward Phillips told Van Hook it had been very helpful.

While that was going on, the Mombasa-bound cargo was being offloaded, and Maersk had people surveying *Alabama* to see what could be done to make it more pirate-proof. Ultimately, they installed razor wire, hot steam lines that could spray over the sides, and LRADs.

The Maersk corporate jet came in to pick up Captain Phillips, and two FBI agents asked if they could fly with him to his home in Burlington, Vermont, to debrief him on the way. Van Hook agreed to give the agents a ride but asked that they wait on questioning him until he'd had a chance to decompress. The agents understood and indicated that they just wanted to establish a personal relationship with him so that he'd be comfortable talking with them later. According to Van Hook, that's pretty much what happened during the seventeen-hour flight—a lot of baseball talk and just a little bit about the recent events, and only because Phillips brought it up.

Since he's a former Navy captain and commander of a destroyer squadron, Van Hook's takeaway from the *Alabama* hijacking isn't surprising.

> Number one, it's all about leadership at sea, and Captain Phillips was a strong leader and he had a plan. It didn't all go exactly according to plan, but a lot of times it doesn't. But he adapted. Then the fact that we maintained this national capability, this particular team of SEALs, their mission is hostage rescue. And the capability that they have and the investment that we've made was a good one. Those guys are unbelievable. They treated it like it was just [all in a day's work]. If you talk to the CO, they came onboard, unpacked their stuff, got set up, did their thing, packed up again and said, "Okay, ready to go."
>
> Other lessons learned out of this—that our company has invested a certain amount in people like me to maintain relationships that are very, very important. When you get on the phone with somebody and you actually know them, they knew who I was, they knew that I had served out there, as [Fifth Fleet commander, Vice Admiral] Gortney said, "You're a member of our tribe," so it's more comfortable.

Before we leave the saga of the *Maersk Alabama* hijacking, I want to pick up on something Gordan said about leadership at sea. I'm a retired rear admiral. I've worked with dozens of young officers in our Navy. I have to say how proud I am of the two young commanders who captained *Bainbridge* and *Halyburton*. Frank Castellano and Michael Huck were classmates in the class of 1990 at the U.S. Naval Academy. They'd never been trained for this kind of mission, yet they took charge, worked out a plan on the fly, and carried it out with great success and very little guidance. That, to me, epitomizes leadership.

One postscript to this story: Lightning may not strike twice, but Somali pirates do. In November 2009, just seven months after pirates were thwarted in their effort to capture the *Maersk Alabama* and hold her for ransom, they tried again. The ship was about six hundred miles off the northeast coast of Somalia, once again on the regular run from Salalah to Djibouti, and on to Mombasa.

Four pirates in a skiff came within three hundred yards of the ship and opened fire. This time, the vessel had more than a few dozen signal flares with which to fight them off. *Alabama* was carrying an armed security team of former U.S. military special operators and was equipped with the LRAD acoustical defensive device. The pirates didn't have a chance.

CHAPTER 11

Chopstick Diplomacy on the High Seas

y command staff moved from the spacious *San Antonio* to the state-of-the-art Aegis cruiser *Vella Gulf* on 4 February, and shortly thereafter we passed near the Russian flagship, the destroyer *Admiral Vinogradov*, as it was escorting one of their merchant ship convoys through the IRTC. Inviting the commander of their fleet over for lunch seemed like the natural thing for me to do.

The Russians had made it more than clear that they understood what working as part of a coalition to fight piracy meant. We'd already had an occurrence that had lots of folks shaking their heads in disbelief. Answering the call of a merchant vessel in distress from a possible pirate attack, the commanding officer of *Vella Gulf* called for air support from *Vinogradov* while it was tracking a suspected pirate skiff. The Russians responded with the helicopter in much the same way that our own organic air assets would have responded.

About a week after I extended the invitation, our flagships were in proximity again, and arrangements were being finalized when I thought it might be a good idea to call back to NAVCENT in Bahrain and tell Vice Admiral Gortney about the plan. It was a casual conversation. I said that "the Russians are coming. The Cold War's going to end. We're bringing down the Berlin wall single-handedly and solving the Cold War's problem of detente."

He came back with, "McKnight, the Berlin Wall is gone." But he said it was a great idea because anything we can do to promote the notion of coalition is a good thing, and getting the Russians to come over to a U.S. ship is flat-out a success story.

It just so happened that at the same time we were hosting NBC News chief Pentagon correspondent Jim "Mik" Miklaszewski and his crew on *Vella Gulf*, and I figured that hosting the Russians would make a great news story for not only the Navy but also for counterpiracy operations. Shortly after my conversation with the admiral, Mik and I were in my stateroom when the phone rang. There's caller ID on that phone, and Mik could see that it read "Vice Admiral Gortney."

Mik said to me, "You might want to answer that." So, I picked up the phone and it's Gortney. He said, "Is NBC News on board ship?"

I said, "Yes, sir."

He said, "Okay, no video of the Russians."

"Yes sir, I got it."

Two hours later, the phone rings; it's Gortney again. "Miklaszewski. Not only don't shoot any video, but get him off the ship." This was embarrassing. Mik thought he'd lucked into being in the right place at the right time and had let his bosses back home know that he'd have a great story for them tomorrow. I walked down to where he and his crew were hanging out and delivered the news. He actually took it quite well. "Terry," he said, "I've been thrown out of worse bars before." So I arranged to transport the NBC team over to *Lewis and Clark* and then began getting ready to greet the Russians, who'd be coming in their own helicopter.

The visit was quite uneventful; the important thing is that it happened, not that we accomplished anything special. The Russians spoke very little English, and we didn't have an interpreter in our crew, but we managed to work out the language barriers and have some good laughs about the Cold War. They appeared to enjoy lunch, and I do recall that they drank a lot, even though the best we had to offer was wine and beer, not the vodka that they are world-famous for serving during their ceremonial visits. We offered to let them purchase items in the ship's store, but a problem arose when it became clear that they were not carrying any greenbacks. Ultimately, to make sure our new friends did not leave the ship disappointed without a few *Vella Gulf* ball caps and tax-free American cigarettes, the CO and XO proudly treated our guests. But why did I have to get Mik off the ship? I still haven't figured that out—which would become even more curious a bit later in my tour when we hosted the Chinese.

One of the major success stories of the counterpiracy operation in the Gulf of Aden has been the coalition against piracy. Yes, many will contend that not all the countries participating in the mission have signed up or formally joined the coalition as members of CTF 151, but it needs to be stressed that they all have contributed forces to defeat piracy, and we were working together.

One of the minor miracles of coalition is the quarterly meeting in Bahrain of what came to be known as SHADE, which stands for Shared Awareness and Deconfliction. Hosted by Combined Maritime Forces, the original notion was to gather everyone involved in the antipiracy effort in a single room to focus on "improving cooperation and coordination of the maritime forces operating in the region, while considering new initiatives and programs designed to disrupt, and ultimately, prevent future pirate attacks." Royal Navy lieutenant commander Dave Bancroft, then the OIC at UKMTO in Dubai, was present at the creation of SHADE in December 2008. He said,

> The great achievement in the SHADE is the fact of who sits at the table. I started my time at sea chasing Russian submarines. If you would have told me that in five years the Berlin Wall would come down then, I would not have believed you. But if you said that before I retired from the sea, I would be seated at a table in the middle of an American base with a Russian admiral and his staff to my left, and a Chinese brigadier general and his staff to my right, then I would have thought you insane—but it happened and is still happening. Seafarers have a code: we are all one family and we always help each other. Politicians build the barriers, but the seaman finds a way around them.

Almost 150 representatives from navies, law enforcement agencies, the shipping industry, and various governments attended the March 2012 SHADE conference.

Bancroft believes the idea for SHADE came from Commodore Tim Lowe of the Royal Navy, who was the deputy at NAVCENT when I was there. He said, "Cdr. Al Whittaker of the Royal Australian Navy actually named it. I believe he very nearly managed to get the name Shared Awareness Group—SHAG—past the powers that be until Commander Lowe saw it and had it changed."

While some State Department people I've spoken with point with amazement at the Turks and Greeks not only belonging to the same group but actually working together on the high seas, it's the active participation of the People's Republic of China (PRC) that fascinates me. In December 2008 Beijing dispatched three of China's newest ships, the *Wuhan*, the *Haikou*, and the supply ship *Weishanhu*, to the Gulf of Aden. The task force was to be commanded by Rear Admiral Du Jingchen. Why is this important? For the first time in years, the Chinese People's Liberation Army Navy (PLAN) would deploy out of area and remain on station.

Over the past few decades, the PLAN has been growing as a regional power, and as recently as the 1980s, the Chinese navy was commanded by a career army officer, General Liu Huaqing. The PLAN deployed to circumnavigate the Pacific in 1997 and sent a two-ship task force to circumnavigate the world in 2002, but they had never operated in the Gulf of Aden (GOA) for extended operations. Now they were coming into waters that were dominated by NAVCENT's Combined Task Force 151.

When I arrived in Bahrain in January 2009—precisely at the same time as Admiral Du's task force began patrolling the GOA—I was briefed that the Chinese would be operating in the Gulf and that "we were all very interested" in their operations. My first question to the NAVCENT/Coalition Forces staff was, how do we communicate with their forces? Silence in the room. Next question, Admiral McKnight? There was clearly no game plan on how we were even supposed to speak with Admiral Du's ships, and I saw that not just as setting us up to miss prospective intelligence opportunities but also as a potential threat to safe operations in fairly crowded waters.

As in the case of all marine and flight operations, there are safety radio frequencies for deconfliction. The last thing I wanted with the Chinese and the rest of the forces operating in the Gulf was a major accident because we failed to inform the other task forces of our intentions, or because we didn't have a clear understanding of theirs. Before I left Bahrain, I tasked my stay-behind-staff to come up with a good answer on the communications problems.

Just prior to my departure, I had the opportunity to meet with Commodore Per Bigum Christensen, Royal Danish Navy, to discuss the situation in the Gulf. The commodore was in the process of turning over Task Force 150 to Rear Admiral Rainer Brinkmann, of the German navy in Bahrain, as well as turning over his flagship, HDMS *Absalon*, to my command. As we were sitting in my office, Commodore Christensen got this little smile on his face and said, "Terry, I have a copy of a letter for you that I presented to Rear Admiral Du on your behalf as the future commander of Task Force 151." After reviewing the letter, I paraphrased the line that Rick said to Captain Renault in the movie *Casablanca*, "I think this is going to be the start of a great relationship." The letter read, in part:

> Dear Commander,
> I welcome you to the Gulf of Aden and the area of responsibility for CTF 150. This is a very challenging area with a lot of criminal activities, not least the piracy being the highest priority for TF 150 at present.
>
> TF 150 is continuously patrolling the GOA to fight the piracy threat and to give the merchant vessels a confidence in their safety. We are broadcasting Maritime Awareness Calls every second hour and we vigorously patrol between the merchant vessels with our ships and helicopters. . . .
>
> TF 150 has taken upon ourselves the coordination responsibility in this area as we have been here for many years and because we have a solid knowledge of the pattern of life. TF 150 is coordinating with all naval forces in the area, including Malaysia, Russian and Indian naval forces. . . .
>
> My Command Authority, Commander Coalition Forces in Bahrain has directed me to exploit every opportunity to coordinate with you. From 12th of January I will be replaced by a new Commander Task Force 151 led by Rear Admiral McKnight, U.S. Navy. He will exercise his command from USS *San Antonio*, and he will continue the coordinating role in the GOA.
>
> I had hoped I could meet with you personally, but since my time in command is running out, I trust my successor will have the honour.

As I quickly read the letter, I realized this was not only my first correspondence as Combined Task Force 151 commander, but it was also to the Chinese! Good thing this did not come from the U.S. Navy;

it would have to have been reviewed by more than twenty-five action officers, the Joint Staff, National Security Council, and the Department of State before being released. And that just highlights one of the great benefits of being in command at sea: you take action and ask for forgiveness later.

When I arrived on USS *San Antonio*, I made meeting Admiral Du, either on my ship or his, one of my top priorities. From January through March we had very little success arranging a visit. Our task forces would pass many times, but our schedules seemed to be always in conflict. The Chinese navy's strategy was to escort their ships through the IRTC in convoy operations. As stated earlier, our strategy was to patrol the areas where we had seen the most pirate activity in the corridor over the past few months.

China has one of the largest merchant shipping fleets and is the home of three of the largest container shipping companies in the world. Ranked in the top ten container companies are China Ocean Shipping Company (COSCO), Evergreen Marine, and China Shipping Container Lines (CSCL). Some of the ships of the COSCO line are the behemoths of the sea. The *COSCO America* is 108,000 gross tons and can hold 10,046 TEU containers. According to the official Chinese Xinhua News Agency, about 20 percent of Chinese merchant ships passing through the waters off Somalia were attacked by pirates in the first eleven months of 2008, with seven ships either owned by China or carrying Chinese cargo and crew hijacked.

Since the arrival of the Chinese navy in the Gulf of Aden in 2008, they have escorted more than three thousand merchant vessels, including upward of one thousand foreign-flagged vessels. It's no mystery why the Gulf of Aden is so important to China. Each year, $3 trillion of global trade passes through these waters, and that includes more than 50 percent of the total energy products that the Chinese import annually. No question, then, that China has a national security interest in the GOA.

In any event, one day in early March, my luck finally changed. I was relaxing casual admiral style—I'd gotten used to wearing flight suits—on the bridge wing of USS *Boxer* when one of my Chinese linguists passed by and I asked her where she was headed. She said the Chinese task force was in close range and they were going to extend our normal pleasantries. I asked her to please pass on to their admiral again that he was most welcome to come over for lunch at any time that worked for his schedule. I listened to the young petty officer as she worked on mastering her Mandarin Chinese skills (one of the hardest languages to master) in conversation with her counterpart on *Wuhan*, who was trying to do the same with his English skills. In the middle of the conversation, she extended my invitation.

"Roger," came the response. "We will pass it on to the admiral." Just about twenty minutes later, the petty officer came out to the bridge wing and said, "Admiral Du has accepted your kind invitation and would like to come over the day after tomorrow." The Chinese had told her that they would finish their easterly convoy transit tomorrow and have a few days before they headed west with another convoy, and if we could meet them at point "B," he would come over for lunch.

Success! It was time for high fives on the bridge of *Boxer*. Besides catching pirates, this was my number-one priority, to meet face to face with the Chinese. I'd had lunch with almost every task force commander, including the Russians, but the Chinese were the gold standard. How many flag officers or U.S. Navy officers have had the honor of hosting a Chinese admiral under way? Yes, it's been done in port, but very few times on the high seas.

Then the realization of what was about to happen set in. I thought, I need to head to the bat cave and call my boss. "Shortney" Gortney is a great naval officer, but he will take your head off in a second. A shoot-shoot-look kind of guy. He'd always supported me, and it was an honor to work for him, but having lunch with the Chinese brass could be a big issue.

There was another more immediate reason why this was a big deal. Even while this proof of detente was happening in the Gulf of Aden, in the South China Sea about seventy-five miles off the coast of Hainan Island, our two countries were involved in a major maritime security incident.

The last time there had been such a dustup was in April 2001, when Chinese fighters had harassed a U.S. Navy EP-3 on an electronic intelligence mission, coincidentally seventy miles from Hainan Island. The fighters made two passes near our plane, and on the third pass there was a collision that crippled the EP-3 and sent the Chinese jet into the water, killing the pilot. Our plane was forced to make an emergency landing at an airfield on the island, and the crew was detained for ten days until what came to be known as the "the letter of two sorries" was delivered to the Chinese foreign minister. It said the United States was "very sorry" for the death of the Chinese pilot and that "we are very sorry the entering of China's airspace and the landing did not have verbal clearance, but very pleased the crew landed safely. We appreciate China's efforts to see to the well-being of our crew."

This time, USNS *Impeccable* was carrying out a surveillance mission off Hainan Island that involved a towed-array system designed for antisubmarine warfare. *Impeccable* was operating in international waters, but the Chinese were not very happy that the U.S. Navy was conducting research so close to their home waters. They dispatched five ships to harass *Impeccable*, one of which sailed to within twenty-five feet of our vessel. This was a very tense international incident for the Obama administration, which had only been in office for two months. And now Admiral McKnight wants to have dim sum and Tsingtao beer on his flagship with a Chinese admiral. This could be a testy phone call with my boss.

I was pleasantly surprised, however, when Vice Admiral Gortney gave me his highest endorsement for the visit. I'll never forget it. He said, "Terry, this is important for the operation, and I will do my best to make this happen." I am pretty sure that Gen. David Petraeus, the CENTCOM CG, and the chairman of the Joint Chiefs were briefed on the luncheon, and the final approval came from the State Department and National Security Council.

Then there was another matter of concern. We were hosting a documentary crew from Military Channel at the time. They'd been shooting a program titled "At Sea," and I wondered whether it was going to be Miklaszewski déjà vu and we'd be ordered to toss them overboard. Surprisingly, no one had any objections to Discovery remaining on the ship and shooting whatever they liked. The luncheon visit was approved, and the TV crew could stay. Like numerous occurrences, it is difficult for me to explain the train of logic on some of the key events of coalition operations.

The other thing that surprised me was the minimal direction I received on how to conduct the luncheon. If this had been taking place back in D.C. or Norfolk, we would have destroyed a whole rain forest worth of trees with the paper used to prepare the script for a PowerPoint to brief the visit multiple times.

During my tour as commandant of Naval District Washington, my wife and I hosted many breakfasts, lunches, and dinners for foreign military attaches in the commandant's quarters at the Washington Navy Yard. Lisa and I became very good friends with the naval attaché from the PRC, Captain Liu Hungwei and his wife, Yun. I learned on my return from the Gulf to Washington that the Chinese navy had sent a diplomatic cable to their embassy in the United States asking for information on one Rear Adm. Terry McKnight. Captain Liu told me he replied to Beijing that this is one naval officer who could be trusted. I have no doubt that this was the key to the positive response to our invitation from Rear Admiral Du.

The logistics for the visit weren't quite as heavy duty as they might have been were the president planning on landing on *Boxer*'s flight deck, but they were considerable. The only practical way for the Chinese to arrive was by helicopter. Should it be a U.S. helo or Chinese? It was decided that our guests would provide their own transportation, but that meant we had to get approval from higher headquarters for their bird to land on our deck. *Boxer* is a *Wasp*-class amphibious ship the size of a World War II aircraft carrier. Forty thousand gross tons full displacement with a flight deck more than eight hundred feet—almost three football fields—long, with nine landing spots. *Boxer* can accommodate the full inventory of Marine helicopters, as well as the AV-8B Harrier.

The *Wuhan* was equipped with a KA-28 Helix helicopter. This is the export version of the Russian Helix and is quite different from the helos seen in the U.S. Navy and NATO. The Helix employs a twin counter-rotating rotor. Looks really strange but seems to work. It turned out not to be a big issue to get approval for the Helix to land on *Boxer*—apparently they've landed on U.S. Navy ships in the past—but both parties requested that the Chinese pilots conduct some DLQs— helicopter deck landing qualifications—the day prior to the luncheon.

The air boss (the officer who controls the flight deck) moved as many aircraft off the deck as possible to give the Chinese pilots plenty of room for their landings. It's not that the landings are difficult, but on *Wuhan* the pilot will come straight in for a stern landing while on *Boxer* the approach is made from the side of the ship at a forty-five-degree angle. The DLQs were conducted with no problems.

Outside of bridge-to-bridge VHF channel 16, communications with the Chinese were somewhat problematic. I'm not sure how it got started, but it was decided that we would send our e-mail traffic to them via my office in Bahrain. Staff there would send the correspondence via a Yahoo account away from the military networks, and send it to another account in China. We were unable to communicate with the Chinese ships using the standard naval messages that were sent to other ships in the task force or to other NATO navies.

We checked with protocol officers at NAVCENT about the menu, but ultimately it was left up to us, so we opted for basic American food under the "when in Rome" theory. The supply officer suggested chocolate chip cookies, and we prepared a gift box for Admiral Du to take with him when he left the ship. As for alcohol, the only thing on board was beer and wine.

Admiral Du arrived on *Boxer* 14 March 2009. From the start, the visit was warm and friendly. As we walked around the ship, we talked about counterpiracy operations and our personal lives. He seemed to understand a little English (more English than I knew Chinese), but, just as I did, he had a translator next to him at all times. The Chinese arrived with a team of about ten, and as we toured *Boxer*, they really enjoyed having their picture taken with American sailors and Marines—especially the young females.

They asked a lot of questions and took a lot of pictures, but their overwhelming interest was in logistics, from fuel to food. I'd been prepped on how I was going to answer the questions about the frequencies of some of our radars or the weapons load out of the aircraft on the flight deck, but the questions always came back to logistics. From how we refueled the task force to where we got the fresh fruit and vegetables, their interest was clearly on extended fleet operations. They wanted to know the what, the how, and the when of resupply on long deployments. It soon became clear that they were planning for the long haul in the Gulf of Aden and beyond as they turned their navy into a true bluewater global force. Being well trained in the art of naval warfare, they clearly took to heart the words of Capt. Alfred Thayer Mahan in 1912, "Logistics—as vital to military success as daily food is to daily work."

As they departed, *Boxer*'s CO gave Admiral Du an American flag, but the gifts the admiral seemed most happy with were the gold Zippo lighter and that box of chocolate chip cookies. His big concern? "How long will they last?" Later that day, we received a thank-you message from the admiral, which read:

Dear Rear Admiral McKnight,

Today I feel honored to have the opportunity to have a face-to-face exchange of views with you on your flag ship, the USS *Boxer*, and we have had a beautiful and unforgettable time together. On behalf of my colleagues, and also in my own name, I would like to extend our sincere thanks for the kind reception and considerate arrangements towards us by Admiral yourself, Captain Cedrun and all the other American friends. We have exchanged views on convoy escort and anti-piracy missions on the Gulf of Aden in a frank and friendly way, which not only increased our mutual understanding, deepened our friendship, but also is conducive to the smooth implementation of our tasks in this sea area.

We have established a good working relationship between us and become good friends as well.

I am quite looking forward to you and your colleagues visiting my flag ship "*Wuhan*" at a convenient time, and let us return your hospitality.

Best Regards,

Yours sincerely,

Rear Admiral DU Jingchen

Commander of Chinese Navy TG169"

For me, that invitation was like hitting the Power Ball Lottery—two weeks in a row. Admiral Du invited us to lunch on *Wuhan*, and believe me, I was going to move heaven and earth to make this happen. My change of command was only a few weeks away, so I immediately had my staff work out a good time for the luncheon.

We reached a mutually agreeable date, 25 March, and surprisingly, it was harder to get approval for me to visit *Wuhan* than for them to come to *Boxer*. Sometimes the way things operate at DOD and State are strange, but we finally got approval for the visit. I can tell that you landing on *Wuhan* had a very special feeling. Commanding Task Force 151 had been a blast from the start to finish, but getting the chance to visit a Chinese warship under way was priceless. It would be one of the hallmarks of my naval career.

Our tour of *Wuhan* was interesting and unsettling. We went through the forecastle with their Special Forces team—who posed for photos guarding me with fixed bayonets. We toured the bridge, the main engineering control areas, the mess decks, and the berthing area, and we ate lunch in the flag wardroom. There was no mention of what was occurring off the coast of Hainan Island at the time, nor of other major issues in the Pacific area of responsibility (AOR). Our discussion was limited to piracy and allowing the free flow of commerce on the high seas.

The ship was spotless—actually, beyond spotless, tending toward sterile. I've been on dozens of navy ships, ours and others, and have never seen anything like this. And I kept wondering where the crew was. That was the unsettling part. We saw very few officers and crew as we walked around the ship.

Then, during lunch, the admiral told me that he had sent a helo to Yemen to bring back prawns for our lunch. Otherwise, rice would have been the main course. We enjoyed Tsingtao beer with our meal, and when I was ready to depart, Admiral Du presented me with the Chinese national flag, a plaque with the writings of Sun Tzu in Chinese, and a very nice bottle of 100 proof Kweichow Moutai, the national liquor of China, which is served at state banquets and always used as a gift for guests of state.

When I returned to *Boxer* I was still consumed with the notion that what I'd just experienced was the chance of a lifetime for a naval officer to visit a Chinese warship under way, and it remains so to this day. When I retired and had the time to do some reading and researching, I looked into the history of America's relationship with China, especially as it was impacted by sea power, and how the use and deployment of naval forces is still an important element of what continues to be a relationship affected by lots of moving pieces.

Nothing in America's foreign policy strategy over the past century has been more confrontational and demanding than its relations with China. The relationship between these two great powers got off to a wonderful start with the Treaty of Wanghia (also known as the Treaty of Peace, Amity, and Commerce) in 1844. This treaty opened the doors for trade in the Far East and gave the United States a most-favored-nation status on par with the dominant world power at that time, Great Britain.

In late 1899 through early 1900, the United States faced its first confrontation with China. A group of Chinese called the Society of Righteous and Harmonious Fists—known to foreigners as the Boxers because its members were athletic young men—that was upset with the outside influences of religion and trade staged a revolt against foreign nationals called the Boxer Rebellion. From our newly acquired facilities in the Philippines as a result of the Spanish American War, the United States was able to send almost 20,000 troops to the rescue and to support the Eight-Nation Coalition (Austria-Hungary, France, Germany, Italy, Japan, Russia, and the United Kingdom). In a very short time, the coalition overpowered the Chinese and forced the government to abolish the society and sign a peace treaty. Two major changes occurred as a consequence of the Boxer Rebellion. First, the United States, because it controlled territory acquired in the Spanish American War, was able to quickly deploy forces and thus demonstrate an ability to play a major role on the world stage. Second, the Chinese, on the other hand, were weakened by the conflict and would fall under the influence of Japan in the Far East for the next half-century.

When Japan attacked China in 1937, the United States sided with China and its leader, Chiang Kai-shek. Prior to the attack on Pearl Harbor and the United States entering World War II, enormous amounts of supplies were provided to the Chinese. Right after the war years, the United States faced a foreign policy concern that would challenge it for decades—the rise of communism. With Russia already totally under communist control, the United States had no choice but to support Nationalist China under the leadership of Chiang. There was no mutual trust between us, but faced with the alternative of total communist dominance in the Far East, the United States put what some would say was limited effort into Chiang's attempt to maintain control of China. In 1946 President Truman dispatched his trusted soldier and statesman (and VMI graduate, I might add) Gen. George C. Marshall to China to try and negotiate a settlement between the Nationalist Chiang and the Communist Mao Zedong. For nearly two years, General Marshall would try in vain to negotiate a treaty between the two. Feeling that he had no chance of success, in early 1947 Marshall returned to the United States without a treaty. Quickly, a civil war ensued, and after two years of heavy fighting, the Nationalists were driven off mainland China and established a government on the island of Taiwan, formerly called Formosa, while Mao established the People's Republic of China on the mainland.

For nearly the next thirty years the United States had minimal relations with what quickly came to be called Communist or Red China, and promised to defend Taiwan against an attack from the mainland. During both the Korean and Vietnam conflicts, Communist China would provide forces and supplies to allies in the north. Even to this day, the PRC has a major influence on the policies of North Korea and Vietnam.

The situation in the entire Asia-Pacific region would change with the arrival of President Richard Nixon in Beijing in February 1972. If you asked the man on the street today what was the most significant event of the Nixon presidency, they would likely say Watergate. However, no other event in U.S. foreign policy in the last half of the twentieth century ranks as important as the opening of U.S. relations with China. Today, while the two countries have not exactly embraced each other, and matters of trust—or the lack thereof—regularly pop up as they did with the harassment of USNS *Impeccable* while I was hosting Admiral Du, the economic landscape of the world has changed dramatically, and it all began with Nixon's visit to China. This was a major step in making the world flat.

In 1970 China was a closed society with very little economic power in the world. Today China has a population of more than 1.3 billion people and is the world's largest exporter. In 2010 China passed Japan as the world's second-largest economy, a ranking Japan had held for more than forty years. In 2001 the U.S. economy was three times that of China. But with China's growth of nearly 10 percent per year, and the United States' marginal growth of 3 percent, leading economists predict that China will pass the United States around 2025. Think about this: the United States passed Great Britain as the world's leading economy in the early 1900s. Talk about a winning streak coming to an end! And it's conceivable—some say likely—that with the growth of India, the United States could fall to third before 2050.

How does all this come into play with counterpiracy operations? In the 1970s the Chinese PLAN had only a few coastal defense destroyers and frigates and was no threat to the mighty U.S. Navy that ruled the Seven Seas. It had no antisubmarine warfare capability, no surface-to-air missiles, and very limited antiship missiles. The U.S. Navy could transit the Straits of Taiwan with impunity. But as the Chinese economy grew and, along with it, the demand for natural resources, so did the Chinese navy, rapidly expanding from a costal force to a blue-water navy.

China's maritime fleet grew as well. Today China is the third-largest ship-owning country in the world. One-fourth of the world's exports in containerized cargo come from China. China is the second-largest oil-importing nation: 70 percent of global oil passes through the Gulf of Aden. Who has one of the largest container shipping fleets in the world? China: 50 percent of the containers that travel across the high seas pass through the Gulf of Aden. Without question, piracy is a national security concern to the second-largest economy in the world. As far back as 1890 U.S. naval officer and historian Alfred Thayer Mahan wrote in *The Influence of Sea Power upon History (1660–1783)* that sea power was decisive in determining national supremacy. He's still regularly quoted as saying that "whoever controls the Indian Ocean will dominate Asia," an observation that both the Chinese and Indians appear to be taking to heart. (It's just a coincidence that when I took over CTF 151, one of the ships in my command was the destroyer USS *Mahan.*)

How does a nation with a rapidly growing economy and rapid growth in its population become a world power? By building a strong blue-water navy. The model has been established for thousands of years. Britannia's Royal Navy ruled the seas. The United States has dominated the oceans for almost a century. The Chinese leaders have read the history books and understand that while they have a large army to defend their homeland, if they want to be a global power, they must build a blue-water navy. Most of their naval doctrine is based on the teachings found in Mahan's seminal work. They know they need to command the seas.

There is no way that the United States can stop the growth of China. Why? Three key issues: population growth, economic growth, and demand for resources. These are all connected and will drive the PLAN not only to get larger but also to become a true global force.

Since I left command of CTF 151 in 2009 we have seen several major developments with PLAN. They've had ships continuously deployed in the Gulf of Aden on counterpiracy operations. In March 2010 their vessels entered the Arabian Gulf and made their first visit to a Middle Eastern port, Abu Dhabi. In May 2011 Pakistan finalized a strategic partnership with China that allows the PLAN to use the Pakistani port of Gwadar as a forward-deployed naval base. In February

2011 China swiftly moved the frigate *Xuzhou* from a counterpiracy mission to assist in the protection and evacuation of Chinese citizens during the Libyan uprising. In August 2011 the *Varyag*, a former Soviet *Admiral Kuznetsov*–class aircraft carrier that had been acquired by the Chinese before construction had been finished, was photographed conducting sea trials in the Yellow Sea. A month later the Chinese hospital ship *Peace Ark* departed China for a one-hundred-day deployment to the Caribbean and Central America. And in December 2011 the PRC worked out an agreement with the Seychelles to establish their first military base in the Indian Ocean in order to be able to resupply warships and provide rest and recuperation facilities for their sailors.

China in the Caribbean—the backyard of the United States? It causes me to think about what China has learned from the U.S. Navy about the doctrine of soft power. Briefly, back to the *Xuzhou*'s mission to Libya: It marked an important milestone because, to the best of our knowledge, this was the first-ever dispatch of a PLA military platform specifically assigned to help protect a noncombatant evacuation operation, in this case, helping PRC citizens trapped in an active conflict zone. (By contrast, evacuation of U.S. citizens in danger during the Libyan uprising was carried out by the State Department and its Diplomatic Security Service, which chartered a ferry that was forced to remain in a Libyan port for two days waiting until bad weather cleared and it was safe to leave.)

Chinese policymakers now have a precedent for future military operations in areas where the lives and property of expatriate PRC citizens come under threat. We expect that the Chinese people's popular support for the mission will be high. This action was a natural sequel to the 2008 decision to launch the antipiracy mission in the Gulf of Aden. On the tactical level, it reflects the PLAN's growing confidence and capacity in conducting long-range operations. The mission is also a booster shot for the PLAN's public image in China and will likely help it secure more funding in coming years.

Successfully protecting Chinese merchant ships from pirates and evacuating Chinese citizens from violent areas are great cards for PLA senior naval officers and civilian supporters of a strong navy to play during internal procurement debates. Having the PLAN consistently answer the call when China's overseas comrades and commercial interests need protection clearly explains the force's value and will smooth the way for advocates of their aircraft carrier program as well as those who seek a more robust long-range naval capability in general.

On the international level, safeguarding the evacuation of PRC citizens provides a positive and peaceful rationale for logistically useful operations that also provide advantageous military training opportunities. I think such contingencies are very likely as China's expatriate workers continue seeking their fortunes in potentially volatile regions such as Africa. *Xuzhou*'s deployment to Libyan waters reflects the reality that Beijing is now more willing to employ military power when PRC citizens overseas are threatened. By demonstrating concrete will and operational capability, a more muscular Chinese foreign military posture such as that shown by *Xuzhou*'s mission may actually be a positive lever for cooperation against nontraditional security threats. Therefore, I think once the dust settles, *Xuzhou*'s dispatch should be discussed with Chinese diplomatic and security officials to explore ways to better coordinate bilateral and multilateral military cooperation.

China is certainly going to continue to grow and deploy. When I initially met with Rear Admiral Du, I invited him to continue to work with us to stop piracy. I also told him that I would recommend to my boss, Vice Admiral Gortney, that the Chinese be invited to the upcoming Shared Awareness and Deconfliction Event (SHADE) conference. In May 2009, shortly after I left the task force, the Chinese attended that meeting and as a result are part of the group of nations including India, Japan, and, most recently, Malaysia that have agreed to exchange piracy-related information to more effectively fight the problem.

This is a small event on the massive issue of dealing with China as a sea power. But we're talking. The only way we'll avoid conflict is to talk. And I believe we need to expand the conversation to include what both our plans are in the waters of the Indian Ocean and the Middle East.

Of course, my friends Peter Pham and Martin Murphy spend pretty much most of their waking hours contemplating things like naval power in general, and in the Indian Ocean in particular, as well as the ups and downs of American influence in that part of the world, and, in Peter's case, focusing on the developing and underdeveloped nations in Africa. So I turned to them to follow up on my historical look at the problem with their analytical examination of what's going on between the Chinese and the Indians, both of whom will defend their right to unhampered use of the shipping lanes through the Indian Ocean.

Before looking at those two powers, Martin Murphy says we must focus first on a more critical question, which is, what will the U.S. Navy's position be on defense of trade and international maritime security? Martin told me, "I think it's one of the missions that they want to drop. I don't think they've ever actually embraced it wholeheartedly, but given the fiscal pressures that are building, the U.S. Navy is focusing on only two AOR's, the Western Pacific and the waters in proximity to Iran." He sees the situation now as being similar to what went on with the Navy during the Cold War, where "anything that distracted the Navy from hunting Russian subs and making sure the Russian surface groups were monitored and controlled, and never did anything bad" was low priority. "We're going to see the same thing happening now," he avers, "and that creates opportunities for other powers to come into the maritime domain, and that's the last bloody thing we want."

Personally, I agree 100 percent with that observation. But can we continue to downsize ourselves and pull out of these missions and say, "Hey, we don't—or can't—care about them"? Look at how much commerce passes each year through the Bab el-Mandeb Straits at the south end of the Red Sea. If something happens there, the world's economy is just going to take a major nosedive. Yet even while I was deployed there, I felt that was not a mission that NAVCENT wanted to go after.

Steve Carmel, the senior vice president of Maersk Line, Ltd., took a position in our conversation on this matter that surprised me. While acknowledging that the United States has traditionally played a role as a guarantor of commerce, he said there's very little U.S. commerce that goes through the heavily pirated areas of the Indian Ocean and Gulf of Aden. "[Cargo bound from] Asia to the United States goes to the Pacific. Eighty percent of the trade through there is actually bound for Europe, not the United States. And so, I have difficulty beyond our leadership role and world stability" seeing it as a commerce issue for the U.S.

> It's a major issue for stability in Africa. This is a big deal for the Africans. But what our direct national interest is, I have yet to get anybody that can tell me that. Now, if you're going to have access out there for the Fifth Fleet burning holes in the ocean anyway—well, it's a pretty good thing to do to keep them busy. But when you're

talking about a constrained budget environment, and the
Navy is going to have to start shedding missions, where
does that [antipiracy] mission end up in the pecking order
of things we should be doing?

Martin Murphy, who has written extensively on this topic and continues to do so, responded by saying, "The U.S., to my mind, is the
ultimate guarantor of maritime security, including freedom of navigation on the world's oceans. It comes with costs, but it comes with huge
advantages, mainly the fact that if you're guarding the sea-lanes, most
other states are not going to challenge the navy. But any opportunity—
as soon as you show signs of weakness—other states are going to have
to step in, if they believe their interests are threatened."

He's clear that those other states are going to be India and China,
a position with which Peter Pham wholeheartedly agrees. Peter says
China has multiple reasons for deploying its navy across the Indian
Ocean, including competition with India.

India has long regarded the western Indian Ocean more or
less as its sphere, and so China is slowly—not directly, and
they'll deny it up and down although I think their denials
ring a little hollow—getting into a competitive situation.
The idea that there's an opening we might create by step-
ping back—China will certainly seek to fill it, especially if
it's right in an area that India is interested in. We see that
with the creation of the de facto Chinese military base in
Pakistan. We see it now in Angola, with this not-quite-yet-
defined Chinese logistics base.

He also makes the point that China is very dependent on oil from
the Middle East and from Africa. "Through the Gulf of Aden flows not
just the oil coming from Saudi Arabia, but also 9 percent of China's
[oil] imports that come out of Port Sudan. And then the imports coming off Angola, although they don't sail through the Gulf of Aden, certainly sail in the Western Indian Ocean waters that Somali pirates have
operated in."

Martin Murphy picks up on that thought with the observation
that India has reversed a long-held position that it wasn't interested
in becoming the policeman of the Indian Ocean, saying that recently

India's defense minister, A. K. Antony, announced that India was going to provide defense for the island nations of the Indian Ocean. "He didn't actually ask the island nations whether they wanted Indian protection, but they're getting it anyway. Why would he say that? I don't know, but India is regarded as a bit of a regional bully, isn't it? And now they're getting more and more agitated about the maritime security situation in the Indian Ocean, they're getting more and more agitated about the Chinese presence. So, in not a typically Indian fashion, they've done a smart about-turn." Whether that reversal means that the Indian navy's status as what Murphy calls "the poor relation in the hierarchy" changes remains to be seen. Currently, he says, the Indian army gets roughly 90 percent of the defense budget, the air force about 8 percent, and the navy only 2 percent. India is currently building its first indigenous aircraft carrier, INS *Vikrant*, which is scheduled to be commissioned in 2014.

CHAPTER 12

Strategy and Tactics

S omali piracy is a strange beast to get a handle on. It's not unreasonable to view it as a game of whack-a-mole on steroids, played out over 2.6 million square miles of ocean. We crack down in the IRTC, pirates go hunting for ships in the open ocean; merchantmen opt to hug the coast of India adding thousands of miles to their voyage, pirates ignore the risk from the Indian navy and pop up close to the coast, operating from hijacked fishing boats turned into mother ships. Or they move into the southern Red Sea off Sudan, or attack on the approaches to the crowded Straits of Hormuz. While the image of a Somali pirate as that of a skinny, uneducated, foolishly brave, barefoot boy barely out of his teens is accurate, we still can't take the pirates for granted. It may not be Darwinian, but they adapt, they struggle, they face horrific odds, and they recognize that success will change their lives in ways unlike anything else available to them. Maybe they're Somalia's version of the Forty-Niners, who weren't always scrupulous about obeying the law in their quest for a huge strike that would change their lives.

The problem that we're facing is that more than halfway through our first decade of dealing with Somali pirates, we don't appear to be any closer to a coherent strategy to fight them than we were at the start of this scourge. I find that curious. Every time I see one of those investment-house commercials on television talking about the global economy, and how "switch grass in Argentina changes engineering in Dubai," it becomes curiouser and curiouser. Because all that world trade is not going to occur only via the Internet or satellite or radio waves. Sooner or later, raw materials and finished goods need to be moved from a continent A to continent E, or vice versa, and unless there are people way above my pay grade who have developed a new method that they're going to spring on us, those goods are going to move on the world's oceans.

What I have noticed since I began paying close attention is that an assortment of antipiracy trial balloons have been floated from a variety of sources—governments, military, and business. They rise up, get a bit of media attention, and then the hot air cools and we're back to where we were. Some of the proposals have merit, others not so much. This chapter contains a sampling of both types, and I'm going to begin with one that I have used—and improved.

The IRTC is one of the most effective defenses against piracy in the Gulf of Aden. The idea was to concentrate merchant ships into a defensible zone, rather than have them wandering singly through the high-risk area where the chance of getting picked off by pirates was much higher.

The IRTC was designed and implemented by the commander of UKMTO from 2007 to mid-2009, now retired Royal Navy captain David Bancroft. It was also during his time at the Dubai-based operation that what has now become known as best management practices were formulated. The first corridor essentially hugged the coast of Yemen in international waters to force the pirates from Somalia to travel extended distances to search for victims. However, the first attempt of the corridor had several turns that did not favor the transit of merchant ships, and there were many false calls of piracy because the corridor was so close to the coast of Yemen and there were fertile fishing grounds off the coast. Additionally, it was discovered that the pirates were actually using the Yemeni coastline as a hiding ground. In February 2009 in consultation with the merchant community and in an effort to improve navigational safety, the corridor was relocated to the south and the transit was configured to a single course setting for the east or west passage.

In January of 2009, prior to my departure from NAVCENT headquarters for the Gulf of Aden, my staff and I had a meeting with Vice Admiral Gortney and Commodore Lowe to brief our proposed strategy for defending the merchants from pirate attacks. We gave the leadership three options: patrol the coast of Somalia; conduct convoy operations; and patrol the area of pirate activity.

In our discussion we looked at the pros and cons of each of the options. Patrolling the 1,200-mile coast would have required a large task force and numerous boarding operations to find the pirates. Since my task force had limited assets, we decided early that this option would not be feasible. However, we were all in agreement that ships and aircraft would periodically patrol the coast inside territorial waters to conduct "presence operations" to remind the pirates that the coalition was watching.

Convoy operations, which had been used to protect merchantmen during World War II and were being used by some coalition navies—most notably the Chinese—in the Gulf of Aden, weren't a good choice in my opinion. There were a number of drawbacks to convoys. We had limited resources to provide protection over the four-hundred-mile length of the IRTC, and convoys can't travel any faster than the slowest ship in the pack. That opens up all the ships to attack by pirates who like nothing more than a slow-moving target.

In the winter of 2009, when we looked at the history of where the majority of the vessels were attacked and pirated, it was clear that it was a concentrated area in the northeastern sector of the corridor. In fact, it was almost a due-north course from the pirate departure point of the port of Bosaso. In my closing remarks I said to Vice Admiral Gortney, "I recommend with only three surface units we patrol the corridor in the area of high pirate activity with the three combatants in 'box operations' and periodically send one of the surface units or aircraft on 'presence operations' or patrol in the vicinity of Bosaso." After a few remarks concerning safety of flight operations in a confined area and deconfliction while operating with the coalition forces that were not under CTF 151, he endorsed the plan and said I should go get some pirates.

Even with two helos on a ship, it was still a stretch patrolling a four-hundred-mile-long corridor with just three ships, each operating in its own box. Consider that pirates have been known to commandeer an unprotected ship in less than ten minutes. Adding protection that slows down their takeover of the bridge, and with proper lookouts providing warning of an impending attack, it's not unreasonable to say that a warship fifty miles away can provide meaningful helicopter support and ward off an attack.

During the course of my research, I learned that there were occasions when just being known as the baddest dude on the block was a successful antipiracy strategy. The related tactic? Flying a Russian flag—and keeping it well lit, even at night—was enough to ward off pirates, who were well aware of the Russian solution.

In November 2011 my co-author, Michael Hirsh, met with the OIC of the UKMTO office in Dubai, and the subject arose of what Royal Navy lieutenant commander Simon Goodes described as a "robust approach" to fighting piracy. He wasn't talking about the Russians. So he asked, "Robust approach is a euphemism for . . . what?" Goodes responded that there are those countries "that don't beat around the bush when they're dealing with pirates. The Indians have been very robust." He went on to say that as a result of such "robustness" in the treatment of captured pirates by the Indian navy, the pirates may have occasionally treated Indian seafarers held hostage differently than those from other nations.

Then there's the proposal from Illinois Republican senator Mark Kirk, who, in early 2011, advanced what he called the "Decatur Initiative," named after Navy captain Stephen Decatur, who recaptured the U.S. frigate *Philadelphia* from the Barbary pirates in 1804 and set it afire so it couldn't be used by the brigands. The senator said in a press release that was widely picked up, "I think we could learn an important lesson from that strategy."

He announced that he was studying the advancement of several antipiracy legislative options, including but not limited to establishment of a "pirate exclusion zone" that would allow immediate boarding or sinking of any vessel from Somalia not approved and certified for sea by allied forces; an expedited legal regime permitting trial and detention of pirates captured on the high seas; blockade of pirate-dominated ports such as Hobyo, Somalia; and broad powers and authority to on-scene commanders to attack or arrest pirates once outside Somalia's twelve-mile territorial limit, including the sinking of vessels if a local commander deems it warranted.

"This effort will recall the spirit of President Thomas Jefferson and the first major mission of the U.S. Navy," said Senator Kirk, a twenty-year intelligence officer in the Naval Reserve. "The open ocean should become increasingly dangerous for pirates to operate against the world's most powerful navy."

Let's take the senator's suggestions one by one, beginning with the notion of establishing what he calls a pirate exclusion zone. This would require the navies to board every single skiff in the Gulf of Aden and, worse, in the Indian Ocean. Pirates don't fly the flag of Somalia on their skiffs or mother ships. Most of the mother ships are hijacked dhows from other nations such as Yemen. What would we do with the fishermen from Yemen who enter the exclusion zone? How can we get legislation in the United States to fight pirates on the high seas, yet we can't even get the Senate to pass the Law of the Seas treaty? The UN would never support this, and there are not enough ships to enforce an exclusion zone. Of course, then there's the matter of what you do with all the seafarers—pirates, fishermen, traders, and others—after you've sunk their skiffs.

As for the expedited legal regime with authorization to try to detain captured pirates, that sounds great, but the senator didn't appear to be offering to fund the construction of courts and prisons so we had a place to put them once they had been captured and convicted. We thought the Seychelles was going to solve that problem, but their new pirate prison is already short on space.

As for the broad powers he suggests, we have all these powers today. In fact, the UN has authorized forces fighting piracy not only to go inside Somalia's territorial waters, but UN Resolution 1816 says we can go ashore to fight piracy, something being considered by a variety of nations.

And finally, as to Senator Kirk's plan that we blockade pirate-dominated ports, consider, if you will, what it really means to blockade a coastline. The last American blockade of a lengthy coastline was the Blockade of the South between 1861 and 1865. President Lincoln ordered the Union Navy to seal off the Atlantic and Gulf Coasts, including twelve major ports. To close 3,500 miles of coastline required five hundred ships. The Somali coastline is roughly 1,500 miles long—the distance from Maine to Miami. While the number of Somali port cities is minimal, pirates can set out to sea in motorized skiffs from tiny villages all along the coast. How many ships—even with UAVs and radar surveillance—would it take to effectively blockade Somalia? And while those ships are on blockade duty, what other naval tasks are going unmet?

I guess I'm displaying pique with politically motivated easy answers and grandstanding. If it were that simple, isn't it likely we would have already done it? (Feels good to be out of uniform and in a position to say things like that.)

Several times since I became actively involved in fighting piracy, stories have surfaced about plans afoot to wipe out the pirate strongholds on the Somali coast. On 23 March 2012 the Council of the European

Union agreed to authorize EU naval forces "to take disruption action against known pirate supplies" on the Somali shore. Not quite two months later, on 15 May, EU forces took action, carrying out their first attack by using what the Operation Atalanta spokesperson said was a single ship-based helicopter to strafe five suspected pirate skiffs as well as fuel supplies and an arms cache on the beach near the pirate stronghold of Harardhere. Boots-on-the-ground had not been authorized by the EU. Initial reports said that there were no casualties. EU officials refused to say from which ship the helicopter was launched. Naval vessels from France, Germany, Italy, Spain, the Netherlands, and Portugal were patrolling off Somalia when the attack took place. Officials of Operation Atalanta, the EU's antipiracy coalition in the heavily pirated waters, said that the mission approved by the EU in March was "totally supported by the Transitional Federal Government of Somalia."

At the time of the attack, Somali pirate groups were holding approximately three hundred hostages. Their practice has been to keep their prisoners aboard the hijacked ships anchored offshore. When I first heard of the EU plans to attack, my concern was that it would put the hostages at risk, perhaps as human shields near pirate facilities on the beach that would be logical targets. Considering the toughness of the individual pirates and their clan leaders, I find it difficult to believe that they won't retaliate in some way.

I'm certain that the destruction of a few pirate skiffs and a fuel depot will not end piracy in the Gulf of Aden. I have a gnawing feeling that rather than this EU action being the beginning of the end, it may result in an escalation of present and future ransom demands. These pirate organizations are only interested in one thing: money. The people running the operations are businessmen. These new offensive measures just might increase ransom demands under a perverted more risk / more reward doctrine.

The EU has promised to step up the intensity of its attacks. We can only wait and see what will happen, but as the guy who had a battalion of Marines and their assault helicopters on his ship, and a Marine colonel just begging for the opportunity to "wipe out those pirate villages in fifteen minutes," all I could do when I first read about EU plans to attack was shake my head. The EU's initial announcement that attacks were going to take place said, "The aircraft would not, however, fire on people." It appears as though on their first go-round they got lucky, but the more aggressive they become, the more likely it is that there will be civilian casualties. I'm not a pessimist, but I've been around long enough to know that when bullets start flying, eventually people get hurt—and not necessarily the people who deserve hurting.

There had been so many calls for wiping out pirate infrastructure on the beaches of Somalia that I sent the first story of the EU plan to attack the pirate enclaves to my friends Martin Murphy and Peter Pham and asked for their analysis. Dr. Murphy's first:

> I am all for effective intervention on land, as you know. Pirates do need to be deprived of sanctuary. The objective would be limited to destroying boats and other equipment, if my understanding is correct. Perhaps they will go after fuel dumps, which would be effective. If they intend grabbing pirates or pirate leaders or to destroy their private property (insofar as this can be reliably identified), I would be surprised given the general reluctance to prosecute and contestable jurisdiction. Will they attempt to free hostages?
>
> If pirate assets are destroyed, this could set the raiders back for months, quite possibly a whole raiding season. If the pirates believe this will become a regular occurrence, it could deter them. What, however, are the potential second order effects? They will look and learn and could take defensive measures, which would almost certainly mean up-arming themselves. They might—stress might—form closer links with al-Shabaab although [al-Shabaab] is in bad shape at the moment. If pirates are killed, and especially if locals not involved in piracy directly are hurt, this will complicate the position. Public opinion within Somalia could swing either way depending on the numbers involved. The action could also be seen to be endorsing Farole and cementing him and other political elites in power, which we may not want. Whatever happens, it will almost certainly be bad news for the hostages. Also it will set a precedent: EU NAVFOR might be capable of conducting a carefully calibrated operation; do we feel confident that the Russians, Chinese, Indonesians, and Malays would be capable of doing the same?

As you can see, I'm not alone in my concerns that when bullets start flying, unintended targets often fall. That's when strategists begin paraphrasing Robert Burns, who said, "The best-laid plans of mice and men often go awry." One obvious problem that immediately crossed my mind with the "attack them and their infrastructure on the beach" strategy: what happens when the pirates move their hostages from the hijacked ships and place them on the beaches amid the infrastructure?

Dr. Peter Pham responded after giving the keynote address at an Intra-European Intel Conference on Somalia hosted by the Dutch Military Intelligence and Security Service at The Hague. Peter said:

> One thing that was clear is that, for whatever reason, our European friends have all of a sudden decided that they want to play on land in Somalia. The Germans, as the report notes, want to go after pirate bases; the Norwegians want to "engage" al-Shabaab and splinter it; the French want to help the Kenyans; the British are convening a Somalia conference next month, etc. Whether they have the political will to actually use force and, if they do, whether they have the expeditionary capability are, however, entirely different issues.
>
> My fear, if my interactions over the years, including last month's meeting, are any indication, is that they just don't know enough and, even if they have the will and the resources, will end up fighting the Puntland president's enemies rather than combating piracy.

The sense that I get from all of this is that there's a movement afoot to do something, almost anything, to make it appear that the problem of Somali piracy is on the front burner and that we're just about ready to move beyond the talking stage. But the only thing I've heard that sounds as though it has potential are murmurings in Washington, mostly around the State Department, that we're beginning to target pirate clan leaders and remove them. Thus far, nothing specific has leaked, but I'm inclined to believe the action may be incidental to prosecuting pirates who have targeted Americans, not that there's anything wrong with that.

Consider the report that appeared in the *New York Times* about thirty-six-year-old FBI special agent Kevin P. Coughlin, the lead investigator in most of that agency's piracy cases. Working out of the FBI's New York offices, he has interviewed two-thirds of the pirates brought back to this country for trial. Thus far, the Justice Department has sought to indict pirates only when an American ship or American sailors have been targeted. Coughlin, who has served as both a Marine Corps lawyer with time in Iraq and as a congressional attorney, has become adept at getting young Somali pirates to reveal how and why they ended up out at sea, stalking merchant vessels.

But the item that caught my eye was that he, along with three other FBI investigators, went to Somalia to retrieve an alleged pirate bigwig, whose arrest had been requested by our government. Somali forces picked up Mohammad Saali Shibin, age fifty, wanted for his alleged involvement in the attack on the American yacht *Quest*, which resulted in the deaths of four U.S. citizens. Shibin, according to the *Times*,

> is the first Somali arrested on dry land to face piracy charges on American soil. And his capture offered investigators an opening to learn more about those higher up the pirate hierarchy, like the financiers who organize the voyages and the negotiators who secure ransom, court documents show. Mr. Coughlin said today's top bosses "will never be on the ship," unlike pirate captains of the Atlantic some three centuries ago.
>
> "You look at it from the perspective of organized crime," Mr. Coughlin said. "The individuals who go out to sea may change, but you imagine the leadership is well in place to continue these operations. If you don't get those guys, they'll just recruit a new group to go out to sea."

Is the Shibin arrest a portent of things to come, of a more aggressive strategy designed to move enforcement activities against those higher up the food chain? No one is saying publicly that this is the case.

One notion that crops up regularly is to create a situation so that the Somalis themselves can police the pirates. Of course, without an effective national government, the task would more likely fall to the governments of the independent states of Puntland or Somaliland. When we handed off pirates to Puntland coastguardsmen who came out to meet us on a boat that would barely qualify to be one of our live-fire targets, I began thinking about the possibility of helping them upgrade. Of course, the thought immediately occurred that there'd have to be some way to ensure that anything we gave them wasn't turned into the best pirate mother ship ever. But the notion stuck with me, and I brought it up when I met with Rear Adm. Thomas Atkin, the U.S. Coast Guard's assistant commandant for intelligence and criminal investigations. He has policy oversight for the Coast Guard intelligence enterprise, and for a period of six months had been at the National Security Staff, where he specialized in maritime safety, security, and stewardship. He knows something about Somali piracy.

Could our Coast Guard help the functioning government of Puntland equip and establish a meaningful counterpiracy coast guard operation? Atkin's answer is yes, if that was the U.S. government's position. "We've done that in a variety of places," he said. "We have an international training division that works under both State Department and Department of Defense to conduct training for foreign governments." He adds that the Coast Guard has an international schoolhouse in Yorktown, Virginia, that trains foreign nationals.

Thus far, there hasn't been a request for them to train Somalis. They've worked with officers from Yemen, Djibouti, Saudi Arabia, Iraq, and Kuwait. "So we have the capability—capability's always a challenge for the Coast Guard. And then, we have our foreign military sales." That program allows the Coast Guard to sell some of its older patrol boats, or small boats, to a foreign government and to provide training in their operation. Similar programs exist in Canada, Great Britain, and France.

The State Department's piracy maven, Donna Hopkins, pointed out another reality-based problem with respect to helping Somalia or Puntland or Somaliland build a coast guard to enforce antipiracy laws. "They don't have laws. How can they enforce what they don't have?" she asked me.

> Piracy is not a crime in Somaliland. That's a big part of the political roadmap for Somalia that we keep trying to push, and they keep getting right to the brink. Just in August [2011], the Somali parliament refused to act on the body of legislation that we thought was on the point of passage, because one of the ministers got up and railed

about the justification for piracy as being illegal fishing and toxic dumping and that whole stupid narrative. So I am not in favor of giving any of those crooks any more stuff, especially not legal stuff, until they get their act together. The Brits have already seen a good deal of their assistance turn into pirate equipment. And I'm just not in favor of doing that any more.

Somewhat sardonically, Donna said there's always hope. But she's a realist.

Money won't solve the problem. It's going to take sustained, complex, and deliberate diplomatic and developmental pressure and assistance for years. My feeling is that there's no incentive for the people in power in Somalia to do anything about this because they're personally profiting from it.

Unfortunately, we're allowing them to continue to profit from it. There are some people who say, "Well, the glass is really half full; it's not half empty. If we keep encouraging and cajoling them to do the things we want to do, they'll eventually come around." I think that's a very Western way of looking at things. These are not Westerners we're talking about.

Returning to my conversation with Rear Admiral Atkin, we moved to a topic that had percolated through a number of interviews. The idea was that the ultimate beneficiaries of anti-Somali-pirate activity of just about any type would be profit-making shipping companies. He saw where I was going and responded,

I can see the logic, and I would argue that it's really so the government [of Somalia] has the ability to form a government that's based on the rule of law. So, is a byproduct of it the economics of the U.S. shipping fleet? Maybe. But everything we do is to boost the economy of the United States. You know, we don't do much that doesn't necessarily have some repercussions back in our own economy. That's why we have a big Navy. It's to maintain the sea lanes of communication. The Coast Guard's International Port Security Program, where we go out and assess foreign ports for antiterrorism standards under IMO—that's all based to maintain the flow of commerce. Private industry benefits from that, and therefore they make money. It's all based on our GDP.

Considering Rear Admiral Atkin's background in intelligence, I switched topics and asked whether he thought the Somali pirates were going to adapt their tactics to defeat the best management practices, including the relatively recent trend toward the use of armed security teams and the conversion of ships so that there's a secure citadel on board where the crew can take refuge and control the ship till help arrives.

He was relatively close-mouthed about the armed guard question, saying he hadn't yet seen the pirates adapt to combat them. But, he said, "you know, they're armed. They have some heavy weapons. They have some responses. I'm trying to think what's open source."

Having hit the security wall, I asked about the citadels, and he was a bit more forthcoming. "I'd say that they're going to adapt to it, and they will try and develop ways to get onboard to prevent folks from getting into the citadel. Or potentially, to do things to drive people out of the citadels." Based on that answer, I'd say that somewhere there's an active research program going on to figure out how to defeat the pirates' next move. While the individual pirates out on the water may not be rocket scientists, they've got brains and money working for them on the beach. And the game being played is clearly chess, not checkers.

While speaking with a number of current and former intelligence officials, it became clear that keeping tabs on Somali piracy was definitely on their to-do list, whether or not it currently had a high priority in the Oval Office or at the highest levels of national security. I was fortunate to have someone discuss the process with me in general terms. What this individual said is worth keeping in mind, because when the day comes that the government takes action against the pirates, it'll help us understand how it might have reached the decision. This was the response when I asked about collecting and analyzing intelligence.

Collection is a process, and intelligence is a process that consists of planning, collection, analysis, and dissemination. All the time. So, if you're not collecting, you're not going to do intelligence. If you're not analyzing, you're not going to do intelligence. If you're not disseminating—which includes packaging, getting the operator's attention, "Hey, listen, this is important"—so the art of intelligence is all those things, all the time. And the difference between intelligence and information is, information is out there and it's data, but intelligence is information that I have collected, acquired, analyzed, packaged for the purpose of supporting my commander, my policymaker's mission—whether it's the president's mission, defend national security, help defend the economy. Do intelligence for that. Or whether it's "go take out a couple of pirates."

So that's intelligence, it's focused on that mission. It's not everything. He doesn't care about all the stuff I know. What he cares about is what he needs to get his mission done. And that's not just information; it's, you know, how do these terrorists operate? How do these pirates operate? What's their command and control? What kind of boat are they on, and how does it work? Everything you need to do the mission, but it's purposefully acquired, purposefully analyzed, and packaged up to support planning, deliberate planning, crisis planning, and tactical execution of the mission.

With respect to the collection of information and dissemination of intelligence about the Somali pirates, Martin Murphy suggests that more assets need to be diverted just to—as he puts it—"hoovering up the sigint" over Somalia (translation: collecting all the electronic signals intelligence that our satellites or other methods can gather). He said, "We can do it if we want to, but we're not doing it." The specialized companies that provide intelligence to private firms doing business in the region say that there's much to be learned from that sort of effort. For all their backward ways, Somalis use cellphones and satellite phones for everything, including bad things. The raw data are there to be hoovered up, as my British friend so quaintly puts it, but it's not being done.

Martin and I also discussed another rather odd problem that hasn't been solved: in the American military, who owns counterpiracy? AFRICOM, headquartered in Germany, has jurisdiction on land.

CENTCOM, headquartered in Tampa, has jurisdiction on the water. As Martin put it, "The very fact you've got an AFRICOM–CENTCOM seam running down the beach is an issue." The pirates live on land, but piracy isn't an AFRICOM priority. The pirates commit their crimes on the water, but CENTCOM can't go on land to fight piracy. Bottom line, it's a mess.

Perhaps the solution lies in what the executive of a shipping company suggested at a program I participated in that dealt with Somali piracy. He said that shipowners had bought about 14,000 miles of barbed wire to string around ship decks to keep pirates from climbing aboard. But he added that it might have made more sense to string a thousand miles of razor wire along the Somali coastline and just prevent the pirates from getting out to the ships. To be clear, there was a lot of laughter in the room.

CHAPTER 13

A Course to Steer

A GLOBAL FORCE FOR COMMERCE

At sea in the Gulf of Aden there was a pretty standard routine that my staff and I followed each night after the evening meal. We would get together to discuss the events of the past day and the plans for the next seventy-two hours. The major items we would focus on were the "vessels of interest" that might be passing through the IRTC. We paid particular attention to U.S.-flagged or -chartered vessels that might be carrying critical supplies for our comrades in the combat zones of Iraq and Afghanistan. I looked forward to being briefed on my upcoming helo rides and visits to one of the coalition warships for lunch. My good friends on the Turkish frigate *Giresun* and the Danish littoral combat ship *Absalon* always prepared something special for my visit. I am not sure how the Danes always had delicious herring and the Turks wonderful desserts on the menu, but they always made the trip special.

When I transferred my flag to *Boxer* in March 2009, I had the honor to work with the battle-hardened Marines of the 13th Marine Expeditionary Unit (MEU) under the command of Col. Dave "Stretch" Coffman, USMC (now brigadier general), and Capt. Pete "Squeaky" Brennan, commander of Amphibious Squadron Five, both real professionals who always had good advice for me in the counterpiracy campaign.

Our nightly briefings went like clockwork. As I went around the room for the "last salvo" of comments, Stretch would always say, "Admiral, you know I can fix your pirate problem in about fifteen minutes." I knew exactly what the CH-46 pilot—a Purple Heart awardee—had in mind. He had reminded me many times to just imagine what a squadron of AV-8B Harriers loaded with MK-82 five-hundred-pound bombs in company with a few AH-1 Super Cobra gunships launching Hellfire laser-guided missiles could do to a beach in Somalia covered with skiffs. And just in case the first attack group missed a few targets, I knew he would follow closely behind in his UH-1Y Super Huey command gunship with the side door open and his 7.62 Gatling gun blazing to finish off the weapons of piracy once and for all. My comment back to Stretch every night: "Let's hold that thought."

In fact, his suggestion was not very far off from plans already on the shelf. I know there is a mega–hard drive in the command center of NAVCENT with a terabyte of PowerPoint slides offering various options on how to attack the pirates ashore in Somalia. As with the first brief that my staff presented to Vice Adm. Kevin Cosgriff in 2007, and with the recommendations that each and every MEU commander has briefed over the last five years, the proposals rest at the "iron bottom sound" of some action officer's inbox. The proposal to strike targets ashore has gone up and down the chain of command, but not a single commander has signed the documents "approved" as of this date. There is no doubt that attacking the pirate villages would disrupt pirate activity for an extended period of time, but the major pushback from our leadership is, "what if we killed innocent civilians or destroyed the livelihood of fishing?" The first issue is a realistic concern, but anyone who mentions "fisherman" and "Somalis" in the same sentence is not well versed on the issue of piracy. The strong majority of the pirates come from the mountain regions and can hardly swim. Additionally, the experts I have interviewed for this book who have spent time in Somalia say it is very hard to find a fish market even in the port city of Bosaso. Somalis rarely catch fish, and the few that do are selling to foreigners living in Mogadishu. There is no livelihood to destroy.

With no real support to attack the pirates' infrastructure ashore, what other options do we have that will stop these menacing buccaneers from attacking the free flow of commerce in one of the busiest shipping lanes in the world? There are several, but they are limited without the total commitment of the world community. While there is very little debate that the piracy problem must be solved ashore in Somalia, that doesn't necessarily mean on the beaches.

Before we consider the pros and cons, let's discuss two very important elements that have been significant in reducing the scourge of piracy in the Horn of Africa region: the coalition navies and the self-protection measures taken by the merchant marine community. When Adm. Jonathan Greenert took over as the thirtieth chief of naval operations in September 2011, he published his "Sailing Directions" to the forces. Under his mission statement he outlined our core responsibilities. The last few sentences relate directly not only to the counterpiracy mission but also to the request for support from our coalition partners: "With global partners, protect the maritime freedom that is the basis for global prosperity. Foster and sustain cooperative relationships with an expanding set of allies and international partners to enhance global security."

Maritime security has always been one of the fundamental missions of our Navy. In the very early days of our nation, just after the Revolutionary War, our merchant fleet faced the growing threat of piracy from the Barbary States. Without a single warship to protect our merchantmen, Congress passed the Naval Act of 1794, which authorized the manning and construction of the six original frigates: the *Chesapeake, Constitution, President, United States, Congress,* and *Constellation.* As in today's environment where jobs for constituents are essential to each member of Congress, each frigate was built in a different shipyard in six different states, and like most defense programs, the project exceeded the original appropriated budget. Nothing has changed over the years.

Today our Navy faces the largest threat it has confronted in the last several years. It is not the threat of another nation-state but our federal deficit. After ten long years of war in Iraq and Afghanistan, many have called for change in our government spending strategy and for focus directed on domestic programs vice defense. Additionally, with a gross federal debt to exceed $16 trillion by the end of the year, many are looking to the Pentagon to balance the budget.

In 2006 then–chief of naval operations Adm. Michael G. Mullen published his thirty-year shipbuilding plan, which called for a fleet of 313 ships by 2020. The ink had hardly dried on Mullen's plan when the Navy published its 2012 shipbuilding plan, which called for only 300 ships in a strategy that centers on the massive Asia-Pacific region. With increased requirements for Aegis missile-defense platforms, defense of the Straits of Hormuz, and the growing Chinese fleet, it is hard to understand why our fleet should not be heading toward 400 ships. We had 281 ships in 2006; today there are 284 deployable platforms. With the growing budget pressures and the Navy's plan to decommission seven state-of-the-art Aegis cruisers and two amphibious assault ships, most people I talk with question if the Navy will have enough ships to meet the current maritime threats in both the Pacific and the Middle East.

The other Navy shipbuilding issue that needs debate in this country is the proposed littoral combat ship (LCS). The plan calls for a fifty-five-ship class of these combatants. The USS *Freedom* entered the fleet in 2008 and has yet to make a major deployment. I am not sure how we can call this a combat ship, because it has very little combat power. A report by the Pentagon's director of operational test and evaluation found that the ship would not "be survivable in a hostile combat environment." With a 30-mm pop gun, a limited electronic support system—some would call it a "fuzz buster"—and a proposed missile system that will only have a maximum range of four miles, the ships of this class have nowhere near the firepower of the missile-guided class of frigates that they are due to replace. Yes, I know they will also replace our aging mine sweeping force with the state-of-the-art mission modules, but this concept has never been proven and is years into cost overruns and delays. It is hard to believe that we have not war gamed the lessons learned from the attack on the Israeli SAAR V-class corvette INS *Hanit* off the coast of Lebanon in 2006 by a C-802 antiship missile.

Compared to what the Danish navy built in its *Absalon*-class flexible support ships, we have fallen well short of our objective to offer the combatant commander the firepower to deal with the threats of the future. I think over the next few years our leadership will be confronted by that famous line from the *I Love Lucy* show: "Lucy, you got some 'splainin' to do."

But how does this digression link to the matter of Somali piracy? Easy. With the need to balance the fleet against the threats, the Navy will be looking for missions to cut. I am sure the question is often asked in the Navy's strategy cells, "Do we really need a ship full time in the Gulf of Aden to fight pirates when we have very few American-flagged merchant ships to protect?" The answer without question is yes! There is not a single nation on the globe that can provide the command and control and, above all else, the leadership to combat piracy. With only seventy-nine commissioned ships in the Royal Navy, Britannia no longer rules the waves. With major budget issues facing the navies of the European Union, and with the size of the EU NAVFOR ATALANTA decreasing since its commissioning in 2008, the U.S. Navy must stay in the forefront of counterpiracy operations.

Some will question if this is in fact a national security matter for the United States. Others have stated that since the arrival of armed security teams on most of the merchant ships transiting the Gulf of Aden the number of hijackings is down and the navies can reduce their presence in the region. With more than 90 percent of the goods that fill the shelves of your local Wal-Mart and 50 percent of the globe's petroleum passing through the high-risk area, including the Gulf of Aden and far out into the Indian Ocean, how could it not be a national security issue?

It is unfortunate that we need to change the history books and disprove Christopher Columbus' theory of 1492, but the world is in fact flat. A financial crisis in Asia or Europe impacts the markets on Wall Street and, most of all, on Main Street. During the course of my research I contacted my good friend and one of the best naval officers I have ever worked with throughout my career, Danish navy captain Dan Termansen, the commanding officer of *Absalon* during my tenure as commander of CTF 151. I asked him, as one of our key coalition partners, if he could relate the importance of piracy to national security.

> Yes, [piracy] is a national security issue for Denmark. Ten percent of all ocean-going trade is controlled by Danish ship owners. It is a substantial source of foreign income for Denmark because of our large merchant fleet. Therefore, Denmark has a huge interest in the free flow of goods at sea, and to be able to maintain order. In addition, several Danish citizens have been held hostage by pirates. Half of the world's oil transits the area. Therefore, we should focus on the impact of piracy on the overall stability in the area. Piracy leads to more instability due to the implications on local trade and fisheries. Instability leads to unrest and fuels illegal trade which leads to erosion of regional power structures, and eventually to terrorism. We have a chance to engage the problems when they still are manageable. If we neglect the signs of regional instability, we might later have to engage in a military effort when things escalate out of control and impact the free flow of oil from the Persian Gulf, and that's at least as vital as the flow of goods between Europe and Asia.

LET'S FORM A POSSE

As you may well know from reading novels, in the days of the Wild West, most sheriffs had limited support from federal agents to track down the big-time bank robbers. To overwhelm the bandits, the sheriff usually mustered a few rough and ready cowboys to form a posse. As early as December 2008, Vice Admiral Gortney, as commander of NAVCENT, spoke to the news media and pressed the maritime community to protect its own ships. He said, "Our presence in the region is helping deter and disrupt criminal attacks off the Somali coast, but the situation with the *Sirius Star* clearly indicates the pirates' ability to adapt their tactics and methods of attack. Piracy is an international crime that threatens global commerce. Shipping companies have to understand that naval forces cannot be everywhere. Self-protection measures are the best way to protect their vessels, their crews, and their cargo."

Gortney, like officials in many of the nations supporting the coalition navies, was calling on the merchant community to provide its own security teams, or, as I prefer to think of them, modern-day posses. In the years since I was out there, this has been one of the critical developments in the best practices against Somali piracy. Private security firms have risen into the limelight over the past decade with the growth of conflict in the Middle East and the increasing use of these contractors by the U.S. military. Prominent among these firms are Academi (formerly known as Blackwater USA and later as Xe Services LLC), DynCorp International, and Triple Canopy, Inc. Since the State Department required extra security measures to counter possible terrorist attacks, the shipping companies turned to these organizations that employed well-trained former members of Special Forces units to provide the security.

About 80 percent of the ships now transiting the Gulf of Aden have embarked security teams, and not one of those ships has been hijacked. However, this initiative has confronted some major challenges over the past few years. Flying a security team to Baghdad or Kabul is relatively easy in comparison to getting an armed security detachment and its weapons to a ship in the Gulf of Aden. Consider a RO/RO car carrier leaving the port of Hamburg with a load of BMWs for a voyage to the Saudi port of Damman. When do you embark the security team? Doing so prior to leaving Hamburg would be quite expensive since you only need the team for about three days of the transit. Until very recently, armed security teams were not permitted to transit the Suez Canal. Saudi officials refuse to allow security teams with weapons to disembark in Saudi ports. This required ships headed to Saudi ports to alter their journey and head to another port of call for disembarkation of these teams. In 2006 the former Blackwater firm purchased the surplus NOAA research vessel *McArthur* from the U.S. government. The vessel was reconfigured with a helo landing platform and the capability to launch rigid raiding watercraft. The closest the vessel ever got to Pirate Alley was the Jordanian port of Aqaba.

There are numerous legal issues that have yet to be finalized with security teams aboard commercial vessels. Who has weapons-release authority? Is it the security team leader or master of the vessel? What are you obliged to do with a pirate you've just wounded? Do you have to take him aboard and see to his injuries, or can you just leave him to die on the high seas? There are dozens of private security teams already embarked on ships transiting the heavily pirated areas, and those questions have yet to be resolved.

During a piracy conference at the U.S. Naval Academy in February 2012 with members of the NATO advisory group, I asked Madeleine Moon, a member of the British House of Commons, her views on the newest developments of arming merchants. She replied,

> We all know the problem. In the next twenty years there will be a doubling of maritime trade while naval power reduces by 30 percent. It will take a long time to tackle poverty and instability in Somalia or any other country where poverty drives people to see piracy as a means of survival. In a time of financial austerity, we are looking to replace military forces with armed guards hired from security companies. It is time for the military within NATO to stand up and stop this. Where are the rules of engagement? What are the legal implications for governments who license these firms? Where do the responsibilities of command and control rest? What comes next if and when we need forces on land? Do we send for the private security firms? We are sleep walking into dangerous territory [with] the privatization of military force.

"Sleep walking into dangerous territory" is exactly what happened to the Italian military security team on the *Enrica Lexie* on 15 February 2012. Thinking the ship was under attack by pirates while steaming off the coast of India, the security team opened fire on an approaching vessel. To the surprise of the security team and many others, they learned that they had opened fire not on pirates but on unarmed Indian fishermen, and they had killed two of them. During the investigation of the shooting it was discovered that the security team actually fired on the fishermen without the consent of the master. While the security team remains in the custody of the Indian authorities, there is debate between the Indian and Italian governments over who has jurisdiction in the case. This landmark case could have major implications on the future of security teams. At the very least, it should remind us that there are no easy answers to complicated questions—even if the easy answers appear to be working.

While the use of private security teams and enhanced best management practices has been successful, it's my belief that private security teams should be a force multiplier and not a replacement for the navies patrolling the region. Advocates of best management practices recommend construction of citadels wherein crews can take refuge until help arrives. But that help will not come in the form of security teams riding shotgun on other merchantmen. The only source of help will be from naval warships that have the ability to assault the hijacked ship, capture or kill the armed pirates, and secure the freedom of the crew hiding in the citadel.

It doesn't come as a surprise to me that there are people who have studied the piracy situation and remain unconvinced that there's a major role to be played by the warships of coalition navies. Their focus is on private security teams as a significantly less expensive option. One such person is Doug Brooks, president of the Washington think tank International Stability Operations Association. Here's his take on the matter:

> We see the corner turning on piracy in the Gulf but not due to any sort of thoughtful, coordinated design from the international community. International navies have proven to be an expensive and insufficient response and thus shipping firms and shipowners have found that pri-

vate sector solutions, especially security, have been vastly more successful. Such measures are an extraordinarily inexpensive answer to piracy, especially considering the significant costs on cargo, ships, and crews that are captured by the pirates, not to mention subsequent legal costs which are still growing. As a result, the pool of vulnerable targets is shrinking and becoming less lucrative, and the large scale piracy that we have seen is likely on the wane. The other part of the answer is land based and less clear, but appears to be moving in the right direction. Puntland has received support from the Gulf countries to address the problem, and the African Union, supported by internationally contracted logistics and training firms, has enjoyed some surprising success with their peacekeeping operations even in chaotic Mogadishu in the south, where the larger international community utterly failed twenty years ago. As most analysts point out, the piracy problem will ultimately require land-based solutions. But while the emerging solutions are uncoordinated, and both public and private, investing in long-term pirate stocks is probably not a lucrative endeavor anymore.

Doug and I have debated the issue and have not reached a consensus. While there's no doubt that armed security guards should be part of the equation, and that they're an inexpensive solution when compared to keeping an Aegis cruiser on station, I believe that without naval vessels in the troubled waters, the pirates will become more aggressive and determined to bring home a prize. Yes, they know the result of confronting SEAL Team Six, but they're not afraid to launch an RPG round into the face of privately contracted armed security personnel.

Imagine for a moment what would happen if all the navies pulled out of the Gulf of Aden. Does anyone really think that all the best management practices, including armed guards, would be enough to contain the problem? I've said it often in this book: one thing we know for certain is that the pirates adapt. Sooner or later, they'll defeat the citadels. And as I've mentioned earlier, a crew of merchant mariners locked inside their citadel is only safe if a warship comes to the rescue. Otherwise, they'll have to emerge sooner or later, and the pirates will be waiting.

The notion of reducing to insignificance the number of warships on scene to fight piracy because we appear to be winning the battle makes as much sense as downsizing a metropolitan police force because the crime rate has dropped. Every shipping company owner yearns to know that his ships can ply the oceans of the world without fear of attack. That may be an unreachable goal, but without a strong navy, that goal will never be approached.

Royal Navy commodore Keith Winstanley, who had been his nation's most senior naval officer in the Middle East and who served as deputy commander of coalition maritime operations for the U.S. Central Command, is—not surprisingly—someone with whom I happen to agree when the subject is the need for navies to play a major role in counterpiracy operations. In 2007 he outlined his position this way:

> I measure success by the continued growth of the Coalition both at the HQ in Bahrain and at sea—already a Coalition of 20 nations, from inside and outside the region: from east and west and I am confident that there are more to come. Increasingly the coalition is being joined by important and powerful regional players—important and powerful NOT perhaps in terms of numbers but definitely important and powerful in terms of vital local knowledge, experience and perspective, both military and cultural.
>
> Despite this success I find myself repeatedly asking nations the question, "If not here, then where? And if not now, then when?" So why here and why now? Against a backdrop of the effects of globalization, the expansion of the global system, the increasing inter-connection and inter-dependency of the world's established and growing economies, against that backdrop, collectively, we have seen total seaborne trade more than quadruple in our lifetimes. One third of the world's bulk cargo and half of the world's containerized cargo must pass through the Indian Ocean. By 2010 only 3 years from now, twenty percent of the U.K.'s liquid natural gas supply will go to the U.K. in ships that must pass through the northern waters of this Region, and sub-region, and I am sure there are similar telling statistics from all the nations here today.

There's one other benefit to coalition operations that actually has little to do with piracy but a lot to do with the future of our world. It was pointed out by Steve Caldwell, the Government Accounting Office expert on maritime security. He described it as a longer-term benefit. "It's the importance of military-to-military contacts and relationships, and in the long run, you know, if there's a dispute between countries and things are escalating, you get the right two people who were operating with each other in a certain environment, who have credibility with each other, that's just the kind of people both governments are looking for to kind of come together and maybe deescalate things or work things out."

RANSOMS—IT'S ALL ABOUT THE MONEY

After almost six frustrating years trying to figure out the solution to end piracy in the Gulf of Aden, there have been many achievements, but the end is nowhere in sight. Billions of dollars have been spent building prisons in the region, including a maximum security facility in the Somaliland capital of Hargeisa funded by the UN, deploying numerous naval task forces, and implementing countless best practices, but these pesky buccaneers still have the upper hand. How can this be so hard? No matter what the solution, all recommendations point to fixing piracy ashore in Somalia.

While the EU nations have approved attacking pirate infrastructure on the beaches, there has yet to be a whisper about putting forces ashore to go after the ringleaders. If we step back and take an analytical approach to the problem, it becomes clear that this is all about ransom payments. We have seen thus far that the pirates really don't care about the cargo of the captured vessels, that there is no apparent link to terrorism, and that in most cases they treat their hostages fairly well (even though thirty-two piracy victims died in 2011, a threefold increase from the previous year). So what does all this mean? Simple. We need to stop the flow of the money to the pirates. Wait a minute—you're thinking that I told you several chapters ago that the merchant community will always pay the ransoms, that paying ransom is the only way it can ensure finding seamen who will sign onto its ships for voyages through dangerous waters. And that's true.

But we know that all the payments are made in U.S. hundred dollar bills. That's a lot of Ben Franklins moving through the Somali economy.

Have you ever gone to a bank with your withdrawal slip, asked the teller for $5 million in crisp hundred dollar bills? I am sure that you would quickly get the attention of not only the bank manager but the U.S. Department of the Treasury and maybe a few law enforcement officials. But funny as it seems, that is exactly what is happening. When the final agreement is reached by the negotiator on the ransom amount, the pirates demand U.S. dollars in one-hundred-dollar denominations. Currently, there is no stopping an individual, a corporate officer, or an insurance firm from withdrawing the money as long as they fill out a form that states that the funds will not be going to a terrorist organization. I hope when you read that, the light came on, as it did for me when a former Special Forces officer who has actually negotiated the release of several hijacked ships explained it to me. Why does the Treasury Department allow this to happen? Our own federal government says we—I guess that means the government—will never pay ransoms, but we allow U.S. dollars to freely flow in the piracy game. So let's try to take this knowledge and make a sound recommendation for putting the Somali pirates out of business.

On 15 March 2011 Kurt Amend, principal deputy assistant secretary of state, Bureau of Political-Military Affairs, testified before the House Committee on Transportation and Infrastructure's Subcommittee on Coast Guard and Maritime Transportation and said:

> One of our most important goals is the disruption of piracy-related financial flows. On March 1st, the Departments of State, Transportation, and Homeland Security convened an Ad Hoc meeting of the Contact Group to develop a strategy and process to undertake coordinated international efforts in intelligence, financial, and law enforcement communities to identify, track, and remove from operation pirate leaders, organizers, and financiers. We will explore options to disrupt these facilitators in coordination with our partners in the Contact Group. We are pleased that the Government of Italy and Government of the Republic of Korea agreed to help orchestrate this effort under the umbrella of the Contact Group, and the United States will lend our strong support and assistance to this important work.

Additionally, when Deputy Assistant Secretary of Defense for Counter Narcotics & Global Threats William F. Wechsler testified before the Subcommittee on Terrorism, Nonproliferation, and Trade, Committee on Foreign Affairs, U.S. House of Representatives, in June 2011, he said, "We need to find a way to make piracy a less profitable choice." It is clearly one of the key goals of both the Defense and State Departments to disrupt "piracy-related financial flow," but it is a certainty that their neighbors in the Treasury Department have not taken all the necessary measures to stop the flow of money to the pirates.

Here's a step-by-step plan: The first thing that must be done is to empty the Somali pirate camps. The last time these pirate camps were empty was in January 2008, and I remember the time very well. During my first tour in NAVCENT as Task Force 51 commander, I called Vice Admiral Cosgriff and told him, "Sir, I am proud to report that the last ransom has been paid and the last vessel is under way and the pirate camps are empty." The joy did not last very long. But it can be done. Whether by force or payment, we need to clear out the camps and announce at the same time that the U.S. Treasury will no longer allow U.S. dollars to be paid to pirates.

It could be done by Executive Order, or by legislation in Congress, mandating that any insurance company or financial institution that paid a ransom with U.S. dollars would be barred from doing business in the United States or with any American company. We have a lot of experience with sanctions against countries. We could label this measure "The U.S. Department of the Treasury Office of Foreign Assets Control—Sanctions against Somali Piracy." What would the pirates do? What could they do? Demand Euros? Good luck with that. Maybe they could go into semiretirement until circa 2025 when China overtakes the United States as the world's leading economy and demand yuan.

If this is so simple, why hasn't this been recommended before? One reason is that restrictions on ransom payments are not in the forefront of counterpiracy operations. Why? Because while piracy is making millions for the pirates, it's actually making a lot more for several legitimate international businesses. There are several very large financial institutions making billions of dollars on piracy. Their names are familiar to anyone with even a passing knowledge of the world of maritime insurance. Over the last few years, while pirates collected on average $160 million in ransom payments, those insurance companies collected five times that amount annually in increased premiums and charges for services.

When I asked a senior State Department official to evaluate my proposal for the U.S. government to forbid the payment of ransoms in U.S. currency, the response confirmed that the primary obstacle to such a ban is the attitude of the maritime industry itself. I was told,

> We have been discussing your idea for a couple of years—it amounts to criminalizing ransom, which is hugely controversial and unlikely to squeak through any administration due to pressure from industry—not to mention impossible to do, given the stashes of U.S. dollars in foreign banks. We have also discussed means of marking currency used in ransom payments to track how they're spent, which is fiendishly difficult if not downright impossible. If you recall, there is already an Executive Order on the book sanctioning any U.S. entity that makes a payment that would end up in either of two [named] pirates' hands, and Treasury has so far steadfastly refused to find that any ransom payment projected would subject the payer to sanctions. This means that the EO is essentially useless, although it has made industry exceedingly nervous about any pirate ransom contemplated, which is a good thing.

For many years, governments have pressed the merchant lines to provide for their own protection, and now they have followed suit with armed security teams. Suddenly—overnight—hundreds of maritime security firms have opened their doors for business, some of them well qualified, many not. With the average cost of $50,000 per vessel per transit of the high-risk area, this has become a very profitable business.

You will read in the press, as you've read in this book, that if we stop the payments of ransom, merchant mariners will not sign onto the vessels transiting the region. There is some truth to this, but during my tour in NAVCENT in 2007 the average duration in captivity was less than ninety days. Today the average is almost six months, and some crews have stayed for over a year while the pirates held out for larger payments and the shipping companies dragged their heels. It's no secret that when the hostages are North Americans or Europeans, ransoms get paid much faster than if they're Filipinos or Indonesians. If concern for the mariners was the primary concern of the shippers, why aren't all the ransoms paid in short order? As of this writing, the M/V *Iceberg 1* holds the record. Hijacked on 29 March 2010, she wasn't released until 25 October 2011, when an undisclosed ransom was paid. The original demand had been for $8 million, which the owners said they couldn't pay. Twenty-three crew members were held captive for nineteen months. One committed suicide seven months into the ordeal. For the record, the crew of this Panama-flagged, Dubai-owned RO/RO consisted of nationals from Yemen, India, Ghana, Sudan, Pakistan, and the Philippines.

In just about every lecture that I have given on the issues of piracy in the Gulf of Aden, I am asked, "How can we stop Somali piracy?" My answer at those events and in this book is the same: piracy begins in Somalia, and it can only be ended there. Our coalition forces have done a remarkable job containing piracy at sea with the limited resources that have been made available. Even the thousand-ship navy would not bring a complete end to the problem.

The large majority of the merchant vessels transiting the region have implemented the best management practices that have proven to be very effective in preventing hijacking. Some of these measures are quite expensive, and some shipping companies cannot afford the more expensive protection program schemes. While it's common knowledge that not a single vessel with an embarked security team has been hijacked, an estimated 30 percent of the vessels transiting the region are not carrying armed guards, in most cases because the average $50,000 cost per transit is more than their owners believe they can afford.

What remains somewhat surprising is that no matter how much money the United Nations and national governments have spent on establishing a functioning judicial and prison system in the region and prosecuting pirates, this very Western-style effort has done little to stop cash-starved Somalis from becoming pirates. In 2011 more than twenty countries arrested, detained, and tried suspected pirates at a cost of more than $16 million. Yet in the interview I conducted with Duke University PhD candidate Jatin Dua, who spent months in Somalia researching the matter, he stated that several pirate leaders incarcerated in Somali prisons were still running pirate activities via multiple cell phones from their jail cells.

Even those pirates apprehended by international naval forces and taken back to the country of the arresting navy for prosecution are either turned loose without going to trial or spend minimal time in jail and are released and allowed to remain in that country. For the pirate, this is an absolute success story: spending time in a European jail, eating three meals a day, being given medical care, and then being freed without having to return to Somalia. Why not be a pirate if you can end up driving a cab in Copenhagen instead of struggling to make a living in the Horn of Africa?

There is no shortage of recommendations put forth to end the piracy problem. They range from making them walk the plank—or the Russian equivalent that makes do without the plank—to bombing every village with boats along the 1,500-mile-long Somali coastline. History buffs are quick to tell me that these measures have worked in the past, but this is the twenty-first century, and rules of engagement have vastly changed from the days of the Barbary pirates or the buccaneers of the Caribbean.

One thing that has not changed in the piracy game is the reason pirate leaders continue to send skiffs full of youthful marauders to sea: that's where there's money to be made, lots of money. And while we've learned that a significant portion of the ransoms, perhaps 40 percent, are immediately distributed to locals as soon as the booty hits the beach, the other 60 percent rapidly begins a journey to pay back investors outside Somalia. It's my belief that if the international community is committed to bringing Somali piracy to an end, it must make the effort to stop the movement of ill-gotten money.

In March 2012 the State Department's leading spokesman on piracy, Assistant Secretary Andrew Shapiro, said, "The State Department last year conducted a review of its anti-piracy strategy and has decided to focus on pirate networks and the flow of money, in an effort to disrupt 'the pirate business process.'" He went on to say, "Often the best way to attack organized crime is to follow the money."

That may be true, but it's a strategy that keeps us behind the pirates when we really need to be out in front of them. Why do we want to follow the money after it's gotten into the hands of the criminals when we could and should prevent them from ever getting the cash? Yes, the State Department has made it clear that, for an assortment of reasons, it doesn't want to criminalize the payment of ransom. But the tools to do so are contained in Executive Order 13,536 issued by President Obama on 12 April 2010, and I believe if we've been given a tool, we should use it. The order is complicated and dense, but the president's language about the profits from piracy is clear as a bell: "(b) I hereby determine that, among other threats to the peace, security, or stability of Somalia, acts of piracy or armed robbery at sea off the coast of Somalia threaten the peace, security, or stability of Somalia." And it says that two Cabinet secretaries are to work together to deal with the problem, which I take to mean they can jointly act to prevent the payment of ransom:

> Sec. 5. The Secretary of the Treasury, in consultation with the Secretary of State, is hereby authorized to take such actions, including the promulgation of rules and regulations, and to employ all powers granted to the President by [the International Emergency Economic Powers Act] IEEPA and the [United Nations Participation Act] UNPA, as may be necessary to carry out the purposes of this order. The Secretary of the Treasury may redelegate any of these functions to other officers and agencies of the United States Government consistent with applicable law. All agencies of the United States Government are hereby directed to take all appropriate measures within their authority to carry out the provisions of this order. (Exec. Order No. 13,536, 75 Fed. Reg. 19871, 12 April 2010)

I believe that there are several practical problems with the Executive Order that may preclude its enforcement. The annex to the EO lists eleven individuals and the al Qaeda–related terrorist group al-Shabaab that may not receive U.S. funds. When ransoms are paid, they are air-dropped to the hijacked ship. Pirate leaders named in the order are not the ones counting the funds when they fall from the sky. So the payments are not really transferred, paid, or exported to the listed persons of interest in the Executive Order. The deficiency is that the order does not explicitly ban the payment of ransoms for piracy, but this can be fixed.

The USA PATRIOT Act of 2001 strictly prohibits the transfer of U.S. funds to terrorists. Why can't it be amended to include piracy? And why can't Treasury be given the wherewithal to follow ransom payments, whether made from the United States or overseas? That way we can stop dollars from leaving this country headed toward the pirates, and we can keep track of dollars coming out of overseas vaults in order to determine precisely who is profiting from this business and eventually put them out of business.

The facts are pretty clear on the global impact on piracy. The One Earth Future Foundation's "Oceans Beyond Piracy Report" of 2011 states that piracy cost almost $7 billion in 2011. The shipping industry bears 80 percent of the costs. This results in increased fuel costs at your local gas station and increased cost of the everyday goods that you shop for at every big box store that imports goods from overseas. The shipping industry is not covering these real costs of piracy. Average Joes are paying them out of their pockets.

The size of the high-risk area of piracy has tripled since I had command of CTF 151. In 2008–9 the major area of pirate activity was the Gulf of Aden. As the coalition task forces became successful, the pirates adapted and hijacked mother ships and extended their reach well out in the Indian Ocean. Now, thousands of merchant ships alter their routes and hug the Indian coastline in an attempt to avoid these newly pirated waters and to remain under the watchful eyes of the Indian navy. This rerouting comes at a cost—and, again, average consumers pay it. Ransom payments have increased from hundreds of thousands of dollars in 2007 to an average approaching $5 million in 2011.

As long as U.S. dollars flow freely to pay ransom, piracy will not end. There is too much ocean for our navies to protect, and even the most rigorous justice system will not stop more buccaneers from heading to sea. There will be tremendous pressure from industry, but the United States government must take all necessary measures to pass legislation and work with the United Nations to stop U.S. dollars from padding the pockets of the Somali pirates. With no money coming in, the pirate camps of Eyl and Harardhere will quickly fade into the past, and the resources saved fighting piracy can be used to aid the people of Somalia in their efforts to become a functional nation-state.

ACKNOWLEDGMENTS

When I graduated from VMI in the spring of 1978, I didn't know that I was going to have the perfect job for thirty-one years. The Navy and all the great adventures of going to sea were made for me. After basic officer training in the great New England seaport of Newport, Rhode Island, I reported to my first command, USS *El Paso* (LKA 117) in Chester, Pennsylvania. There were only five built in the *Charleston* class LKA, and they were often referred to as the "fifth wagon wheel" of the amphibious ready group. They carried tons and tons of marine equipment, but to offload the ship took hours and hours. I hope you caught that I reported to *El Paso* in Chester, Pennsylvania. Why there, you ask? Overhaul. An overhaul is when a ship goes in for major repairs. The overhaul period was scheduled for six months, but I reported in the eighth month of an eventual thirteen-month overhaul conducted at Sun Shipbuilding and Dry Dock Company. The only reason I need to mention Sun shipyard is that it was famous for converting the Hughes *Glomar Explorer* to USNS *Glomar Explorer*. If you are a real naval history buff, you will remember Project Azorian. If not, here's the story: the project was a top-secret mission funded by the CIA and Howard Hughes to recover the sunken Soviet Golf II ballistic-missile submarine K-129 from the depths in the middle of the Pacific Ocean. Other than that, it was a lousy place to report to your first command.

The *El Paso* was a very important stepping-stone for my naval career. I had three completely different but outstanding commanding officers on that ship who taught me early in my career the keys to leadership and taking responsibility. The first was an F-4 Phantom pilot by trade turned nuclear-trained officer, Capt. Ed Clexton, who would later retire as a vice admiral. Captain Clexton was on *El Paso* for one reason: to learn the trades of commanding a ship and then move on to command an aircraft carrier. For an aviator, ships like *El Paso* were the "training wheels" for those heading off to bigger and better ships such as the mighty aircraft carrier. I had two major encounters with Captain Clexton. I had only been on *El Paso* for a very short time and I was about to receive my first operational fitness report in the Navy. In those days, you made it a point to avoid the commanding officer at all cost; there was not a lot of TLC from COs in the late 70s as there is today.

So I approached his stateroom scared to death and knocked on the door. After a few—very few—words of wisdom, he handed me my fitness report. It could have labeled me the worst officer since Ensign Roberts, but I knew the only thing I could say was, "thank you, sir," and be on my merry way. Actually, it was not bad for a very green naval officer. I remember to this day him telling me that I had great potential, and that the Cs and Bs should turn to As with a little hard work. I am not sure why I said it, but I told him that I was very happy, and if I would have had these grades at VMI, my parents would have been much more proud of me. He looked at me, bewildered that an ensign would say anything at all, and just laughed.

The other lesson he taught me was to always be prepared for your watch. After we left the shipyard, we were conducting underway replenishment drills. It was my turn to take the conn and bring her alongside the oiler. As I was standing there giving the helm orders, Captain Clexton asked me to explain the radian rule. The radian rule is a simple math formula to tell you the separation distance between your ship and the oiler. I had no idea. Captain Clexton said, "Terry, go back and learn the radian rule and then you can conn the ship alongside." With my head hanging low I went back to my stateroom and went over my notes on ship handling. Even to this day I remember the formula: $R \times N$ over 60!

My next skipper aboard *El Paso* was a crusty A-6 Intruder pilot, a chain-smoking, fun-loving captain named Rick France. During his tour we sailed almost half the world. After departing Norfolk, Virginia, in August 1980 we set sail for a major fleet amphibious exercise in the fjords of Norway. During the Cold War, the Marines had a mission to defend Norway from Soviet aggression into Northern Europe, and we were off to rehearse that mission. The deployment would eventually take us to Diego Garcia and Mombasa, Kenya, two of the places that the U.S. Navy did not frequent in the early 80s. During this deployment, Captain France would award me my surface warfare pin and trust me to be his officer of the deck in some very demanding situations. For a guy who struggled through school most of his life, under Captain France I learned two of the key elements of leadership: responsibility and trust. He was a true master and commander.

My last commanding officer on *El Paso* was a real merchant mariner and my first surface warfare commanding officer, bird-watching Capt. Andy Conklin. After a few months aboard he selected me as his navigator. Aside from being a commanding officer, this was one of the most rewarding assignments I've had in the Navy. He sat me down in his stateroom and said, "Terry, I am going to take you off the watch bill, but I want to see a complete daily navigation picture when the ship is under way. To include morning and evening stars, sun lines during the days and local apparent noon." All this really meant was that I would be on the bridge for long hours with a sextant in my hand. Under the leadership of my leading chief quartermaster, Joel "Haze" Gray, we had a blast running down to the captain's cabin each day showing off our skills as real mariners. I can never thank him enough for demanding the best out of me and teaching me the real art of seamanship and navigation.

My first assignment when I boarded *El Paso* was the signals division officer. It's a naval art that you can only read about in the history books—signal flags and flashing lights. With the assistance of my leading petty officer, SM1 John McVey, a salty veteran with experience in Vietnam, I would learn the real tricks of the trade for leading sailors. He made my transition from college kid to a naval officer very easy.

During that tour I also learned the values of friendship. Two guys, CWO Bill Chadwick and Capt. Tom Kennedy, took me under their wings and have always provided a sounding board for me throughout my career. These are two big guys with big hearts and an abundance of leadership skills. Chadwick was an all high school football player from Philadelphia who joined the Navy to help support his mother. He served in the toughest times of our Navy, on the toughest platforms, and in the toughest assignments. Just listening to him talk about his tours on battleships, heavy cruisers, and patrol boats in Vietnam was invaluable in the development of my career. With my lifelong friend Tom Kennedy I learned the true value of taking care of your people and always preparing yourself each and every day that you wear the uniform. I would never have stayed in the Navy without the guidance and support of these great officers and the real "fun" of going to sea that I experienced serving on USS *El Paso*.

I would like to thank thirty-one years of sailors and Marines who served alongside me, from the hurricane waters of the North Atlantic to the tense transits of the Straits of Hormuz. Without the likes of such battle-hardened mariners as John McKay, Craig Diffie, Richie Enrique, Rich Landolt, Gil Kirkland, Rich Natonski, Luke Parent, Dana Weiner, and many others, I never would have made it through the first midwatch. All of you have been inspirational shipmates.

To the staff of CTF 151, without your insights and tactical knowledge, the task force would not have been nearly as successful as it was. I never thought that a lawyer and a public affairs officer would be the most important advisors on my staff. But Pete Koebler and John Fage proved to be two of the very best and real pros in their professions. To the commanding officers of CTF 151, Dan Termansen, Cenk Dalkanat, Tim Henry, Kevin Cash, Mark Genung, Todd Rostock, Mark Cordon, Steve Murphy, Pete Brennan, Dave Coffman, Greg Cox, and Greg Ponzi you came ready to fight as a team and demonstrated how coalition operations can be successful.

I must acknowledge several lifelong friends who took care of my family during those long deployments, and who always answered my calls for assistance and provided cheerful words of wisdom: Vice Adm. Dan Holloway, Steve Johnson, Michael Hoffmann, John Marshall, Wads Bugg, Harry Siegfried, Jack Snyder, and Chuck Zingler. You guys are a very special group of friends.

Writing a book for the first time reminds me of the day I reported to *El Paso*. I had a clear understanding of the difference between the bow and the stern, and I knew it was important to render a proper salute to the National Ensign, but after that it was a totally new adventure. Writing *Pirate Alley* has been a remarkable journey, but without the support and expertise of so many extraordinary individuals this book would never have been possible.

While writing *Pirate Alley*, I had the pleasure of working with several authentic experts on piracy and Somalia: Peter Pham, Martin Murphy, Jatin Dua, and Claude Berube. You have been so helpful on my journey in completing this book, and I have really enjoyed your insights and discussions with you on the key issues of piracy.

As commander of the task force, one of my biggest challenges was figuring out how to get the press embarked back and forth from Djibouti. They came from all over the globe—the *New York Times*, *Wall Street Journal*, *Economist*, and ABC News, just to name a few.

One of the most remarkable reporters that I had a chance to meet was Jim Miklaszewski of NBC News. This is the guy you want to sit next to on a trans-Pacific flight. Mik has done it all, from chasing the Ronald Reagan motorcade after the president escaped a security threat while playing golf at Augusta, to drinks at the table next to Ben Hogan's at Colonial Country Club in Fort Worth, to sitting down with the elders in the caves of Afghanistan. He has covered the most formidable assignments in this unpredictable world over the last several decades, and he never let a childhood disability restrict him from being one of the best in his business. It means a lot to me that he has written the foreword to this book.

I also would like to thank a very special group of people who must remain anonymous. They provided me with hard-to-come-by information about several operations reported in this book and talked with me about the thinking behind our government's counterpiracy strategy. Their assistance in getting the story straight was invaluable.

When it came time to pick a writing team, there were outstanding players in the field, but I had the real honor to work with a group of first-round draft picks. My agent, Doug Grad, worked tirelessly to get the book published. A lifetime full of thanks goes to my co-author, Michael Hirsh. He sorted through volumes of material on the centuries-old epic story of piracy, participated with me in interviewing most of the experts quoted in this book, and helped bring to life a book with a unique perspective on the challenges of fighting the modern-day pirates of Somalia.

Also to be thanked is Kathy Kirkland, who had the tough assignment of transcribing countless interviews and trying to figure out all those puzzling and often-mumbled military acronyms.

To Pete Daly and his team at the Naval Institute Press, from the very beginning you always expressed an interest in my material and were out front in your desire to get the book published. It has been an honor to work with a real group of professional naval historians, including my editor, Tom Cutler. A special thanks goes to Rick Russell, Susan Corrado, Judy Heise, and Claire Noble of the NIP team. They were able to teach a career naval officer the "inside baseball" requirements for making a successful book.

To my brother, Harry, I thank you for leading me in the right direction and pushing me to make that difficult decision to go VMI, which eventually changed the course of life. To my two sisters, Mary and Kathie, who never gave up hope and who overcame life-threatening ill-nesses—thanks for your inspiration. I was blessed with two loving parents who taught me the two most important virtues in life: love for God and love for family. Thanks, Mom and Dad, for all you did for me over the years. Serving as the CTF 151 commander was a real honor for me, but the pinnacle of my career was standing on the tarmac at Dover Air Force Base to receive the dignified remains of numerous of our fallen service members for their families and the nation.

This book is dedicated to my loving family, Lisa, T, and Tyler, who provided me with the support and motivation to make this book a reality. Many thanks for all your love.

We miss you, Rio.

INDEX

ABOUT THE AUTHORS

Rear Adm. Terry McKnight, USN (Ret.), is a thirty-one-year veteran of the U.S. Navy who, as a surface warfare officer, rose to command USS *Kearsarge*, an amphibious assault ship carrying nearly three thousand sailors and Marines. He was selected to serve as the first commander of Combined Task Force 151, a multinational unit formed to combat piracy in the Gulf of Aden. He currently lives in Fairfax Station, Virginia, with his wife of over thirty years, and they have two wonderful sons.

Michael Hirsh is a journalist who has produced documentaries and specials for PBS, CBS, ABC, and HBO. He's received the Peabody Award, a Writers Guild Award, and multiple Emmy Awards. Among his television specials are *Memories of M*A*S*H* for CBS, *A Program for Vietnam Veterans—and everyone else who should care* for PBS, and a five-program PBS series on the prevention of child sexual abuse. He's written six nonfiction books, including *None Braver—US Air Force Pararescuemen in the War on Terror* and *The Liberators—America's Witnesses to the Holocaust*. He and his wife, Karen, live in Punta Gorda, Florida.